The Origin
of
Thought

A New Essay
on the
Origin of Ideas

THE ORIGIN
OF
THOUGHT

by
ANTONIO ROSMINI

Abridged, edited and translated by
TERENCE WATSON
and
DENIS CLEARY

ROSMINI HOUSE
DURHAM

Translated from Nuovo Saggio
sull'Origine delle Idee,
vol. II, Intra, 1876.

Front cover picture ©AA.

2nd edition 1989

Typeset by Litho Link Limited, Welshpool, UK.
Printed by The Camelot Press, Southampton, UK.

ISBN 0 9513211 2 9

Foreword

We live in an age of uncertainty. Even the great strides towards domination over nature taken during the past two centuries have contributed in bringing western civilisation to intolerable mental indecision. Inevitably we look for salvation, and find it at best in a strong ruler, at worst in any distraction promising relief from the need to accept our individual responsibilities.

The chief factor leading to our disorientated living is widespread scepticism about the value of human reasoning. Not long ago, such an attitude would have been found only in philosophical circles, but greater instruction, better communications and the loss of our ability to concentrate on sustained argument have enabled it to spread throughout society at great cost to objectivity. Subjectivity, however, affords no solid basis on which to found a consistent way of life and fulfil human longing for freedom and dignity.

Rosmini's work on the problem of knowledge places 'the *light* of reason', not reasoning itself, at the centre of thought. Revealing itself to human beings as the objective source of all knowledge, this light is the sure element upon which all reasoning depends. Without this illumination, even scepticism would be at a loss to express the contradiction inherent to its affirmation of universal doubt.

The light of reason is not a transient feature in human life. It shines before individuals unchangeably, whatever use they make of it and even when they endeavour to turn away from it. As a stable feature it allows human beings to share unceasingly in its eminent characteristics; without entering their existence as part of their subjective being, it is the fount of their dignity, their duties and their rights. As something seen by all who share human nature, it is the source of their unity and brotherhood. And it draws all human beings above themselves, inviting them to search for that of which it is an image. Finally, it offers not only a basis for certainty, but a criterion by which we may judge whether we do in fact possess certainty, defined by Rosmini as 'a firm and reasonable persuasion which conforms to the truth.'

Rosmini's investigation into the source of human knowledge offers much more than the brief synopsis we have attempted here. It also provides, amongst other things, an examination of the relationship in the human person between the light of reason and feeling, or sensation, and shows how these elements contribute objectivity and subjectivity to human existence. Account has been taken of this in the abridgment of the whole work.

We have omitted Rosmini's evaluation of philosophers who before him had considered the problem of the origin of human thought, and from whom he drew so much of his own work. Rosmini's critique, which forms the first of the three volumes which make up the *New Essay on the Origin of Ideas* in Italian, would have to be considered in any attempt to assign him a place in the history of philosophy, but is dispensed with here so that we may take a closer view of his own principles. The last of the three volumes, *On Certainty*, will however form an accompanying volume to the present translation.

But even in this edition of volume two, we have in great part omitted Rosmini's reflections on the history of the problem of knowledge, and placed lengthy footnotes, which sometimes form essays in their own right, as an Appendix to the book. We hope that in doing this we have not betrayed his thought, but made it more accessible.

DENIS CLEARY,
TERRY WATSON,
Durham.

May 23rd, 1987.

NOTE

The paragraph numeration used by Rosmini throughout the three volumes of his complete work has been retained in this translation to enable easy reference to the Italian edition.

Paragraphs omitted in the translation are indicated by omitted numbers.

[. . .] indicates an omission from the text of paragraphs.

° indicates an omitted footnote.

App. no. indicates that a footnote has been moved to the Appendix.

[text] indicates an addition by the editors.

Contents

Contents

Contents

Contents

Contents

Contents

Contents

Contents

Contents

Contents

Contents

Contents

Contents

Contents

Contents

Contents

INTRODUCTION.
THE PRINCIPLES DIRECTING
THIS INVESTIGATION

1

THE TWO PRINCIPLES OF
METHOD IN PHILOSOPHY

26. Our investigation must be directed by two principles.

First: 'When explaining facts about the human spirit, we must not take into account less than is necessary for the explanation.' The reason is clear: as long as we take into account less than is needed, it is impossible to posit a sufficient explanation of the facts. In a word, we have not explained them. Let us suppose, for example, that someone observes colour and sound sensations, two facts of human sensibility, and claims to explain them both by allowing human beings one sense only, either sight or hearing. In this case, the facts remain unexplained because their reduction to the single sense of sight cannot show how the eye hears, while their reduction to hearing alone cannot show how the ear sees.

27. Second: 'In our explanation of these facts, we must not take into account more than is required.'[1] Non-essentials are superfluous to the explanation and, as entirely gratuitous, can be gratuitously denied. Two human senses, for example, may be posited to explain one kind of sensation. This is obviously ridiculous because two causes, one of them superfluous and without foundation, have been assigned to a single kind of fact.

28. Meditation on the human spirit must lead us, therefore:
1. to recognise and uphold everything necessary for explain-

[1] It is easy to see that these two principles, taken together, are only the principle of sufficient reason divided into its parts.

ing all characteristic facts obtainable through careful observation; 2. to accept only the minimum required to explain these
facts. In other words: 'Of all the complete explanations of the
facts about the human spirit, the simplest and that requiring
the fewest suppositions is to be preferred.'

2

MATURE AND POPULAR PHILOSOPHY,
AND THEIR OPPOSITE DEFECTS

29. The two principles governing an exact, genuine method
in philosophical investigation are matched by two, and only
two, basic defects in theories concerned with the human
spirit. Some theories offend against the first principle by not
taking into account sufficient to explain the facts, others, by
too easily accepting matters inessential to the explanation of
facts provided by observation, offend against the second principle and give rise to superfluous hypotheses.

30. Avoiding these hazards is difficult, and philosophy is
near perfection when it succeeds in negotiating them carefully. It will not achieve this, however: 1. without full and
complete observation of the facts; 2. without accurately and
wisely identifying and isolating specific, characteristic facts;
3. without recognising and weighing the difficulty of explaining the facts on the one hand, and the force of preferred
reasons on the other. If philosophical understanding neglects
accurate consideration and penetration both of the difficulty
and of the force of the reasons given, the arguments will
either be invalid or superfluous without our being aware of it.

31. Errors in popular philosophy originate in the absence
of one or all of these three conditions, and usually offend
against the first of the two principles mentioned above. Popular philosophy[2] is never based on complete observation. It is

---

[2] What I call 'popular philosophy' is the imperfect philosophy found in the general
body of thinkers despite the deep, speculative acumen presented in books handed
down for generations. In the last century, marked by a move to forsake our entire
tradition, philosophy relapsed into an infantile state. I call this 'popular philosophy'
because, like the man in the street, it continues to deal with initial problems which

incapable of classifying observed facts, or of distinguishing characteristic from non-characteristic facts. Having collected many facts, it thinks it has made progress, without realising that the success of observation depends upon the number of characteristic facts, that is, upon those distinguishing a species, and not upon the number of common, repetitive facts. Finally, it does not penetrate the interior nature of the fact, nor feel the force of reasons explaining it. Popular philosophy is marked by all these imperfections and defects.

32. Anyone accustomed to reflection can easily recognise the imperfections of popular thinking through contact with people in general, amongst whom the absence of the three conditions already mentioned gives rise to evident contradiction. For instance, people generally show no surprise at what is in itself amazing. If you ask them a reason for the marvel, they imagine that their natural, easy answer is satisfactory, and they may even be amused at your ignorance. They ask few questions, and solve their difficulties with reasons, or gross suppositions, that leave them without misgivings. But when you cast doubt on their answers, or point to some snag they can comprehend, their first reaction leads them to the opposite extreme. Previously they had solved the difficulty by not seeing it but, as soon as they understand the objection, the reasons you rightly offer for its solution are as hard for them to follow as their previous acceptance of the matter was easy.

I mention this to show that the theories of those who take too little into account coincide with simplistic thinking in so far as both lack sufficient reasons. On the other hand, those take too much into account who, after serious investigation, have encountered difficulties without being able to discover any fundamental explanation for them. This requires time, because the first reasons suggested, although hypothetical and involved, are accepted by our impatient mind which, unable to discover better reasons, will not tolerate its own lack of them.

34. As a consequence, we can outline three periods of philosophy. First, *popular* philosophy, lacking self-criticism, later may have changed their nature and status as a result of deeper and more mature philosophy. [. . .]

which if it succeeds in seeing difficulties explains them by confused or shallow hypotheses. In the second period philosophy, having gained *experience*, is aware of the difficulties inherent in former hypotheses, and comes to despise the old, popular theories. Ingenious and difficult systems are devised, but they offend by excess as much as popular philosophy offended by defect. In both periods, philosophy is defective: in the first, because it is new to difficulties; in the second, because it is new to solving them. But as it progresses, defects are corrected and theories simplified and completed. Philosophy has now entered its third period, that of its perfection.

40. If I have to justify myself, therefore, for positing what I call *the form of truth* as the sole form of human reason, I can only succeed by showing that there is no other way to avoid the two hazards on which modern theories have foundered. [. . .] I have to prove that the theory postulating *a single form of reason* takes account of both dangers, while offering the simplest and most complete explanation of the fact I have before me. This theory will take into account and presuppose less than any other.

However, I do not wish to provide a theory of everything observable in the human spirit. I simply want to explain the origin of ideas. To do this, I shall first have to indicate as briefly and clearly as possible the essential nature of the fact. This will enable the reader to penetrate the problem, and understand why its solution is so difficult.

3

THE DIFFICULTY OF EXPLAINING

THE ORIGIN OF THOUGHT

41. The fact I wish to explain is the existence of human thought or ideas.[3]

[3] Every idea provides some knowledge, although it could be denied that pure ideas, which give no knowledge of real things, form *knowledge* properly so-called [. . .]. Nevertheless, the word 'knowledge' can be applied in a broad sense to all kinds of ideas. In fact, ideas are the formal part of every kind of knowledge, as we shall see later.

Human beings think of different things, know, and have ideas. For the time being, I am not asking what these ideas are; I am satisfied that common knowledge supposes that every person has them. Whatever they are, my question is: what is their source? or, what causes them in the human spirit? Everyone can put this question to himself, although not all are equally capable of answering it. It is the great problem of the origin of ideas which in every age has divided philosophers and their schools.

42. Let us formulate the difficulty as briefly as possible. To form a judgment, we need universal notions. When we say, for example: 'This sheet of paper is white', or 'This man is wise', we must already possess the universal idea of whiteness and of wisdom. Otherwise, we could not attribute such predicates to some subjects rather than others.

It would take too long to show this about all species of judgments through induction, although it could be done. It can be demonstrated that a judgment is an operation by which we unite a given predicate to a given subject. Through this operation of our mind: 1. we take subject and predicate as mentally distinct things, in the sense that we can fix our attention exclusively on one of them, and thus distinguish it from the other; 2. we recognise that these two entities are united naturally speaking, and we fix our attention not on each of them taken separately, but on their relationship in the subject.

This analysis of judgment shows that we must first conceive a predicate distinct from a subject. Otherwise we could make no judgment. But a predicate distinct from a subject always contains a universal notion. Until joined to one subject, it can be joined to several, or even to an infinite number of possible subjects. This is what we mean when we apply the word 'universal' to ideas.

If the human mind cannot carry out the operation called 'judgment' without first being in possession of some universal notion or idea, how does it form universal ideas?

43. It is easy to observe that the mind can form a universal idea only in one of two ways: 1. by *abstraction*, 2. by *judgment*.

Through abstraction, we can form a universal idea from a

particular idea[4] by the following operations of our spirit: 1. the *common* element in the particular idea is separated from the *proper* element; 2. the proper element is abandoned; 3. attention is fixed solely on the *common characteristics*, which are precisely the universal idea we are seeking.

We have to note, however: 1. that these three operations of the spirit are carried out on a particular idea already present to us, however we may have acquired it; 2. their only purpose is the observation of a single, common characteristic, which they neither bring into existence nor generate in our spirit. But if we observe the common, universal element affirmed to be present in our particular ideas, we must grant that it is already there to be observed; otherwise we could neither observe this pure idea nor fix our attention upon it.

Abstraction, therefore, will not serve to explain the formation of ideas which of themselves are *common* and *general*, although this is the method adopted by some schools of philosophy. Abstraction only enables us to observe these ideas when they are already present and, by purifying them of all foreign elements, presents them to our attention in perfect isolation.

44. Judgment alone remains as the way of forming common or universal ideas. We have already seen, however, that every judgment presupposes a universal idea (cf. 42). Judgment is only an operation of the mind applying a universal idea to a subject which it places, as it were, in a class of things determined by the universal idea. Judging, for example, that someone is good, I place that person in the class of things formed by the universal idea of goodness. The same can be said about any other judgment.

Therefore, if judgment can begin only through a universal idea, it is obviously impossible to explain the *formation* of all universal ideas through *judgments*. We must suppose that

---

[4] The phrase 'particular idea' needs some explanation. An idea is particular only in so far as it is connected in my spirit with some real individual. Mentally separated from such an individual, it acquires or rather manifests universality, and can be applied freely by me to an infinite number of equal individuals. Only the real individual is absolutely proper or particular in an idea, to which it adheres without forming part of the idea itself; it is not joined to the idea by nature, but by the work of the human spirit. 'Pure idea' is, therefore, equivalent for us to 'universal idea', as we shall explain fully in the course of our study.

some universal idea pre-exists all judgments in human beings, enabling them to judge and, through their judgments, gradually to form all other ideas.

45. This is a brief explanation of the difficulty facing those who endeavour to explain the origin of ideas without learned prejudices or popular presuppositions. The difficulty will become more obvious as we proceed with our study. [. . .]

PART ONE.
ORIGIN OF
THE IDEA OF BEING

1

IT IS A FACT THAT WE THINK
OF BEING IN GENERAL

398. I begin with a simple, very obvious fact, the study of which forms the whole theory of this book: we think of being in a general way. This fact, no matter how we explain it, cannot be called into doubt.

To think being in a general way simply means thinking of the quality common to all things, while ignoring all other qualities, generic, specific or proper. I have the power to fix my attention on one element of a thing rather than on another, and in concentrating exclusively on being, the quality common to all things, I am said to be thinking *being* in general.

To deny that we can direct our attention to being as common to all things, while ignoring or rather abstracting from all their other qualities, contradicts what is attested by ordinary observation of our own actions; it would mean contradicting common sense and violating ordinary speech. When I say: reason is proper to human beings, who have feeling in common with animals and vegetable life in common with plants, I am thinking this *common being* independently of everything else. If human beings did not have the ability to think *being* separately from everything else, this statement would be impossible.

This fact is so obvious that to mention it would be sufficient, if it were not for the doubt prevalent in modern thinking. Yet it is the foundation of the entire theory of the origin of ideas.

399. To think being in a general way means that we have the idea of being in general, or at least presupposes that we have it; without the idea of being, we cannot think being. Our task, then, is to identify the origin of this idea. But if we are to discover its source, we must first examine its nature and character.

2

THE NATURE OF
THE IDEA OF BEING

Article 1.
The pure idea of being is not a sensible image

400. Because the argument has to be free from every possible ambiguity, I must first point out that in affirming human capacity for possessing the *idea of being*, isolated and separate from all other ideas [. . .], I do not wish to say that we form for ourselves a *sensible image* of that idea. A sensible image cannot be formed of anything unless the thing itself is: 1. determined and individualised; 2. corporeal, and perceived by the senses.

401. Some modern philosophers have denied abstract or indetermined ideas simply because it is impossible to form images of them, but this is a material reason unknown to true thinkers who understand the necessity of observing nature and acknowledging all it presents. The existence of something cannot be denied just because it does not conform with laws imposed *a priori* on the nature of things by our fantasy. Simple, unprejudiced observation would have easily recognised three series of thoughts within the human spirit:

1. thoughts representing *indetermined ideas*, that is, objects which cannot be presented under the form of images, nor exist in reality on their own, but which can nevertheless be considered on their own;

2. thoughts about spiritual beings which have everything required for *subsistence* but offer no basis for sensible images;

3. thoughts about bodies or corporeal qualities which alone are capable of being expressed by sensible imagination.

The existence of these three classes of thoughts is a fact, independent of any system and must be admitted even by those who deny the *existence of spiritual beings*, an altogether different question from that implied by *concepts of spiritual beings*. To establish gratuitously the principle: 'What we cannot imagine sensibly, we cannot even think', and to draw from this gratuitous assertion the consequence that 'Hence, universal and abstract ideas do not exist', is a false method. Its starting point is a prejudice to which we wish to subject the facts; it implies a determination to dictate laws to nature, rather than a desire to listen to nature, and interpret it wisely.

Article 2.
The idea of anything must be distinguished from the judgment about its subsistence

402. We must also distinguish *the idea* from the *judgment about the subsistence* of things. This is a cardinal distinction in epistemology.

When our spirit forms the *idea* or *concept* of anything, we can possess a perfect concept of that being, with all its essential and accidental qualities, without *judging* that it really exists. This is sufficient to assure us that our spirit, when intuiting the *idea*, performs a different operation from that involved in making a judgment about the subsistence of a being.

Let us take the idea or concept of a horse containing every individual internal and external feature necessary for its existence (body, head, neck, legs, and so on), and imagine that this could really exist, if I were capable of creating it, without need of any addition to the particulars contained in the idea that serves me as its exemplar or type. If I wished to bring this horse into existence, and were capable of doing so, and if my concept still did not present all the minute particulars of the individual horse I intended to make, I would be obliged as I went ahead with my work to think of the parts lacking to the concept, which I would gradually perfect as the external reality was formed. Let us imagine now that the concept has been perfected, and the horse brought into being in such a way that it corresponds exactly with the concept used to bring it to this state and make it exist. There is no doubt that the material horse would depend upon the thought and concept from which I had copied it.

403. The next step is to ask whether my perfect concept has received anything from the real subsistence of the horse. Undoubtedly, it has not. The concept had to be perfect before the horse could exist, in order that I might have a standard or exemplar from which to produce and forge it. The concept derives nothing from the perfected horse, nor can it do so, because its own perfection first comprises without exception all the particulars of the horse. So much is evident.

404. This fact throws light on the nature of ideas which are independent (as far as their nature is concerned) of the *real* existence of individuals in such a way that they can be perfect irrespective of the real existence of individuals. Moreover, when individuals come into existence, their subsistence adds nothing to their idea or concept. Whatever grade of perfection the individual has is already contained in its concept.

405. This truth concerning the independence of the idea of an external thing (we are speaking about the nature of the idea, not its origin) enables us to grasp the difference between possessing an *idea*, and *judging* that the thing of which we have the idea really exists. Our second operation of thought is a *judgment* on the subsistence of the thing we are thinking about and as such is entirely different from its *idea* or concept. As we said, our *idea* of anything is equally perfect and complete whether the thing subsists or not, whether we judge of its real existence or not, whether we make this judgment in one way or another.

The *judgment* of a thing's subsistence supposes the *idea* of the thing. The judgment, therefore, is not the *idea*, and does not add anything to it. Such a judgment forms within us only a *persuasion* of the *subsistence* of the thing we judge to exist in a real way. *Persuasion* is only *assent*, an operation in its own right which must not be confused in any way with the *intuition* of the idea.

Article 3.
Ideas of things never contain the subsistence of these things

406. I call the *subsistence* of anything its real, actual existence.

407. The heading of this article is, therefore, a corollary of the preceding article which affirmed the essential distinction between the *idea* and the *judgment* we make on the real existence of things. In fact if the *idea* is complete and perfect without its containing any thought of the real, actual existence of things (cf. 399-400), it cannot help us in any way to know things as *subsisting*. It presents them to us only as *possible*. The subsistence of things is known by means of another operation of our spirit, called *judgment*, which is essentially different from the intuition of the idea.°

Article 4.
The idea of being presents only simple possibility

408. 'Idea of being' does not mean the thought of some subsistent being whose qualities, apart from actual existence, are unknown or abstract, like *x*, *y* and *z* in algebra. Nor does it mean judgment or persuasion about the subsistence even of an indetermined being; it simply means *idea of being*, mere possibility. This is a corollary of the preceding article.

After the last possible abstraction on a being as thought, *possibility* remains. If we think of a subsistent being without knowing its qualities, we can still abstract from it the persuasion of its subsistence while retaining the thought of its possibility.

409. The most universal idea of all therefore which remains after every other abstraction, is *possible being*; we can call it simply the *idea of being*.

Article 5.
We cannot think of anything without the idea of being

Demonstration

410. This obvious statement needs little consideration yet few people have given it sufficient attention. Modern philosophers [. . .] have been at pains to analyse the *faculties* of the spirit although few have analysed their *product*, that is, *human knowledge*. Faculties are known only by their effects which therefore must be analysed first; we examine the faculties after investigating knowledge. The opposite way is taken by [. . .] those who begin by examining the faculties and then move on to knowledge. This inversion of the process is possibly the principle source of their errors. I have started from the effects and tried to analyse a known fact. By doing this I have endeavoured to find the cause of the fact, that is, to determine the faculties necessary for all human knowledge.

411. Now the analysis of any knowledge we have always gives the same result: 'We cannot think of anything without the idea of being.' Indeed we have no knowledge or thought separate from the idea of being. Existence is the most common, universal quality of all.

Take any object you wish. First abstract its particular qualities, then its common qualities, then its more common qualities and so on. In the end the last quality will be existence by means of which you can still think something, a being, but without its mode of existence; the object of your thought is a perfectly indetermined something, unknown as regards its qualities, an *x*. But it *is* something; it is not nothing, because nothing has no existence, not even possible existence in your mind. Either you are thinking that a being exists, or can exist, with all the qualities necessary for its existence although these remain unknown to you, or you are not thinking at all. What you are thinking is indeed an idea although totally indetermined.

On the contrary, if you finally take away *being*, the most universal of all qualities, nothing is left in your mind; all thought has disappeared and along with it any idea of the being.

To give an example. Let us take the concrete idea of a particular person, Maurice. Now when I take away from Maurice what is particular and individual to him, I am left with what is common to human beings. Next, by a second abstraction, I remove the human elements such as reason and freedom, and now I have a more general idea, that of an animal. Abstracting animal qualities I am left with a body that has vegetable life without feeling. After this I take away all physical organisation and vegetable life, fixing my attention on what is common to minerals; my idea is now that of something material. Finally I withdraw my attention from what is proper to matter; my idea is now of anything that exists. But during this process of abstraction, my mind has dealt with something, and has never ceased thinking; it has always had the idea as an object of its action, although this idea has become consistently more universal until my mind arrived at the most universal of all ideas, the idea of *being*, indetermined by any quality known or fixed by me. I can finally think that this being is a being solely because it has *being*. Abstraction can go no further without losing every object of thought and destroying every idea in my mind. The idea of being therefore is the most universal idea, and remains after the last possible abstraction; without it, all thinking ceases and all other ideas are impossible.

Article 6.
No other idea is necessary for the intuition of the idea of being

412. This statement is the converse of the preceding statement and follows naturally from what has been said (cf. 406). We have seen how the idea of anything can be broken down, as it were: first, the particular qualities are removed, then the more common and finally the most common. After reducing it to its bare minimum, we are left only with *being* as the basis of all the other qualities and the most abstract of ideas: take this away and every other thought and idea becomes impossible. Yet this single, bare idea, revealed by our abstractions remains in the mind as an object of contemplation. Able to be intuited and known of itself, it needs no other idea for its intuition.

3

THE ORIGIN OF THE IDEA OF BEING

413. After establishing the existence and learning the nature of the idea of being, we must now investigate its origin, that is, how it comes to be in our mind. We will first indicate where it does *not* come from and then where it *does* come from.

Article 1.
The idea of being does not come from bodily sensations

414. To see the truth of this statement clearly, we must examine the special characteristics of the idea of being, which are very different from anything sensations can present to us. Because each of these characteristics is inexplicable in any system claiming to derive the idea of being from sensations, they provide an irrefutable demonstration of the invalidity of this claim.

§1. *Demonstration 1.*
From *objectivity*, the first characteristic of the idea of being and its first element

415. When we think of any being in general or even of some particular being, we are thinking of it only in itself. Its relationship with us or with anything else is not part of our thought;[5] we think of it absolutely. This way of perceiving things as they are in themselves, independently of any relationship with anything else, is common to everything our mind can conceive; we perceive things impartially, as it were,

---

[5] If this way of conceiving things in our mind, that is, as they are in themselves, were only apparent because their existence was in fact relative to us, the argument would still be valid. But apparent or not, we would still have to explain the fact that things seem to be perceived in themselves, objectively. On the other hand because the discussion is solely about the way we perceive things, the difference between the apparent and the true is irrelevant. We cannot deceive ourselves about the way we conceive an object in our mind: to say 'I conceive the object in this way' means only that I conceive it in the way I do and nothing more. Whether the external thing corresponds to my concept or not, does not concern us here. [. . .]

just as they are and with their own grades of being. The thought by which we perceive them as they are can be reduced to the following formula: 'This thing (that I conceive in my mind) has such a grade or mode of existence.' Existence, the sole term of reference of our mental conception, is common to everything we perceive and is also the term to which everything experienced in our feeling is related. Let us now suppose that through our senses we perceive and conceive all things as beings possessing existence in the grade or mode indicated.

416. I maintain that sensation is incapable of making us perceive *obectively*, in the way characteristic of intellectual perception. In fact sensations are only particular modifications or experiences in our own make-up; what is felt exists as such only relatively to us.

Sensations therefore can make us feel only the relationship to us of external things (if there are any, but I am not discussing this yet), and the power they have to modify us. If we were limited to sensations alone, the *subject* of this power could never be present to us in itself. Existence in itself is not felt by us because the expressions 'to exist in itself' and 'to be felt' indicate what is absolute and what is relative, opposite concepts which directly exclude one another.

In fact, the mere existence in itself of a thing does not require or imply a sensation produced in some other thing, while a sensation, which does not include the idea of something *existing in itself*, indicates only our experience and its term.

Sensations therefore cannot make us perceive a thing as it is in itself but only in relationship to us: *sensation* means simply some modification in us, while *idea* means *mental conception of something that exists*, independently of any modification or experience in another being. Therefore the idea of being is not given to us in any way by sensations.

> *Observations* on the difference between sensation,
> sense-perception, idea and intellective perception

417. To avoid confusion, we define our use of certain words:

1. a *sensation* is a modification of the feeling subject;

2. *sense-perception* is a sensation (or more generally any feeling) considered in so far as it is united to a real term;

3. an *idea* is being, or a possible being, intuited as object by the mind;

4. *intellective perception* is the act by which the mind apprehends a real thing (something feelable) as an object, that is, in the idea.

Sensation therefore is *subjective*, sense-perception is *extra-subjective*; an idea is an *object*, intellective perception is *objective*.

418. It is difficult for us to separate sense-perception from intellective perception because, as reasoning beings, we habitually make the second follow immediately on the first; the two are naturally linked in us and taken as one so that very accurate observation is needed to distinguish them.

419. Another reason for our extreme difficulty in separating *sensations* from *ideas* and forming an exact concept of each without confusing them, is our need for an intellective perception or an idea in order to know or reason about anything. If we have no idea of a thing, we cannot know, think or talk about it. Hence we need an idea or intellectual perception of *sensations* which are of themselves unintelligible, objects neither of thought nor of reason.

Every time we intend to talk about sensations, therefore, we must have an idea accompanying them. This necessity of thinking about sensations by means of an idea makes it very difficult for us to understand the need to isolate a sensation from its idea in order to gain a clear concept of it.

420. It is a fact that we particularly resist the strenuous mental effort of isolating whatever is foreign to sensation, even the idea by which we conceive it, because sensation by itself is unintelligible.

This rarely perceived difficulty is due to our knowledge of material beings, or of any being that is not an *idea*. In themselves such beings are obscure and incomprehensible; separated from ideas, they have an existence impossible for us to understand.

421. In addition to the difficulty we meet in forming a clear concept both of bodies and of sensations, there is a special difficulty connected with the concept of sensations.

Sensations, once separated from the ideas by which they are conceived, are unknown, as we have said. But this fact is very hard to accept. Because sensations, as modifications felt essentially by our spirit, are always accompanied by pleasure or pain, it seems impossible for them to be unknown. This great difficulty comes precisely from what we said earlier about our habit of perceiving sensations intellectually as soon as we have them; we are beings endowed with intellect and reason, and what we feel is also apprehended intellectively.

Furthermore, even if we were to have a pure sensation without any accompanying idea — as seems to happen when we feel something without being aware of it because our mind is occupied with other things — such a sensation could not help us form an exact concept of itself because we would have neither understood it nor considered it; relative to our understanding it would not exist at all, and could not, therefore, be thought or reasoned about.

422. The concept of a sensation unaccompanied by an idea can be formed only indirectly as follows: 1. we perceive a sensation intellectually, for example, the colour red; 2. in this sensation we have joined intimately the idea and the sensation: the idea is essentially *knowledge*, the sensation something made *known*; 3. we then analyse this act of our intellectual perception, that is, we analyse our *idea of the sensation of red* and separate the *idea* that makes the sensation known from the *sensation* known through the idea; 4. we conclude that the *sensation* without the *idea* can only be an *unknown entity*; it is known only through the *idea*, and by separating the idea, we have removed what makes the sensation present to our mind - in a word, we have removed the *form* of the cognition and left only its *matter*; 5. finally we direct our attention to this *matter* and see that it is a *sensation*, a *modification* of our spirit different from external bodies which, as such, are not only *not* known in themselves but *not even felt*.

§2. *Demonstration 2.*
From *possibility* or *ideality*, the second characteristic of the idea of being and its second element

423. The simple idea of being is not the *perception* of some

subsistent thing (cf. 406-409), but the *intuition* of possible beings, the possibility of things. Our sensations provide only modifications of our spirit coming from subsistent things; merely possible things have no power to act on our organs and produce sensations in them. Sensations, therefore, have nothing in common with our idea of being and cannot in any way furnish us with it. [. . .] The same reason determines the impossibility of any *image* of the idea of being.

Observations on the connection between the general proofs, already given, of the inability of sensations to provide us with the idea of being

424. The idea of being comprehends or at least implies two elements so united that the idea could not exist without either of them. These elements are: 1st. *possibility*; 2nd. *some indetermined thing* to which possibility can be referred.

Just as it is impossible to think of *any thing* which is logically *impossible*, it is also impossible to think of *possibility* alone, without understanding it as the *possibility* of *some thing*. Hence the idea of being, although perfectly simple and indivisible in itself, has or implies two *mental* elements, that is, elements indicated by the mind alone.

425. Examination of the nature of one of these elements (existence, or something indetermined) has provided the first demonstration; examination of the other element (possibility) has provided the second demonstration.

The first element, *existence*, or anything whatsoever in so far as it has a mode of existence, cannot be perceived by sense which perceives a being not in so far as it exists, but only in so far as it acts. The second element, *possibility*, cannot be perceived by sense because what is merely possible cannot produce sensations: that which does not yet actually exist cannot act.

§3. *Demonstration 3.*
From *simplicity*, the third characteristic of possible being

426. We must now consider *possible being* on the one hand and *sensation* on the other. Every organic sensation, with its

root in an extended organ, will be found to have some extension. On the contrary, every *possible being* intuited by the mind is perfectly *simple* and free from bodily solidity.

Simplicity consists in the absence of anything material or of any likeness with matter, and in the absence of anything extended or of any likeness with extension. It is directly opposed to the nature of real sensation which cannot therefore be a source in any way of the extremely simple light of the mind.

§4. *Demonstration 4.*
From *unity* or *identity*, the fourth characteristic of the idea of being

427. We shall continue our comparison between *possible being* and concrete *sensations*. Every concrete sensation resides in a single place, cut off from and incommunicable with other sensations. For example, the pain I feel in one of my fingers has nothing to do with a similar pain experienced by someone else in the same finger. The two sensations are separated by the limitations imposed by place and real subsistence.

On the contrary, being, or a being which shines before the mind in a state of mere possibility, is not in one place rather than another. It can be actuated in many places if its reality is such as to occupy space; it can be multiplied indefinitely even if its nature is not subject to the limitations of place.

For example, the mind can contemplate the human body as something possible. This body remains present to the mind even if its subsistence is actuated in various places, and multiplied indefinitely. *Real bodies* are multiple, while the *concept* or idea of body remains constantly one. The mind — several minds, if you wish — sees it as identical in all the infinite human bodies that can be thought of as subsisting.

The nature of real things, therefore, to which *sensations* belong, and the nature of the *simple* idea are opposed to one another. The latter cannot be found in the former, nor can it be produced by them.

§5. *Demonstrations 5 & 6.*
From *universality* and *necessity*, the fifth and sixth characteristics of possible being

428. Every being, considered in its logical possibility, is *universal* and *necessary*. There is no repugnance in the thought of an indefinite number of real, subsistent beings, all in conformity with my one idea. Every idea is a light in which I can know any number of beings that subsist or will subsist in correspondence with it. This light therefore is universal, *infinite*. On the other hand, every single sensation is particular: everything I feel in it is limited to that sensation. It is impossible to find the universal in sensation, or to draw the universal from it.

429. Something similar can be said about *necessity*; what I contemplate as possible is also *necessary*, because it is impossible to think that what is possible could ever be impossible. Real sensations, however, can be or not be. They are accidental, contingent, and without any element which would prompt the mind to think of some absolute *necessity*. Consquently, the idea of being, or possible being, cannot be drawn from sensations.

Observation 1. Being is the source of *a priori* knowledge

430. The two characteristics of *universality* and *necessity* [. . .] are not the ultimate criteria of *a priori* knowledge. They are partial criteria, derived from an exact analysis of the *idea of being*, the unique form of knowledge and the source of all *a priori* knowledge.

Observation 2. The idea of being in general and all other ideas without exception possess the characteristics indicated, especially *universality* and *necessity*

431. This proposition, a corollary of what has already been said, is very helpful for making known the nature of ideas. We have already seen that possibility alone is the object of

thought in the pure idea, which indicates nothing about the subsistence of things. Subsistence is proper to another faculty of the human spirit, different from that of ideas (cf. 405-406). We have also shown that the possibility of something extends to its unlimited repetition, which our thought cannot deny. The characteristics of *universality* and *necessity*, therefore, are contained in that of possibility (cf. 428-429). Every idea is consequently universal and necessary.

It is always the idea of being, clothed with determining qualities drawn from experience, which provides us with a quantity of more or less determined ideas or concepts that represent, however, merely possible, non-subsistent entities.

For example, generic and specific ideas, such as the concepts of *human being, animal, tree, stone,* and so on, which do not indicate individuals in any way, are only the idea of *possible being* clothed with the determinations and qualities common to human beings, trees, stones, etc. Although such ideas are given to us through experience, and perhaps clothed with every quality needed for their subsistence, they remain void of the act of subsistence itself, and as such are merely possible. All these more or less general ideas, therefore, represent merely possible beings, not real beings, and share: 1. *universality* and 2. *necessity*, the characteristics of possibility.

In fact, every idea is both *universal* in relationship to the possible, infinite individuals that can be formed on the model offered by that idea, and *necessary* for the same class of individuals because no individual of the class can exist without representing what is contained in the idea. It would be absurd to imagine an individual in a given class without attributing to it the constitutive qualities of the same class. [. . .]

§6. Demonstrations 7 and 8.
From *immutability* and *eternity*, the seventh and eighth characteristics of possible being

433. The mind which contemplates *being*, or any *possible being* whatsoever, cannot think of it in any other way, and

thus change it. It can only turn its attention from one possible being to another. All possible beings, therefore, present themselves to the mind as *immutable*. It follows that the mind cannot think of any time in which a possible being might not have been what it is now and always will be. The impossibility of thinking of change or limitation of time in a possible being is what we call the *immutability* and *eternity* of *possible being*. Changeable and passing sensations offer no sign of such characteristics, and cannot therefore enable the mind to think of them.

§7. *Demonstration 9.*
From *indetermination*, the ninth characteristic of possible being, and its third element

434. By analysing the idea of being, and separating two elements within it, we have shown that it cannot come from the senses. These two elements consist of: 1. the notion of *any thing*; 2. the notion of the relationship of *possibility* (cf. 415-422). Our analysis shows that the idea of being is furnished with the characteristics of *simplicity, identity, universality, necessity, immutability* and *eternity*, each of which allows us to demonstrate that the idea of being is not given to us by sensations (cf. 426-431). The same conclusion can be deduced from the third constitutive element of the idea of being in general, that is, its total indetermination.

The arguments used hitherto are indeed valid for all ideas, and show that none of them, considered *purely* as an idea, can derive from sensations. Every idea is a being intuited in its essence or possibility, without concrete existence (cf. 402-407), but furnished with all the characteristics we have indicated and distinguished (cf. 440-441). However, the idea of being in general provides another argument, which can be deduced from its *indetermination*.

435. A pure idea is constituted when the mind intuits a being without reference to its *subsistence*, although the being can have qualities which posit it in any particular *genus* and *species*. *Being in general*, however, is not only devoid of subsistence; it is also free of any differentiation and determi-

nation dependent upon *species* and *genus*. While other ideas
are universal because they respond to an infinite number of
equal, possible individuals, being in general is even more
universal because it extends without any determining limit to
all possible *species* and *genera*.

Our real sensations cannot possess any likeness whatsoever
with this kind of ideal being because they are all perfectly
determined. Sensations are produced by real, existing things
which, like their effects, must be furnished with all the
particular determinations and qualities necessary for their
real, actual existence.

The idea of being in general and sensations are, therefore,
contrary to one another and mutually exclusive. Perfect *indetermination* is essential to the idea of merely possible, universal being; perfect *determination*, without which they would
lack individuation and subsistence, is essential to sensations
and the agents producing them. A stone, for example, could
not exist without determined form, weight, and so on. On
the other hand, when we think of being in general, we
prescind from all such accidental and essential qualities of
particular beings. The being I have in mind is not particular,
but universal to the highest degree. It is, in other words, only
the possibility of various beings, the possibility of infinite
modes and grades of real existence which we do not enumer-
ate, reflect on, or reach out to. Thinking of their possibility,
we are in fact thinking of *existence* without reference to its
modes, although we are satisfied that these modes, whatever
they may be, will be found in the really existent beings.

436. Nor can it be said that I am in possession of *indetermined being* if I abstract the special determinations which
individuate a particular agent from the qualities perceived by
the senses alone. As we have seen repeatedly, sensations
enable me to perceive only what is particular and proper,
without any relationship, without what is common considered as common.

Sensations, therefore, do not bring me to know feelable
things as beings, that is, as existing in themselves with their
own grades of existence, nor as related to the common existence in which they share. With my sense-faculty I perceive
only the action of their feelable reality upon me, and the

effect left in my sensory make-up where particular agents are separated from one another. Moreover, each action of an agent stands on its own, separate from every other action, because sense, which cannot refer an action to anything else, cannot experience an action except in isolation nor extend itself beyond the limits of an action. If I had only sensations of feelable beings, without simultaneously perceiving them with my understanding, and then wished to abstract everything particular from the sensations, I would find myself left with nothing at all, rather than with indetermined being. As the sensations and their causes vanished, I would remain bereft of everything. We have to understand this fact carefully, and consider it attentively, if we wish to form a correct idea of the human spirit and its way of acting.

But, as I said, this is extremely difficult because we never possess sensations alone (cf. 417-420). When we experience them, we perceive what is real and external with both sense and understanding. We do not analyse our *sensations*, therefore, but our *ideas* of bodies, and through abstraction find in them the existence, possibility and determination of being. Although we think we find these things in pure *sensations*, they are found only in our *ideas*. We are not aware of having put them there because our understanding, as we have hinted elsewhere, perceives feelable things and all other beings in themselves, that is, in relation to the being in which they all participate. This cannot be achieved by feeling. Because of the outstanding importance of this truth, we shall deal with it again later.[6]

§8. A synopsis of the proofs already stated, together with a hint about other special proofs showing that *a priori* knowledge cannot be deduced from sensations

437. So far, our analysis of the idea of being has shown it to contain three inseparable elements, interconnected in such a way that one cannot be thought of without the others. These elements are: 1. *any thing* (being); 2. the *possibility* of any thing, of being; 3. *indetermination*. We have seen that none

---

[6] In passing, we note that *determination* is the effect of our imperfect vision of being; it is not something inherent in *being itself*.

of these elementary concepts, or elements of a single idea, can be profered by sensations because they are essentially different from them, to the point of mutual exclusion. On this basis, we gave three fundamental demonstrations of the following proposition: 'the idea of being cannot be derived from sensations' (cf. 414, 424, 433, 435) [437 in text]. Further analysis of the first two elements, especially that of possibility, showed it to contain other characteristics, all equally impossible to be deduced from sensation (cf. 426-433). [. . .]

Article 2.
The idea of being does not come from the feeling of one's own existence

§1. This proposition follows from what has been said

438. If the *idea of being*, and consequently all other ideas, cannot come to us from *external sensations*, it follows that it cannot come from *the feeling of oneself*, which is simply a permanent, interior sensation. Although feeling is characterised by special qualities, the arguments already employed to prove that the *idea of being* cannot come from bodily sensations are applicable to it.

§2. The distinction between the feeling and the idea of 'myself'

439. The internal feeling of 'myself', therefore, has to be distinguished from the idea or intellectual perception of 'myself'. The feeling of 'myself' is simple. The idea, on the other hand, is made up of: 1. the feeling of 'myself', which is the matter of knowledge; and 2. the idea of *being*, the form to which the mind refers the feeling of 'myself' and thus knows it, that is, it considers 'myself' as a *being*, and thinks it objectively, as it is in itself.

'Myself' is subject, and as such is wholly particular, related only to itself, a real, determined being. In order to know this subject or have an *idea* of it, I must conceive it objectively - as referred to being, not to myself - just as I consider any other particular, feelable thing. Being is the common measure, and when I have referred what I feel to this standard, I *feel*, and I *know* what I feel.

§3. The feeling of 'myself' gives me only my particular existence[7]

440. The feeling of 'myself' gives me, therefore, the sensation of my existence, but not the idea of existence in general. This feeling is indeed my own existence, but not therefore the intellective perception of my existence. This arises early within me, but comes about through an act by which I consider my own feeling as a being with the same impartiality with which I would consider anything else. Classifying myself amongst beings, I find myself in their midst, and distinguish myself from others through the feeling of 'myself' that marks me. Through the judgment made by my reason, I refer the idea of existence to this feeling.

§4. My own feeling is innate; the intellective perception of my existence is acquired

441. Hence, although the feeling expressed by the monosyllable 'myself' is innate (because I must be innate to myself), the intellective perception of myself is acquired, and cannot be confused with my subsistence nor with the feeling constituting it.

§5. The idea of being precedes the idea of 'myself'

442. The idea of 'myself' in general is formed through the intellective perception of my own 'myself' which, in turn, is formed through the idea of being (cf. 436). In the order of ideas, therefore, the idea of being precedes the idea of 'myself'. The former is necessary for the production of the latter. This is a corollary following immediately from what was established when we showed that the first thing understood by our intellect in any object is *being* [App. no. 1].

---

[7] Here 'myself' expresses the proper, substantial feeling of a person, not the additions provided by reflection carried out from the moment when the human being pronounces the monosyllable 'I'.

Article 3.
The idea of being does not come from Locke's reflection

§1. *Definition.*

444. By *Locke's reflection* I understand the faculty by which our spirit fixes its attention on our external sensations or internal feeling (feeling includes here all the *operations* of our spirit felt by us). Such attention may be directed to the whole or any part of sensation and feeling, without however adding anything to it and creating a new object.

445. This way of explaining Locke's *reflection* is justified by comparing what he says about reflection with what he says about innate ideas. Indeed, Locke's definition of reflection as 'the perception of the working of our spirit on ideas received from the senses,' (cf. *Essay on Human Understanding*, bk. 2, chap. 1, §4) is too equivocal to be of any systematic use. If it is simply the perception of the working of our spirit on ideas given by our senses, presumably ideas are already formed; and because we cannot have ideas without the idea of being, this awkward idea must also be presumed, which is the point at issue. The difficulty has been overcome by a simple supposition, or rather has neither been seen nor faced. As a result Locke's reflection can proceed without trouble. But let us go back and look for a moment at the path it has taken.

The first *ideas* were formed by *sensation*, but Locke does not tell us how and he is in no hurry to explain; he finds it enough to say: 'Our senses make all these ideas enter our spirit,' adding as his only words of explanation: 'By that I mean our senses make the act that produces these perceptions pass into our spirit from the objects' *(ibid.,* bk. 2, chap. 3, §3). This is not a satisfactory explanation; it is not even a satisfactory description of the fact of sensation. Locke is not interested in justifying how our sense-faculty causes the act by which our spirit has first a sense-perception and then an intellective perception. It is as if he were saying: 'Our sense-faculty produces the act by which our spirit feels and also the act by which it understands and forms ideas; I have no intention of shaming myself by showing you the difference between *feeling* and *understanding*, or by seeking what is needed for understanding to follow feeling. Whatever is required for producing these two facts and the difference between them, I start from the principle that all ideas come from sensation and reflection!' — this principle is the fundamental postulate of all Locke's philosophy. He seems to be saying: 'Let me use these two words, *sensation* and *reflection*, without having to define them accurately. Let them express all the causes of ideas with any meaning necessary for doing this. So, starting from this postulate, let us list all the ideas we have and refer them all to their source, *sensation* and *reflection*.' A genuine analysis of Locke's *Essay on Human Understanding* shows that the preparation of such a list is the sum total of the volume that has caused such a stir in the world.

446. Our analysis shows the whole question of innate ideas to have been eliminated by Locke, as he would seem to have intended, had he not introduced matter extraneous to his argument and used the whole of the first book to refute every innate idea and principle. What he says at such length in his first book, however, gives us the right to determine the sense of his equivocal, inconclusive definition of reflection. If there is no innate idea or principle in the human spirit, reflection, without adding anything to sensations, can only fix its attention on them to discover what they contain. And, as we said in our initial definition, this is characteristic of Locke's reflection.

§2. *Demonstration 1.*

447. I have already shown that the idea of being does not come from Locke's reflection. I pointed out: 1. that the idea of being is not contained in any way in external sensations (cf. 414-436); 2. nor in our internal feeling (cf. 437-443); 3. that Locke's reflection is a faculty for observing and finding what is in our sensations or feeling without adding anything to either (cf. 444-446).

It follows, therefore, that Locke's reflection, which cannot discover what is not present in our sensations or feeling, is incapable of finding the absent *idea of being*. Consequently, this idea has to come from some other source.

§3. *Demonstration 2.*

448. If I show that Locke's reflection is in fact impossible, I also show that the idea of being cannot come from it. If we recall the definition (cf. 444), it is not difficult to prove that his reflection is impossible. We have seen that it is 'the faculty by which our spirit fixes its attention on the whole or parts of our external or internal sensations, without adding anything and creating a new object.' It is true our attention can be held at random by the pleasure we have in sensations, but this is not Locke's reflection, whose aim is to acquire ideas, not to experience pleasure or enjoy it more easily. His reflection is a force of our spirit directed to and fixed on a part or complex of our feelings with the intention of finding new ideas in them. But can our spirit come to reflect in this way on its internal and external sensations without already possessing the universal ideas it is looking for?

Any similar reflection purposing to analyse sensations and extract ideas from them, has to divide, compose and find similar and dissimilar parts; in a word, it has to classify. But we cannot classify anything unless we presuppose the presence of the general idea constituting the class: it is impossible to compare and know what is similar or dissimilar in two individuals without first having the abstract idea common to both of them. Without this idea we would perceive two similar individuals, e.g. two red flags, but we would not think or reflect at all about their similarity. The two red sensations, perceived by our sense-organs, would remain separate, at least in time and place, as long as they were simply sensations with different, incommunicable existence. [...] Locke's reflection, therefore, is impossible. How can we reflect on our sensations for the purpose of extracting ideas from them if we have no ideas to direct our spirit, or enable it to unite and analyse sensations, and to move its attention freely from reflection to sensation?

449. When our spirit has only sensations but no ideas, *instinct* enables it to concentrate on any sensation for greater pleasure. This is not reflection properly speaking, but a reinforcement of attention on the part of our senses, rather than of our understanding. In fact, rather than *attention* it would

be better to call it *an application of instinctive, animal force*, naturally captivated by the pleasant sensation. I do not have time to take this further, but what has been said is sufficient to distinguish it from *intellectual attention*, the sole source of reflection. In passing, let me add that *sensible attention* does not differ from the feeling faculty, and could, if necessary, be called a natural actuation of this faculty [. . .].

450. We conclude that it is impossible to conceive mentally any reflection directed to the formation of ideas which begins to act before there are any ideas to direct and regulate it. Reflection of this kind contains contradictory elements because it requires the formation of ideas without ideas.

But if Locke's reflection is impossible and absurd, neither the idea of being nor any other idea (which will always contain the idea of being) may be derived from it. This is what I intended to demonstrate.

Article 4.
The idea of being does not begin to exist in our spirit in the act of perception

§1. *Demonstration 1.*
From observation of the fact

451. Bodily sensation does not contain the idea of being (cf. 409-433), and cannot therefore offer it for our reflection, which only notes what is present in sensation without adding anything to it (cf. 444-450). We have yet to see whether the idea of being presents itself to our spirit in the act of sensation or reflection in such a way that its sudden appearance to our mind draws us to conceive and possess it.

452. Before dealing with the possibility of such an extraordinary phenomenon, we must note carefully whether it actually occurs or not. Reid [Scottish philosopher, 1710-1796] insists that he wishes simply to describe the fact of human knowledge without attempting to explain it. Having separated its parts, and taken all its circumstances into account, he has no doubt that, related to the existence of bodies, knowledge is composed of three unconnected parts: 1. an *impression* on our bodily organs; 2. *sensation*; 3. *perception* of the

existence of bodies which follows immediately upon sensation [. . .]. He believes he has observed a law of constant
succession between these three occurrences: given the first,
the second follows; given the second, the third follows. But,
he continues, the first is unlike the second, the second unlike
the third; moreover, they are not connected as cause and
effect. Having described the fact, he now affirms that it is
inexplicable and totally mysterious. This description of the
perception of bodies certainly indicates philosophical concern
and effort, but we may doubt whether it is rigorous and
complete. Let us examine it briefly.

453. I have no doubt that the three events are successive,
and have to be distinguished from one another [App. no. 2].
Reid's account leaves no room for doubt here. I agree that the
events bear no likeness to one another, and that one cannot be
impressed on the other. Certainly, the *impression* made on
the bodily organs is of its nature essentially different from
sensation, while *sensation* has no likeness whatsoever with the
perception of being proper to our understanding [App. no. 3].
One event cannot therefore cause another by reproducing its
own impression or copy. But does this entitle us to say that
the fact under consideration is entirely inexplicable and
mysterious in all its parts [App. no. 4]?

454. Reid maintains: given the *sensation*, I have a *perception
of existing bodies*, although sensation is totally different from
perception. This is inexact. Although we have seen that *existence in general* is different from and opposed to *sensation* (cf.
402-429), our previous analysis of perception (cf. 411-417)
shows that intellective perception is not totally different from
sensation.[8]

I am not speaking here of the way in which a sensation
takes place in us on the occasion of an external impression.
That is outside our scope at present. I want to insist on the
last part of the fact, that is, on the way in which the *perception
of bodies* as existing things arises in the soul on the occasion of
sensations. Reid considers this inexplicable, because he has
not submitted it to sufficient analysis. Let us try to complete
his work.

---

[8] I include in *sensation* here what I have called corporeal *sense-perception* (cf. 417,
[App. no. 4]).

Thorough analysis indicates that intellective perception is not simple, like sensation, but made up of distinct parts. If it were simple, an inexplicable appearance would offer the only possibility of understanding its presence in our souls; a creation would be carried out in our spirit whenever a sensation occurred. But if it consists of different parts, it is not sufficient to declare it inexplicable. First, it should be split up into its parts; then, the relationship of the parts should be examined. Are they simultaneous or successive? How are they connected and so give rise to our perception of bodies?

I. As we have already seen, intellective perception is composed of three parts: 1. *sensation*, in which particular feelable qualities, separated from the predicate of quality and every other abstract notion, are terms of our sensory capacities; these feelable qualities establish the sign to which our thought turns its attention; 2. *the idea of existence in general*: to conceive of a body mentally as something means classifying it amongst existent things. This in turn presupposes the idea of existence in general which forms the class, as it were, of that which exists; 3. *judgment, the relationship between sensation and the idea of existence*, in which existence, known in the idea (predicate), is attributed to the *force acting* in the sensations and drawing them together in a being. This final act of the spirit is the proper source of the *intellective perception of bodies*. We also saw that the spirit achieves this in virtue of its perfect unity, that is, of the identity between the feeling and understanding subject. In a word, the same subject, on receiving sensations and seeing being in them, possesses the energy to turn towards itself where it beholds what it undergoes in its feeling related to the agent whose existence it affirms. In this way it sees the thing in itself, *objectively*.

II. If we now ask whether these parts are of their nature simultaneous or successive, we can see that naturally and temporally they have to be found in the following order. First, the idea of being must be present; this is followed by the sensation; finally, judgment, by joining the idea of being and sensation, generates the perception of the existence of bodies. Such perception is simply the application of existence (a quasi-predicate) to bodily agents which, in the self-same application, become objects.

It is surely obvious that no judgment can take place unless it is preceded by its two terms (subject and predicate). Moreover, careful observation of these terms of judgment will show that the idea of being must take precedence over sensation. Most obviously of all, we see on reflection that the idea of being must be present in all our ideas, and therefore in all our judgments (cf. 405, 417). Granted that we have made a judgment or obtained an idea, it must also be granted that we have made use of the idea of existence which we must already possess.

456. Observation will clarify the matter further for those wishing to undertand it better. The question 'Does the idea of being precede the sensation or not?' can only be asked about the first judgment we make on entering this world. By noting the *essential* laws governing judgment, which must be applicable to our first judgment, we shall be in a better position to answer the question.

In every judgment made as we feel something, we think of the existence of a particular, feelable thing; this is a constitutive law of judgment. But what does 'thinking of the existence of a feelable thing' mean? It does not mean receiving, but making use of, the idea of existence. Using the idea, however, presupposes it. How can one make use of something which is non-existent?

457. Whoever takes observation as a sure guide to the presence of facts in nature will notice something relevant to our argument in the way he makes use of the information he already has about existence. He is certainly not conscious of receiving this information by suddenly passing from a state in which he does not possess it to one in which he does. He is conscious, however, of using it as something already stored in his mind when he comes to employ it on the occasion of some sensation. He is not surprised that he knows what existence is, nor has he any new awareness as he uses it. He sees it as something already familiar to him, and understood independently of other things. Careful observation of the act by which we affirm to ourselves the existence of external things [. . .] shows precisely this. Although in judging the existence

of things we unite existence to the bodily force we feel, the idea of existence is so well-known that it escapes our attention. This, of course, makes it very difficult to observe.

It seems to me rather rash, therefore, to maintain that the *perception of bodies* succeeds *sensation* in a mysterious, inexplicable manner. In saying this, the possibilities of explanation are restricted to the limits of one's own observation. But are these limits the ultimate criterion? We do not always have to believe philosophers who declare on their own authority that philosophical investigation can go no further simply because they themselves can make no progress. I have no doubt that there is a mystery involved in intellective perception, but it is not to be found where Reid put it.

458. The intellective perception of bodies is only the application of an idea, that is, of some information known prior to bodily sensations. Confirmation of this may be obtained from the very expression we use [. . .], in which our words are an analysis of our thoughts. 'Perception of the existence of bodies' includes and expresses *the idea of existence* applied to *bodies*. The perception of the *existence of bodies* is therefore generated by the preceding idea of *existence*, then applied to sensations. The resulting object is called 'body'.

459. We may conclude: the idea of being does not begin to exist in our spirit in the act of *perception*. Self-observation provides no awareness of any sudden presence of this idea in us, nor of any instantaneous illumination; it tells us nothing of the immense leap necessarily required if our spirit is to pass from non-possession to possession of this idea; it provides no recollection of a time when we did not possess it and when we did. On the contrary, we are conscious only of the continual use made of this idea which we have always considered as our own. We have no right, therefore, without further proof to assert as fact the extraordinary, interior, instantaneous creation within us of an idea which bears no relationship to exterior, corporeal things.

§2. *Demonstration 2.*
From absurdity

460. Let us now suppose that the idea of being did occur to our mind either on the occasion of a sensation or immediately

afterwards, and that we perceived the existence of bodies by applying this fortuitous idea to the bodily force felt in the sensation. Such an occurrence would be a miracle: an idea unconnected with sensation and appearing to our mind is either a creation or at least a unique, isolated event, without analogy in nature. This consideration would be enough to exclude the hypothesis as unnecessary, since there is an easier, more ordinary way to explain the origin of ideas.

461. In any case, the idea of being, if created instantaneously in our soul could result from only one of two causes: either from a being outside us (God) producing the idea on the occasion of sensation, or from the nature of the soul itself emitting and creating the idea according to some necessary, physical law. [. . .]

462. The supposition [. . .] that human beings lack a complete faculty of thought and that, on the occasion of the sensations, God himself has to create in our mind the idea of being, which makes us thinking beings, is a strange, unsupported hypothesis, unlikely to attract many followers, especially today.

463. However is it any more true to say [. . .] that the soul is capable of drawing the idea of being from itself when sensation occurs? Such an extraordinary occurrence would be an emanation or creation, both of which are inexplicable and gratuitous.

If the idea of being were indeed an emanation, it would already be present deep in the soul and therefore innate; the soul would unveil the idea to itself as sensation occurred, although the idea as pre-existing in the soul could not then begin to exist at the moment of revelation. How this emanation takes place does not concern me; what concerns me is that we are dealing either with a pre-existing idea and this would seem to be the real case, or with the soul as producing the idea, an absurd hypothesis unsupported by observation.

If the idea of being is entirely different from sensation, how can sensation give rise to it? [. . .] Moreover, if sensation cannot present the idea of being to the subject but only move it naturally to see the idea immediately before it, would we not be aware of such a change?

464. But the fallacy of the hypothesis is shown above all by the following consideration. If the idea of being does not pre-exist, the subject cannot produce it of itself. A subject is particular, contingent and real, like all bodies and the sensations deriving from them; the idea of being is universal, necessary and possible. In a word, they are opposites: a subject is *subject*, the idea is *object*, (cf. 415-416).

465. Let us consider this last point for a moment. 'Myself', *subject*, sees the idea of being, *object*,. This is the undeniable result of observation which tells us that our mind is indeed conscious of *seeing* but not of *producing*, what it sees.

When we produce something, we are conscious of the effort made in producing it. When we simply gaze, we are conscious of not acting: the object of our vision is independent of us and has not been placed there by our eye. Similarly the idea of being stands before us as something seen, not made or produced: its essence is as independent of our spirit as a star is independent of the astronomer.

466. Finally, it is not difficult to show by means of the sublime characteristics obtained from our accurate analysis of the idea of being that the production of this idea is beyond the strength of any finite being, even of the human mind. But I think I have said enough to prove my point. I shall return later to this second, more rigorous, demonstration.

Article 5.
The idea of being is innate

§1. *Demonstration*

467. That the idea of being is innate follows from what has been said already. For:

if the idea is so necessary and essential to the formation of all our ideas that the faculty of thought is not possible without it (cf. 410-411);

if it is not found in sensations (cf. 414-439), nor extracted by reflection from internal or external sensations (cf. 438-447);

if it is not created by God at the moment of perception (cf. 461-462);

if finally its emanation from ourselves is an absurdity (cf. 463-464);

then the only possibility left is that the idea of being is innate in our soul; we are born with the vision of possible being but we advert to it only much later.°

468. This proof by exclusion is final if no other case is possible. That there is none, is shown by the following:

the fact to be explained is the existence of the idea of being in general;

if it exists, then either it was given to us by nature or was produced later; there is no middle term;

if it was produced later, either we produced it or something else did; again there is no middle term. Production by us is excluded; anything else producing it must be either feelable (the action of bodies) or unfeelable (an intelligent being different from us, God, for example, and so on), and again there is no middle term. But these two cases are excluded.

The list of possible cases therefore is complete because it has been reduced to alternatives with a middle term excluded as absurd. But if all the cases which consider the idea of being as given to us after we come into existence are impossible, it remains that the idea of being is innate and not produced. This is what we had to prove.

§2. Why it is difficult to be aware that the idea of being is
continually present to us

469. People unused to reflecting on themselves, usually make the following objection: 'How can we have the intuition of the idea of being without being aware of it, without knowing we have it or without stating it?' [. . .]

Such an objector should first ask himself what happens when he thinks about something that absorbs his attention; does he simultaneously reflect on all the other ideas acquired during life and stored in his memory? Is he actually aware of having them? He would say, I believe, that he can think or talk only of one thing at a time. Yet all kinds of topics and arguments are stored in his mind, ready to be taken out when needed. This fact implies two things: 1. many ideas can be in our mind without our giving them a thought or actually being aware of them, as if they were not there at all; 2. we cannot turn from one idea to another without some act on our part by which we disregard what we are now thinking of in order to attend to what was indeed stored in our mind but lay neglected and unnoticed.

I do not need to explain here how this is possible; observation tells us it is, and this is sufficient for the present. Nor do we need to discover the nature of facts or ideas lying unnoticed in the memory — this is irrelevant. Nothing more is required than ordinary observation which attests to the two points we have noted.

But if we need a new act of attention in order to be aware of and enuntiate new ideas, it follows that some ideas must remain unobserved and unnoticed in our spirit until some stimulus directs our attention to them. It is neither absurd nor strange, therefore, that the *idea of being itself*, lies in our soul unobserved and unenuntiated in the first moments of our existence. It cannot be otherwise, for what in fact do we observe about ourselves when we are born? So even the idea of being remains unnoticed until our reflection is stimulated to find it and contemplate it. But after reflection has sufficiently distinguished it, the idea can be enuntiated and stated without hesitation.

470. This is what happens in fact. In the first moments of our existence, our spirit has nothing to excite and direct it to reflect on itself; it has no interest nor stimulus in turning inward. In fact everything that affects a human being draws him away from himself by directing his attention to external, feelable things. From the beginning his sense-organs are struck from all directions by countless new impressions; the baby's eyes are enchanted by light, his palate and stomach cry out for nourishment; he has no interest in his spirit; he is totally unaware of his thoughts and ignorant of his nobler part. Philosophy and profound self-knowledge do not begin in the cradle, where even the body remains in great part unknown. Yet the baby has an intellect and heart as well as a body.

As the child grows, and reflection is stimulated, he begins to philosophise (philosophy is nothing but a kind of inner reflection). The philosopher's very effort to discover what takes place within him is sufficient to confirm that feelings and ideas take place unnoticed in our soul and intellect where they do indeed exist, although we pay no attention to them nor mention them to others.

In fact, to be aware of an idea in our mind, we must not only note it attentively but be drawn to do so by some special need or curiosity, although even when stimulated in this way we do not find and determine the idea quickly, always or effortlessly. If ideas and events in our spirit were continually present to us, human philosophy would be a waste of time; everybody would be a philosopher or, rather, would be intimately informed about the spirit without the accurate, philosophical meditations required to ascertain what is in us. No philosopher would know more than another, nor correct another's observations, nor affirm about our spirit what a colleague had denied. To sum up, no matter how strange it may seem, observation forces us to conclude that an idea may exist in our mind without conscious advertence, awareness, affirmation or declaration on our part; we could be unaware of it and unable to affirm it to ourselves or others.

This objection, therefore, does not dissuade us from positing the idea of being as innate. It is certain that in the first moments of our existence, and for a long time after, we are unable to observe this idea because: 1. our attention lacks a reason or stimulus for concentrating interiorly on our spirit rather than on external matters, or for focusing on what is happening within when everything draws it outside; 2. even when our attention is sufficiently stimulated in early adulthood to search for what is present and taking place in our spirit, it cannot easily discover this idea of pure being. If we wish to see the idea directly as it is, there is nothing to draw our attention to it; if we want to find pure being in the ideas we already have, which are ideas of bodies, a very difficult abstraction is required to isolate it from the other elements composing these ideas. We reach this idea only through a final abstraction, after all the accidents, forms and modes of being of an object have been distinguished and separated from it (cf. 408-411).

The spirit needs much practice to be sufficiently capable of prolonging a series of abstractions to the final point where it discovers the idea of being. Very few people have the ability and time to do this. Many give up, abandoning the path that would lead to the discovery of the reflex idea, if only they had the courage to follow it. [. . .]

PART TWO.
ORIGIN OF ALL IDEAS
IN GENERAL THROUGH
THE IDEA OF BEING

1

GIVEN THE IDEA OF BEING, THE ORIGIN
OF OTHER IDEAS IS EXPLAINED BY
ANALYSIS OF THEIR ELEMENTS

Article 1.
The link with what has been said above

473. In explaining the origin of acquired ideas through the idea of being bestowed by nature, I have not been guilty of empty theorising. My first step has enabled me to prove the existence of this one idea, which would then serve to explain all others.[9] Because all ideas are derived from the single idea of being, I now have to show that, granted this idea, all other ideas are readily explained.

Observation itself tends to indicate the idea of being in general as the source of other ideas. Of all ideas it is the

---

[9] Newton notes that two conditions are necessary if a hypothesis is to explain facts: 1. the cause of the facts really exists, and is not itself a hypothesis; 2. the real cause is *capable* of producing the facts it is intended to explain.

In addition to Newton's two conditions my own way of explaining the origin of ideas fulfils a third condition enabling it to be classed as solid theory rather than as an hypothesis. Not only do I prove that the idea of being exists with its capacity for generating all other ideas, but I also show that it does in fact generate them. Careful analysis demonstrates that the *formal* part of ideas consists only in the idea of being. But while I prove that this idea is the (formal) cause of all other ideas, I also show that this cause is a *fact*. My teaching on the origin of ideas can therefore claim a place amongst the rigorous sciences.

simplest and, as we have seen, the least innate element that can be admitted if we wish to explain the origin of ideas.

Article 2.
Analysis of all acquired ideas

474. A careful analysis of our ideas has led us to the following conclusions: 1. all contain essentially the mental conception of being in such a way that we can have no idea of anything without first conceiving *possible existence* (cf. 408-409), which constitutes the *formal a priori* part of our knowledge [. . .]; 2. if an idea contains something other than the mental conception of being, this can only be a *mode of being*. It follows that any idea whatsoever is either being, conceived regardless of mode, or being more or less determined by its modes. The determination forms *a posteriori* knowledge or the *matter* of knowledge.

Article 3.
A twofold cause is needed to explain form and matter, the two elements of all acquired ideas

475. In order to explain the origin of ideas, two things have to be accounted for: 1. the mental conception of being; 2. the different determinations of which being is susceptible.

Article 4.
The twofold cause of acquired ideas is the idea of being and sensation

476. Having shown that the mental conception of *being* is naturally innate in our spirit, there is no difficulty° in indicating *sense* as the source of the determinations of being. Let us imagine that we have to explain how we think of a corporeal being of a given size, form and colour — a football,

for instance. When I think of a football, I think two things in my idea: 1. some thing that can *exist*, because I could never think a football without thinking at the same time some possibly existing thing; 2. some thing possessing a given size, weight and shape. Granted I have the idea of possible existence, what have I to do now to explain the way in which I begin to think this football? I have to show how the possible being I intuit is determined, by means of weight, shape, size, colour and so on. This is not difficult; it is clear that such determinations of being are suggested to my spirit by the exterior senses which perceive them, and that I remember what I have perceived.

Article 5.
The true interpretation of the Scholastic dictum: 'There is nothing in the understanding that did not first exist in the sense'

478. Sense [. . .] provides only *matter* of human knowledge; *form*, the second element, depends upon the intellect. Hence, to interpret the Scholastic dictum, 'There is nothing in the understanding that was not first in the sense', as though it meant that sense were the only source of human knowledge, is to misunderstand the saying. This is the error of modern sensists. The authentic meaning of the saying, as it must have been understood by the great Scholastics, could only have been: 'Everything *material* in human knowledge has its source in sense.' I have already explained what is to be understood by 'everything material' when I said that in all our ideas we think: 1. being, as the *formal* element of ideas; and 2. a *determined mode* of being as their *material* element. The meaning of the Scholastic dictum, therefore, must be: 'The understanding cannot think a determined *mode* of being unless it is administered to it by the sense.'[o]

479. As long as we think indetermined being alone, we are not thinking anything that subsists or merits the indication *real thing*. All knowledge of what is real is suggested by the senses; *subsistence* determines being in such a way that it merits to be called *real thing*.

2

ANOTHER WAY OF EXPLAINING THE ORIGIN
OF ACQUIRED IDEAS: THROUGH THE
FORMATION OF HUMAN REASON

Article 1.
The idea of being present to our spirit forms the intellect and human reason

480. We receive the *matter* of our knowledge from sensations (cf. 476). This *matter* is not of itself knowledge, but becomes such when the *form*, or being, is added to it. This means that our spirit, simultaneously feeling and understanding, considers what it feels with its sense in relationship to being which it sees with its intellect and then discovers in what it feels something (a being) that acts upon it.

481. We have defined *intellect* as the faculty of seeing indetermined being, and *reason* as the faculty of reasoning and hence primarily of applying being to sensations. Reason sees being determined to a *mode* offered by the sensations, and unites *form* to the *matter* of knowledge. But if *being* is the essential object of both intellect and reason, these two faculties (intellect and reason) can exist in us only through our permanent vision of being.

482. *Being* as object, therefore, draws our spirit to that essential act we call *intellect*, making it capable of beholding being itself in relationship to the particular modes provided by sensations. We call this capacity, *reason*. In a word, the idea of being joined to our spirit is that which forms our *intellect* and our *reason*; it makes us intelligent beings, and rational animals.

Article 2.
Corollary: all acquired ideas depend upon the innate idea of being

486. All philosophers agree that ideas belong to our faculty of knowledge. But this faculty receives its existence from the

union of the idea of being with our spirit (cf. 470-485).[10]
Therefore, the idea of being, the principle of the faculty of
knowledge, is also the principle of all the ideas acquired by
this faculty — which is what we had to prove.

3

THIRD WAY OF EXPLAINING THE ORIGIN OF
ACQUIRED IDEAS IN GENERAL: BY THE
FACULTIES THAT PRODUCE THEM

Article 1.
Reflection

487. I have said that *reflection*, which can produce ideas,
differs from sense-instinct, found also in irrational animals as
the means by which the animal responds to sensations with its
power of feeling, seeking and concentrating on a pleasant
sensation so as to enjoy it fully (cf. 448-450).

Reflection is a function of *reason* and differs from simple
perception[11] in the following way. *Perception* is limited to the
object perceived and does not go beyond it; in so far as I
perceive a thing, I know nothing outside it. In *reflection*
however I direct my attention to things *perceived*. As a result
my reflection is not limited to the object of a single
perception; it can review many perceptions at once and make
a single object of several objects and their relationships.
Relative to *perception*, *reflection* is *general*, because it is not
limited to any number of perceptions for its object;
perception, relative to its corresponding *reflection*, is
particular. Hence *reflection* could be called a *general
perception*, a *perception of many perceptions*. Therefore when
I *reflect*, I act at a higher level than when I perceive. From this
vantage point I observe the objects below me as I

---

[10] The way in which the idea of being in general adheres to our spirit will be
explained later (cf. 534-535).

[11] I recognise two kinds of *perception*: *sense-perception* and *intellective*. [Cf. App.
nos. 2, 3, 4].

contemplate, compare, join or separate my different perceptions, creating natural or absurd compositions as I like.° I am reflecting when I turn my attention to the ideas in my mind and say to myself: 'I have ideas' and then reason about them, put them in some order, deduce one from the other, and so on.

488. If I concentrated on only one of my ideas, would I be *reflecting*? We must distinguish. If I have some definite *purpose* for concentrating on that idea, my concentration is an act of *reflection*. However such a case is contrary to the hypothesis which says: 'If I concentrate on only one idea.' When I concentrate for a purpose, I am no longer concentrating on one idea because the idea of the purpose is also present: I am considering both the idea on which I concentrate and the purpose to which the idea is directed. I am considering the idea and its relationship with the purpose.

On the other hand, if I concentrate on the idea involuntarily, captivated by the pleasurable action of its light in the same way that sense-pleasure delights and instinctively captures the activity of my feeling, then my concentration is not *reflection*, but simply direct *attention* drawn to and held naturally in a more intense act. This *heightening* of activity must be carefully distinguished from *reflection*.

'*Reflection* therefore is a *voluntary attention* to our concepts,' an attention governed by a purpose, which supposes an intellective being capable of knowing and pursuing a purpose [. . .].

489. *Reflection* therefore enables us to form *ideas of relationship*, grouping them together (synthesis) or dividing them (analysis). When I use *reflection* to analyse an idea, separating what is *common* from what is *proper* in it, I am carrying out an *abstraction*. All these actions are functions of reflection.

Article 2.
Universalisation and abstraction

490. *Abstraction* is quite different from *universalisation* and many errors have been caused by confusing them. In *abstraction*, something is subtracted from the concept, for

example, its particular characteristics; in *universalisation*, something is added [App. no. 5], and therefore the concept is universalised. Subtraction and addition are opposites.

491. In *universalisation* we add *universality* [. . .] which, as I have shown, is only the *possibility* of the thing (cf. 418-419). A precise description of universalisation would be: I receive a sensation; I add the idea of a being that is causing the sensation *(intellective perception)*; I consider this being as possible; it is therefore universalised *(pure idea)*. For example, let us suppose the being is a dove. When I universalise the dove acting on my senses, I certainly do not remove anything from it: while I still have a vivid image of the dove before me with all its physical features clearly defined, I can add the possibility of other real doves corresponding in every detail to that image. My representation of the dove is universal although it has remained what it was before I universalised it. It has the essential and the accidental characteristics of doves; only the reality is missing.

492. But if I had mentally taken away its colour, shape, movement, in fact, all its accidental qualities, replacing them with only what is essential to the genus dove, I would have also carried out an *abstraction*. My representation of the bird would be pure, abstract thought; it would be incomplete, imperfect and deficient.

493. Bearing in mind this distinction between *universalisation* and *abstraction*, we can say that all ideas are *universal* but not *abstract*. It is helpful to keep this distinction clear so that we may distinguish ideas which, because of their affinity, can be easily confused.

Observation 1. Why the faculty of *abstraction* has been confused with the faculty of *universalisation*

494. The reason for the confusion is that in every *universalisation* we set aside the judgment on the *subsistence* of the thing; this resembles *abstraction*.

495. However I think it is clearer not to use the word *abstraction* in this sense, because universalisation does not take anything away from the representation. It will help if I clarify the matter further.

The difference between the *idea* of a thing and the

judgment on its subsistence (cf. 402-407) has been pointed out: I can have the full idea of a thing without judging that it subsists. But when I judge a thing to subsist, I have at the same time the *idea* of it, and the *judgment* of its subsistence. The *idea* of the thing accompanied by the *judgment* is what I call *intellectual perception* of the thing (cf. 417).°

Intellectual perception certainly requires the *idea* of a thing but it also determines and fixes the idea on an individual actually felt. The idea, applied to something felt, *illuminates* it [App. no. 6], perceiving in it a being we call body.

If we consider the *idea* alone (one of the elements of *perception*), we see that it is *universal*; this *universality*, considered as an element of *perception*, exists in the idea. But the *universality* lies unnoticed in perception because it is considered in its relationship to the particular thing perceived by sense.

When I detach an *idea* from complete perception in order to consider it by itself, I seem to have abstracted it because I have removed its bond with the image and with the thing felt in reality; I have dismissed the *subsistence* of the thing. In this action, as I have said, there is apparently a kind of abstraction which could be called *abstraction from subsistence* or judgment.

When, in *intellectual perception*, I separate judgment about subsistence from an idea, I do not remove the core, as it were, of the idea but only those things that are not its own and adhere to it without forming its nature. The persuasion of the subsistence of the thing represented by the idea is not the idea nor anything belonging to it. So the idea itself does not undergo the slightest abstraction or change; it remains just what it was when joined with the persuasion of the subsistence of the thing.

Strictly speaking, therefore, *abstraction* has not taken place; what abstraction there was concerned only the *intellectual perception* and not the *idea*, a part of the perception. If we wish to keep the word *abstraction* in this case, we must say that the idea was obtained by abstraction carried out on the perception.

496. Again, if nothing is abstracted from the idea which is an element of intellective perception, the nature of the idea does not change when considered separately. If it is universal

when contemplated separately from the perception, it was also universal in the perception, and not universalised through abstraction. Universalisation took place at the moment of the intellectual perception before the apparent abstraction [. . .].

497. This process, inappropriately called *abstraction*, concerns the *perception*, not the *idea*. In it the following three steps must be noted:

    1. corporeal *sensation*, phantasm, sense-perception;

    2. *union* of what is felt corporeally with the idea of being in general; this takes place in our own unity, as thinking subjects (intellective perception); thus: a) a *judgment* about the subsistence; and b) the intuition of the particular being or *idea* of the thing take place in intellective perception simultaneously and with one operation;

    3. *abstraction*, or separation of the *judgment* from the *idea* that gives the pure idea alone. Although the idea was *universal* from the first moment of its existence in the perception, it was considered still bound to the subsisting individual; dissolved from this bond, it stands alone in its universality.

498. *Universalisation* therefore is the faculty that produces ideas,° while *abstraction* is a faculty that changes their form and mode of being.

Observation 2. Universalisation produces *species*, abstraction
genera

499. The ancient world classified things in two ways, as *genera* and *species*. Such a universal consensus suggests that the classification was not arbitrary but followed a distinction actually found in the faculties of the human spirit. This is in fact the case; close investigation shows that *species* and *genera* correspond to the faculties of *universalisation* and *abstraction*. The faculty of *universalisation*, which is the faculty of forming *ideas*, is the faculty relative to *species* (hence *species* are also called ideas);[12] to form *genera*, the faculty of *abstraction* is also needed.

---

[12] Originally 'species' meant 'aspect', 'something seen', 'representation', 'idea', etc., but it came to mean certain classes of things because every *idea*, being universal, is the foundation of a class.

Observation 3. Plato's theory on *genera* and *species*

500. We now have the key to understanding an important theory of Plato on *ideas*. We must note that *ideas*, which he understood to be substances separated from things and subsistent in themselves, were *species* and not *genera* [App. no. 7]. This makes me suspect that he had some notion of the difference between *universalisation* and *abstraction*.

Plato included *types* of individual things among his *ideas*. Now the type according to which a craftsman, for example, models his product must be complete in all its parts (cf. 398-401): it must have not only what is essential but also all the accidents due to it. The accidents may vary, but the product must have at least some of them - were the craftsman to have only the idea of an abstract thing without being able to add anything to it mentally, he could never produce it in reality.

501. But such an explanation would still not be enough for a proper understanding of Plato's *ideas* or for forming a true concept of the nature of *species*. We have to know more than that. Plato noticed that every being in the universe is capable of greater or less perfection; he said that we can mentally assign to any being its final and complete perfection, or at least that it is not absurd for us to be able to do that. Every being, therefore, has a *concept* that can represent it in its full, natural perfection without defect. For Plato there could be only *one* such full and absolute *concept*; no being could be thought of as having its final perfection except in one way only. This sort of intellectual *optimism* does in fact seem probable. However, leaving aside an investigation into the truth of the matter, which is the subject of ontology, I offer the following consideration.

If a being has two forms of natural perfection, it has two *primitive concepts*, two types, two ideas, which form two *species* of things. In this sense, the opinion that the individual of a species has only one form of natural perfection is true; if it had two, it would be two species or would belong to two *species*. All the *ideas* then that represent some defective being, are reduced to this *idea* of the being that constitutes its ideal perfection; they are all the same idea more or less deficient and imperfect.

502. If a craftsman had in his mind the perfect idea of the product, he could produce a perfect object from it, and produce even more easily imperfect objects, since these are relative to the perfect idea, as everything imperfect is relative to its perfect form.

503. We can now see how the *species* of a thing originates. It is constituted by the most perfect idea, which contains all the accidents of the thing. This idea, being the type of perfection, requires and determines these accidents because, from among all accidents, they are demanded by its perfection. However, the idea also has an infinite number of other ideas subject to it, which represent the being in its various states of imperfection without forming a new species. They are not truly other *ideas*, but the most perfect idea without some part or endowment which lessens but does not change it.

Article 3.
Synthesis of ideas

504. Besides the faculties mentioned above, we also have the power to devote our attention to several ideas at once and reduce them to unity by means of their relationships. This means we can form *complex ideas*.

4

FOURTH WAY OF EXPLAINING THE ORIGIN OF
ACQUIRED IDEAS IN GENERAL: BY MEANS OF A
SUMMARY CLASSIFICATION OF THE IDEAS
THEMSELVES

Article 1.
Classification of our intellections

505. I define *intellection* as every act of the mind
terminating only in an idea or in an idea joined to something
else or forming a mode of an idea.

506. Our intellections are classified as follows: 1.
intellective perceptions; 2. *ideas* properly so-called; 3. *modes
of ideas.*[13] *Intellective perception* is the judgment I make
persuading me of the *subsistence* of something (cf. 491). It
springs from two elements, *judgment* on the subsistence of
the thing, and its *idea*.

507. It will be helpful if we distinguish *modes of ideas* from
ideas, retaining the word *idea* for the *complete species* [...],
and the phrase *modes of ideas* for *abstractions* and *complexes
of ideas*.

508. Normally, however, these modes are also called ideas,
whether *abstract* or *complex*. Thus there would be three
classes of ideas: 1. ideas properly so-called; 2. abstract ideas;
and 3. complex ideas. In this case, the sources of the three
classes are the three faculties already listed: the faculty of
universalisation, which produces *ideas* properly so-called,
one of which is the perfect idea (cf. 503); the faculty of
abstraction, which produces *abstract ideas*; and the faculty of
the *synthesis of ideas*, which produces *complex ideas*.

509. However, *abstract* and *complex ideas* do not contain
more than *full ideas* (cf. 507). All three kinds of ideas are
distinguished only by the different way in which our mental

---

[13] *Memory* and *imagination* form part of these intellections. Memory is concerned
with past intellections, the imagination with intellections formed in the likeness of
others already experienced. But examining them here would complicate matters.

attention focuses upon them. Ideas are *full*[14] if we think of them as they first show themselves; *abstract* when we consider any part of them, disregarding other parts (abstraction, analysis); *complex* when they are considered as joined to other ideas (synthesis). These phrases indicate three *modes* of intellectual attention, and hence three *modes* of the ideas which are objects of attention; but strictly speaking, they do not indicate three classes of *ideas*.

Article 2.
The basic difficulty in explaining the three listed classes of intellections

510. Our mind carries out three successive operations: 1. it perceives intellectually; 2. it separates the idea from the perception; 3. it draws abstracts from ideas, that is, the bonds which unite ideas and produce complex ideas.[15] The first operation is carried out by means of *universalisation*, the second by an *abstraction exercised on the perceptions*, the third by an *abstraction exercised on ideas* already formed.

511.   No   faculty   of   *reflection*[16]   is   necessary   for

[14] *When first generated*, the ideas of things are *full species* (that is, they possess all the substantial and accidental constitutives of things), but they are not *perfect species* because they are not produced by perfect things. Species are perfected by another operation of the spirit which I call *integration*.

[15] Complex ideas are brought about by reflection after the formation of *abstract ideas*. After explaining *reflection* and *abstract* ideas, it is not difficult to understand how *complex* ideas come about, and hence unnecessary to explain them further at this point.

[16] *Universalisation* has no need of reflection if we mean by reflection the *aptitude possessed by the understanding for turning its attention toward the products of its own operations*. On the one hand, we have *sensation*, a direct act of our spirit; on the other hand, the intuition of being, another direct act. Between the two lies the unity of the spirit reaching out simultaneously to the sensation and the idea. The subject's awareness of feeling sensation and intuiting the idea is *universalisation*, almost whole and complete. But if reflection were to mean an aptitude of the spirit *for turning towards its own operations*, there could be a partial *reflection* in the primitive synthesis, and in the universalisation it contains. The subject, joining the idea of being to its sensations through the unity of its feeling, turns towards its *sensations*, but by means of a very different kind of act which of itself is direct and straightforward. In this case, one could distinguish between *reflection upon direct sensations* and *reflection* upon ideas. Reflection upon sensations is a *direct* act relative to the understanding to which alone it belongs, but a *reflexive act* relative to the spirit, to which it belongs in equal manner, and to the sensations towards which it turns. I note this in order to avoid all ambiguity. For the rest, I generally use the word *reflection* to indicate reflection carried out by the understanding, not by the spirit. [. . .]

universalisation. Universalisation is a direct, natural action of our spirit which, abandoning the judgment on subsistence that forms part of perception, retains the *determined ideas*, that is, the union between what is felt and the idea of being, brought about by the work of a sentient subject intuiting the idea of being. The determinable idea of being and the thing felt that determines the idea happen to find themselves together in the same subject.

512. *Abstraction* on the contrary is an operation belonging to the faculty of reflection. It is clear that I cannot abstract anything from my perception unless I turn back to it, just as I cannot abstract anything from my idea until I consider it reflexively.

513. The *primitive synthesis* containing *universalisation* is not deliberately thought out, although it is bound up with an external element. It is carried out, or at least helped, by the careful watch set up in human beings by nature. It is as though the human being, through his essential understanding of being, had an eye open to everything passing before him. In this case, it is not difficult to understand that, given the sensations, the primitive synthesis is achieved spontaneously by the soul which, relative to the synthesis, is already active by its own power. There is no need for me to explain how the spirit moves towards universalisation once its first, essential activity has been demonstrated and established. It would be like explaining at length how the sun illuminates an object on which it shines when it is already known that the sun radiates light continually on everything around. But it is still necessary for me to describe universalisation accurately, and analyse it into all its parts.

Abstraction, on the contrary, is an act of reflection, and consequently depends upon the *will*. Like its faculty, it is voluntary , and of itself remains motionless until activated by the will. We have to find, therefore, a *sufficient reason* to explain the will's desire to reflect upon perceptions and ideas, to abstract ideas from perceptions, and to draw abstract ideas from ideas. Lack of a sufficient reason for the movement towards reflection would leave unexplained the acts of the faculties, the origin of abstract ideas, and the complex ideas springing from them.

In attempting the explanation, we suppose that the *perceptions* are already formed. But we shall come back to them later, and show how they can be brought about by means of the primitive synthesis.

Article 3.
Our intelligence needs language as a stimulus in forming abstracts

514. Our reasoning faculty has no energy of itself independent of external stimuli. This truth can be shown from experience, and from the nature of human intelligence. 'If we were left solely to ourselves and to the internal forces arising from our nature, without our being affected in any way by forces foreign to us, we would be incapable of activating ourselves or carrying out any intellective operation. If the Almighty were to keep us in this state of isolation from other beings for thousands of years, we would remain motionless without a single thought. We would be totally at rest, with inactive minds, because stimuli and terms would be lacking; our life could be compared only to non-existence. This kind of life, may I say in passing, is a worthy object of philosophical consideration, and a key for explaining marvellous secrets in the study of human beings' (*Theodicy*, no. 90).

Summing up, therefore, we have to see what kind of stimulus is needed for: 1. perception; 2. ideas; and 3. abstract ideas. We must also discover how the reason is activated relative to all three.

§1. Our spirit is drawn to the act of *perception* by feelable things

515. Our spirit cannot perceive anything not present to its perceptive faculty.[17] Thus the human being can neither feel nor think unless some term is presented to this faculty; without this term, he remains immobile, bound by one of the limitations of human intelligence. It follows that the action of

[17] Not as bodies are present to one another, but as the terms of acts are present to the spirit that carries them out.

our spirit is limited by its term. But although it is the term that draws our intelligent spirit to act and to find rest after acting, we also have to say that the presence of a term provides an explanation only for the special activity of the spirit to which it gives rise and offers repose. A term is incapable of explaining any activity of a nature or higher grade than it can absorb.

516. According to these principles, bodily elements experienced by our senses can move the spirit only to *perception*, not to abstraction or some other act. Sensations present feelable things to our spirit and give rise to a new activity beyond the innate capacity for seeing being, but the activity of our spirit is limited and finalised by the terms themselves. The activity of the spirit stimulated by feelable things cannot exceed and surpass feelable things. Thus feelable things cannot provide suffcient explanation for the formation of abstracts, which are insensible objects, by the spirit.

If sense presents me with something corporeal, I have no difficulty in understanding how my intelligence can be attracted and moved to see such a corporeal being. Because my intelligence is naturally awake and active, the appearance of a term is sufficient to stimulate attention and vision. But what meaning is to be attached to 'the presentation of such a term to the intelligence'? What is it that presents the term to the intelligence? Only feeling; nothing else can do it. As sensitive beings we receive the action of corporeal agents in us by means of our sense organs. Because the agent is in us through its activity on us, it is present where it can be seen by our understanding. It is not difficult to grasp how we see that which is in us. As I have said, we have already opened the seeing eye of our intellect to the vision of all that takes place within us, in so far as it operates through the senses[18] (cf. *Theodicy*, no. 153).

In a word, we can understand how feelable things are capable of attracting our spirit to themselves, and how what is felt can be grasped by us. Everything needed by our mind for such an operation is present. We have: 1. the *faculty*,

---

[18] We are speaking of external sensations. The same can be said about feeling.

intelligence; 2. the terms presented to us, which stimulate our intelligence to an act terminating in them. Granted sensations, there is no difficulty in understanding that intelligence forms for itself perceptions of corporeal individuals. In other words, what is felt requires nothing more than itself in order to be perceived by us intellectually.

517. We can go a step further. People do not always mistake the *corporeal images* of what they see for subsisting things themselves; they understand the difference, whatever it may be, between real things and their images. It is at least probable, therefore, that these *images* stimulate us to form *pure ideas*, devoid of any *persuasion* of the actual presence and subsistence of beings. Thus, just as *sensations* occasion *intellectual perceptions*, so weaker images occasion *ideas* of corporeal beings, devoid of persuasion and judgment about their subsistence. This kind of *abstraction*, which separates *ideas* from *perceptions*, seems to find its explanation in *phantasms* or *corporeal images* in the same way that *perceptions* of bodies have their explanation in *sensations*.

Observations. The limits of development attainable by human beings outside society if sensations and bodily images were the only stimuli of their reason

518. *Intellective perceptions* and full, specific *ideas* follow *sensations* and *phantasms*, and *phantasms* follow *sensations* and other phanstams. Feelable things, therefore, granted their presence, provide sufficient explanation: 1. for all the *activity* unfolded in human beings through *feeling* and *corporeal imagery*; 2. for all the activity manifested in human beings through the laws of *animal instinct* corresponding to those two faculties; finally 3. for all the activity shown in the formation of *perceptions* and *full, specific ideas* of corporeal things.

Let us consider briefly the nature and limitation of this third kind of activity. *Intellective perceptions* and *full, specific ideas* of material things are such that they follow and are indivisibly joined to *what is felt* and *what is imagined*. *Intellective perception* contains a judgment about the *subsistence* of what is felt, but nothing more. It terminates in a particular felt thing, and is therefore an *idea* accompanied by *sensitive perception*, to which it adds *judgment about subsistence*. *Idea* and *sensation* are bound together in *intellective perception* and obliged to move in harmony like a pair of human eyes. More accurately, we could say perhaps that the idea is like an impetuous horse yoked to a plodding ox whose lumbering pace it has to maintain.

An *idea* joined to a *sensation* cannot extend beyond the limits of the sensation; by this kind of idea human beings are confined to the sphere of movements and actions common to animal sense and instinct. This explains why people separated as infants from society and left without human companionship or language are in a pitiable state when found later after years in which their only stimulus has been sensations. They have been unable to rise above the feelable things comprising animal life, and their only guide has been instinctive behaviour. They are not without reason which, however, follows instinct instead of guiding it. Their way of life could not be called human in the sense used of life amongst people born and reared in society. The same is true, more or less, of the uneducated deaf and dumb, and is what we would expect on the basis of the principle established above: 'The action of our spirit is limited by its term' (cf. 515).

As long as the term of the spirit is limited to corporeal elements (which in this case we presume not to have reached the status of signs), the human being, whose activity is limited to and completed by them, can think only of *bodily, individual* things. His ideas are tied to sensations and images, from which they cannot be separated. The spirit can go no further; sensations and instincts are its sole guide.

§2. Corporeal images are sufficient explanation of the spirit's activity in forming *ideas* separated from perceptions

519. *Abstraction* is carried out in two ways on what is present in our intelligence. Broadly speaking, it is exercised on our *perceptions* by separating *ideas* from them; strictly speaking, it is exercised on *ideas* from which it produces *abstract ideas* (cf. 494-498). Both operations may be carried

out by *reflection*, which is however indispensable for the second.

Abstraction exercised on *perceptions* consists in fixing one's attention solely on the *apprehension* of a thing (idea), to the exclusion of the *judgment* on the thing's subsistence. Exercised on *ideas*, abstraction consists in *reflecting* upon them while fixing attention on a single part of what is contained and thought in the idea. The part reflected upon may be an essential or an accidental element of the whole being considered in the idea. The first type of abstraction leaves the idea whole and entire, still a complete object with all its parts; only *persuasion* about the object's subsistence is lacking.

520. *Persuasion* about the subsistence of any thing can be disregarded not only through reflection, but naturally, as we have indicated, by means of the *corporeal images* remaining in us and reactivated according to certain animal laws governing our internal sensibility. Such images are not always sufficiently vivid, complete, consistent and coherent to prevent human beings from knowing them as different from the real, present beings actively impressing themselves on our external sensory organs.

§3. Language provides sufficient explanation of the spirit's activity in forming abstract ideas

521. How is the reason activated to form abstracts? If *sensations* and *images* are incapable of activating it for this purpose, what other stimulus will draw it to the growth and development implied in its possession of abstracts?

First, in order to remove possible objections, we must note that 'the natural act of the intelligent spirit in focusing on being is totally insufficient to turn the mind to abstractions.' Being is the ever-present *object*, holding our spirit in a *first act* constituting human intelligence. But the spirit's activity ends and comes to rest in its object, not outside it (cf. 515). The object, *being in general*, instigates in the spirit only the activity terminating and coming to rest in itself. The primitive activity of our spirit, therefore, is an immanent act, unmoved by any accidental disturbance; it is a firm, uniform, continuous vision of being, and nothing more. As an immobile, direct act, it provides no explanation of the spirit's activity in applying itself to particular beings and their (abstract) modes.

As we shall see immediately, abstraction is explained by signs. An *abstract idea* is only *part of an idea*. Hence, our spirit's activity in forming *abstract ideas* will be explained if we can show what motivates it to suspend its attention from the idea as a whole and concentrate exclusively on a part of it. It is this discriminatory activity which needs causal explanation.

Let us take as our example the abstract idea of *humanity*. *Sense* offers our understanding the matter with which to perceive *real human beings*. The general notion of *humanity*, however, deprived of all the accidents proper to single individuals, does not fall under our senses nor possess any feelable elements. *Images* of human beings already perceived will be activated in us (with varying degrees of vividness) by similar sensations either accidently or through some internal movement in the nerves. They will provide some impetus for my intelligence, but only enough for me to form a full *idea* of one or more human types. The idea of *humanity* is altogether different: it is not a sensation, not a corporeal image, not an object of perception, nor an idea detached from perception. How then can it be explained?

The law we have discovered and established about forces that move our attention may be stated thus: 'Our spirit is drawn to the act of perception by the terms presented to it' (cf. 515). But can *humanity* which is not real and does not exist be presented to us in person? Obviously some *vicarious sign* of it is needed. Humanity has no existence outside the mind and cannot draw the mind's attention to itself except through a feelable *sign* which, existing outside the mind, can take the place of that idea and in some sense cause it to subsist. The mind cannot be stimulated to think *abstract ideas* which have no corresponding realities, unless feelable signs replace, represent or activate such realities in our minds. But how can *signs* perform this task?

Both *natural* and *conventional signs*, especially words, express everything added to them by tacit or express agreement. They are equally suitable for indicating a subsistent thing, a sensation, an image, a complete idea or part of an idea, or a single quality common to several objects and isolated from them, even though this quality does not subsist outside the mind in which it has its existence as an ideal object. If words can do all this, as we see they can, it is obvious that in the same way as they draw our attention to what subsists by indicating and expressing it, so they can draw our attention to any other meaning they may have. When they are used to indicate abstract ideas, they can draw us to them in such a way that our attention is limited to and concentrated upon the abstract qualities signified by the words; anyone listening wants to understand what the word says, and nothing more.

522. Note that I do not intend to deal with questions of fact about the divine or human origin of language, nor with the philosophical question of the possibility of language.° I take language as it is transmitted by the society in which we are born, and proceed to affirm that it is suitable for stimulating the attention of the child, who hears language from the moment of its birth, to discover the meaning of the sounds, and to find amongst the different meanings the ideas of qualities and relationships continually named and expressed by the words.

Nor is it my intention to describe in detail the fact I have in mind, or show how *natural language* is the child's first key to its understanding of *artifical and conventional language*. Daily experience is sufficient to show clearly that children first understand words expressing subsistent, real things related to their needs, instincts and affections, and then come to understand and speak the whole language. This is enough to remove any doubt about language's capacity for drawing attention to abstract ideas, that is, to forming them, because in every language and reasoning and judgment, the most noble and important part is formed by abstractions.

If language can achieve what is impossible to sensations, images, and the idea of being, it follows that the child's development towards the use of *abstractions* is totally dependent upon the assistance provided by language. A good negative example of what I mean is found in human beings lost as children, and later rediscovered as adults incapable of speech. They give no sign whatsoever of having conceived abstractions mentally, nor of being raised in any way above the level of material, individual objects. The same can be said about uneducated deaf-mutes.

Observation 1. An objection drawn from human freedom

523. It may be objected that free, human activity, which renders the human being master of his own powers, can direct attention where it wills, and specifically to ideas in their entirety, or to parts of ideas. This intrinsic activity, by which a human being deliberately restricts his attention to part of an idea and to a single common quality, could enable him to form abstract ideas without need of *signs* determining and fixing these qualities and parts by removing and separating them from the whole.

524. Careful observation of the laws and conditions according to which our free activity is employed is sufficent to overcome this objection. I am certain that human activity is stimulated in two ways, *instinctively* and *deliberately*. So far we have spoken of the *instinctive* stimulation of activity: the act is drawn out physically, as it were, by its term when the *impression* made by an agent draws the sense to feel, and the sensation stimulates the imaginative faculty. All this depends upon sense-instinct. But there is also *rational instinct*,[19] drawn naturally by sensation to the perception of the corporeal agent, and by the *phantasm* to the *idea*, that is, to the object, without added persuasion of its subsistence.

I grant that instinct also leads human beings to express outwardly, by words, gestures and even sounds, what they feel and understand inwardly. Moreover this instinct, in so far as it is sense-instinct, generates inarticulate noises and exclamations, expressive of feeling; in so far as it is rational instinct, it will profer a few articulate words, signs of perceptions and ideas. But such instincts will never bring human beings to express what they have not yet mentally

[19] The active faculty of *rational instinct* corresponds to the receptive faculty of being (intellect). *Spontaneity* properly speaking means the mode of operation of sense-instinct, rational instinct or moral instinct.

conceived, such as abstractions. *Sense-instinct* and *rational instinct* have their limits beyond which they cannot progress. Can the free will make these instincts go further, without the stimuli and assistance human beings receive from the society of their fellows?

Free will is conditioned by a law requiring it to have a purpose as sufficient reason for its acts. Free, intelligent will cannot therefore do anything without having an end in view that enables it to be active and mobile. The aim bringing me to restrict my intellectual vision to a quality common to many objects, whilst ignoring all other qualities, is my natural desire to produce *abstract ideas*. But can I propose to form *abstract ideas* for myself if I do not have or know any, and am unable to see how they can help me, or what value they have for me? It is certain that no one can propose for himself an aim of which he is ignorant, and in which he sees no advantage or need. In our case the necessary *condition* enabling the free will to impel itself to discover abstract ideas is lacking. The sufficient reason, the *end* from which it gains its motivation, is unknown, as is the *good* obtainable from this end. Thus there is no knowledge to interest and move the will to abstract ideas. My free will cannot urge and direct my intelligence to *abstract mental concepts* without first possessing some abstract mental conceptions. It cannot *move* the intelligence to an abstract idea if it is ignorant of all abstract ideas: *voluntas non fertur in incognitum*; it lacks all *stimulus*. Nor can the free will *direct* the intelligence because it lacks the notion of an object to serve as a *rule* with which to guide the intelligence. But if our free will needs abstract ideas before it can form abstract ideas, we have to conclude that it is impossible to explain the formation of these ideas by free, human activity without language.

Observation 2. Human development by means of society and language; the necessity of language, if human beings are to be masters of their own powers

525. We have seen that signs are needed if human free will is to motivate itself to form abstract ideas. We must now add that *abstract ideas* are always necessary to our will if it is to be

able deliberately to move its other powers. The will does not, in fact, decide to move its powers, the attention, for example, except for some *good* which it understands. But activating oneself for some good presupposes an abstraction, that is, some *relationship* of end to means, which of its nature is an abstract idea.

526. Moreover, how can I deliberately move my attention from one idea to another except through a relationship binding together in some way the ideas to which I successively move my attention? Every relationship between two things or ideas is an abstract, that is, neither the one idea nor the other, but a connection that each has with my mind as it thinks them; every *relationship*, therefore, is an *abstraction*.

Let us imagine that I decide to take a holiday for health reasons. As I deliberate, I think of the *suitability* of the holiday for a cure; I think of the journey in front of me, and the *means* I shall need to reach my destination. This *suitability* and these *means* are both abstract ideas.

I could also imagine myself thinking through all the new knowledge I have gained from conversation with some cultured person. What binds together the series of thoughts running through my mind? I can distinguish them from all other thoughts, and look upon them as a class in themselves only through an abstract idea, a *relationship* common to all the knowledge acquired through my conversation. This common quality or relationship enables me to review on its own the knowledge acquired in this conversation. If I make up my mind to think, and decide to choose one argument from the many which could presently exercise my intelligence, I must be acting for a purpose, for a reason, for some idea bound up with that argument; and this *bond* is an abstract.

Without *abstracts*, therefore, I cannot use my free will, nor can I direct my intelligence in one way rather than another. *Abstracts* bind together my particular ideas, and provide a passage from one to another. Without abstracts, ideas would remain totally divided and separate from one another. My attention would be fixed upon each of them individually without its being able to turn towards them as a group and embrace them collectively in a single glance. There would be no reasoning because the whole operation of understanding would end where feeling itself ends. Abstractions are of the utmost importance.

527. We have seen that abstracts are obtained with the help of language coming to us through human society. The proposition I set out to demonstrate is, therefore, true and irrefutable: 'Language is necessary to make us masters of our own powers'; and every great advance made by mankind is due to this immense benefit we receive from the society of our peers.

Article 4.
Intellective perception explained

§1. The only intellective perception we have is of ourselves and of bodies

528. At our birth, nature endows us with the intellective perception of ourselves and of bodies. In fact the only way we can *perceive*[20] *the subsistence* of a being, is when we feel its action in us. *Feeling* therefore is necessary for the intellective perception of some subsistent thing. Now the only *feeling* we have is: 1. of ourselves; 2. of bodies. Therefore we have *intellective perception* only of ourselves [App. no. 8] and of bodies.

§2. Explanation of the perception

529. If one of the two kinds of perception is explained, the explanation of the other will follow. Let us take the explanation of the perception of bodies. We recall that we are affected by *sensations* which immediately tell us some thing exists (*judgment*) and is determined by the way it affects us (*idea of bodies*). There is no need to explain the *sensation* (the first part) in this sequence because we start with it as a simple, basic fact. Nor do we need to explain the nature of the *idea* of bodies (the third part), that is, the *way* some thing judged to exist is limited and determined by sensations. I shall try to do this in a later chapter when I examine our idea of bodies.

---

[20] We can *believe* and be persuaded that other beings subsist but this must not be confused with *perception*, which takes place directly through our external and internal senses.

What must be done here is give a satisfactory explanation of the *judgment* we make as a result of sensations that: 'Some thing different from us exists.' This judgment gives rise to the *perception* of bodies, that is, the persuasion of their actual, particular existence (subsistence).

§3. Explanation of the judgment generating the perception of bodies

530. The idea of being in us does not by itself make us know any particular being but only the possible existence of any being. *Existence* means actuality, because the concept of existence is only the concept of a *first action* [. . .]. So it is impossible for me to conceive existence mentally without conceiving an *act of existing*, since both these expressions mean exactly the same. The *act of existing* can be thought in two ways, either by not applying it to what is real or by applying to something real.

If I think the *actuality* of existence without applying it to anything real, I think the *possibility* of beings and nothing more, which is the idea given us by nature. If I think the *actuality* of existence in something real, I think of what I call *subsistence* or real being, which is the *judgment* that produces *intellective perception* and is what I want to explain.

When I make this judgment I add nothing to the idea of existence (cf. 402-407); all I do is concentrate on the existence I have thought of in something real. Such an action of my spirit takes place when I think of actual existence in general. To think of actual existence means to think a first *action* (cf. 530). Sensations are *actions* in us of which we are not the authors. As *actions*, sensations suppose a *first action*, an existence. Sensations are also determined actions and therefore suppose a *determined first action*. A *determined first action* is a being existing in a determined way. If we compare the *experience* we have (through sensations) with the *idea of actual existence*, we find that this *experience* is a particular case of what we were thinking previously with the idea of *existence*. We were thinking an *action* with this idea but not affirming or determining it. In the sensation, or more correctly in what is felt, we know a determined being, a certain body.[21] But because we naturally think of the *action* in itself (existence), so in experiencing an action (a sensation) our spirit notes action itself in its limitations. We recognise it precisely through what we were previously thinking by saying to ourselves: 'This is one of the actions (or a grade and mode of action) that I was thinking with my spirit.' The act of noting this particular case, of recognising what is happening in us as part of what we were previously thinking, forms the perception of the real thing, that is, the judgment we are examining.

In this judgment we focus our spirit (which previously had nothing to concentrate on but rested quietly and uniformly in *possible being*) on some particular, limited being in which it finds being realised. It notices what it already knows, it finds, we may say, what it was seeking. This explains how we make a comparison and judgment between *what is felt* and the *idea of being*. It also explains how what is felt becomes the *subject* in so far as it is contained in the idea of being, the *predicate*.

To understand this more clearly, let *sensation* and *indetermined existence*, the two things we wish to compare, be reduced to the same terms. Both are *actions*, but *indetermined existence* is *action* void of real conditions; *sensation* is *action* limited by real conditions and determinations. There is nothing extraordinary then in my noticing and recognising a *particular action* when I already possess the notion of *universal action*. From *action* it is easy to come to a *being*, which, as I have said, is nothing but *first action*. If there is an action there must be a first action, for no second action can exist without first action.

Article 5.
The necessity of intellective perception

535. Must our spirit immediately perceive some being when it has sensations? This question of fact is not relative to my purpose at the moment; I am concerned with a different kind of necessity relative to *perception*. I maintain that if our spirit understands something, it must understand in the way I

[21] Thus it is very easy for a child to pass from sensations to making a judgment on subsisting beings. This judgment is only an intellective perception carried out by the very nature of the child's intelligence. In many theories the judgments made by children in their early years on the existence of substances are inexplicable.

have described, that is, by the primitive judgment through which it recognises that the being it is thinking has a subsistence in the way determined and limited by sensations.

What I have said so far demonstrates this necessity. I have shown that the essence of understanding subsistent things is nothing other than giving such assent or forming the judgment I have described.

In fact, granted that our spirit has the idea of being and necessarily sees it always; granted that this idea is what forms our intellect and reason (cf. 480-485); and granted therefore that the nature of the intelligent spirit consists in intuiting being, then the law of intelligence is: 'To conceive nothing mentally except as a being, a thing.'⁰

536. This law of intelligence is neither *subjective* nor arbitrary; it is necessary in the sense that its contrary cannot be thought. Indeed, it would be a contradiction in terms to say our spirit knows things presented to it without its conceiving anything. But to conceive something is the same as conceiving a being. The general formula therefore that expresses the necessary nature of intellectual perception is: 'Judging, affirming, being persuaded that a being subsists with its determinations.'

To clarify the matter further, let us suppose that we have received sensations from bodies but do not have the interior power to see being and therefore could not consider the sensations in relationship with being. In this case our spirit would have been modified by the corporeal sensations without their appearing as determinations of being; we would not perceive a determined being, a subsisting thing, a body. To perceive a body is to perceive a determined being. The sensations would not be perceived by our understanding; they would remain only in our feeling, and therefore we would know nothing. To be able to know the *body* (the name 'body' itself was invented as a result of intellective perception) as well as feel it, we must have the power to see a determined being where the sensation is.

The intelligent spirit therefore does not know except by means of the idea of being it has. To know is only to conceive a *determination* of possible or common *being*, a determination that makes it a being in its own right.

5

THE INNATE IDEA OF BEING RESOLVES THE GENERAL DIFFICULTY OF THE PROBLEM OF THE ORIGIN OF IDEAS

Article 1.
The difficulty solved

539. I have reduced the difficulty contained in the problem of the origin of ideas to one, simple question: 'How is the first judgment possible?' In Locke's hypothesis, which derives all ideas from the senses, the difficulty is insuperable. But granted and proved that a completely universal idea naturally exists before we experience sensations, there is no difficulty in understanding how the first judgment is formed.

Article 2.
Objections and answers

§1. First objection

540. Nevertheless, we have to examine objections to our conclusion. First: the judgment said to be necessary for the formation of ideas was shown to be the same as the mental conception of ideas, which must be brought about through judgments. If this is true, an innate, competely universal idea offers no solution to our difficulty because it too requires a judgment in order to be conceived mentally. To say that this idea is innate resolves nothing; it can only mean that it is conceived mentally by us through our natural powers from the first moment of our existence. If this is the case, all ideas will be conceived mentally through judgment, and we find ourselves face to face once more with the difficulty: 'How can we make the judgment enabling us to conceive mentally the most universal idea?'

Reply to the first objection

541. The objection depends upon the false supposition

that: 'A judgment is necessary for the mental conception of all ideas.' It is true that a judgment is needed for *ideas which we form*, such as those of bodies, which unite predicate to subject. Here we find two elements, one of which must be universal. But it is not the case with an idea comprising one element only, which does not require a judgment in order to be possessed and conceived. Judgment, we remember, is always an operation of the mind bringing together two terms. The presence of one term alone would not require any kind of *judgment* which would indeed be impossible because pre-empted by an immediate *intuition*.

Amongst the ideas we possess, only one, the idea of being, has the unique characteristic of utter simplicity. Not composed of predicate and subject, it is the one idea needing no judgment in order to be conceived mentally. It cannot, therefore, be *formed* by means of some mental operation, but only *intuited*. Equally, it cannot be intuited unless present to our spirit. Thus we have a new, very clear demonstration that the idea of being is given to human beings by nature.

§2. The first objection renewed

542. Nevertheless, I accept that it is very difficult to understand how the idea of *being* can be intuited without admixture of some kind of judgment in the intuition itself. At first sight, it would seem that the idea of being could be expressed in the following proposition: 'Any thing can exist.' But this is a judgment. We conceive this possibility mentally by judging: 'Any thing is possible.' Such a judgment, however, would be included in the idea of being, as our own analysis of it shows (cf. 424). There we found the idea of being to comprise three elements, two of which are: 1. the idea of any thing; and 2. the possibility of any thing. In these two elements we seem to have come across the kind of predicate and subject necessarily expressed in the proposition: 'Any thing is possible.' The *possibility* is the element providing the predicate, while the indetermined *thing* is the element forming the subject.

We must now confront this difficulty.

A further reply

543. The difficulty rests upon the uncertainty presented by the concept of *possibility*, which requires further analysis. We first note that we must not confuse this *logical possibility* of which we are speaking with *probability*. The two things are quite different.

What is *logical possibility*? By a *possible* entity we mean an entity that *can* subsist, that is, can be thought as subsisting. Everything not involving contradiction is said to be possible. The mind can always think it exists, and can imagine it to exist whenever it wishes.

For a thing to be declared *impossible*, the mind must possess a necessary reason excluding the possible existence of the thing, so that either the reason must be shown to be false or the thing must be declared impossible. A reason acknowledged as necessary cannot be false, and the thing under discussion must be declared impossible.

The contrary of *impossible* is *possible*. When we rightly state that something is impossible, we must possess a necessary concept contradicting the very thing we are considering. On the other hand, the *possibility* of something requires only the absence of any concept rendering it incoherent and contradictory. If there is no necessary reason to the contrary, everything is *per se* possible.

It is characteristic of our mind and language that the word *possibility* takes on a positive meaning. Language expresses both positive and negative beings by words, that is, positive signs. This makes for confusion. For example, when we say *nothing*, we exclude the existence of everything, although we think we have said something because the sign for *nothing* is a word.

The same cannot be said of *probability*. While *possibility* indicates only the absence of contradiction, *probability* adds some positive reason to the mental entity which renders the entity's present or future existence probable. The reason may be the number of times the thing has happened, or the knowledge of a special, subsisting power capable of producing it.

It is clear that we take *possibility* in its absolute, logical sense, not in the approximate sense of ordinary conversation. People say: 'It is impossible for this tree to be in the garden without the presence of a seed from which it grew.' This is physical impossibility, and as such clashes with the physical law requiring plants to grow from seeds. Again, people say: 'Granted the risks you take, it is impossible for you to escape serious injury.' This so-called impossibility is in fact improbability, because in the ordinary course of events it clashes with the chances of remaining uninjured. But we are not thinking about impossibility that clashes with physical laws, nor about the impossibility of avoiding the natural consequence of actions, nor about the impossibility of breaking moral laws; we are dealing with impossibility that conflicts with the laws of thought in such a way that one term of a given proposition cannot be mentally conceived as existing along with the other term. Everything not involving such a contradiction we call possible.[22]

544. The *possibility* of a thing is not, therefore, positive in itself, outside the thing. It is, as they say, a mental entity or an observation made by the mind about some essence in which it cannot find intrinsic repugnance. We express this lack of ideal, intellectual repugnance through the word

[22] Certain things contain a hidden *logical impossibility*, not immediately evident. This situation arises when the idea we have of something is defective because too extensive. We do not consider the thing in itself but take it indiscriminately as forming part of a genus or species. In this case, we have to sift it thoroughly by examining both the thing itself and its characteristics. It is not sufficient to consider only its common qualities in order to be sure of its possibility. A mathematical example may be useful here. 'What is the square root of 2, expressed in a finite series of numbers?' The answer to this problem seemed possible before mathematicians started to work on it. They concluded, however, that there could be no answer, and produced a demonstration of the impossibility of expressing the square root of 2 in a finite series of whole numbers or fractions. A similar demonstration is applicable to all *recurring* numbers. In our example, it was necessary to demonstrate the *impossibility* of the problem because the impossibility was hidden and not immediately obvious. The reason for such mental imperfection, which obscures the impossibility of certain things and consequently impedes certainty about their *possibility*, lies in what we have said about the *indetermination* of the idea of being. This idea is a *tabula rasa*, in mere potency relative to determined beings. The mind cannot form a judgment about them or their possibility: 1. without thinking of determinations; and 2. without confronting the determinations with the idea of being, their supreme norm. In a word, the *rule* for judging the possibility of things is innate, but the *judgment* about their possibility, and the matter required for such a judgment, is not innate. The judgment has to be made, and often not without considerable difficulty [. . .].

possibility, giving the impression of something separate from the mental entity, although this is not the case.

All mental entities are in fact the fruit of observation indicating some lack, or relationship, or quality, etc. Considered separately and of themselves, they cannot be present to our mind from the beginning of our existence; they can be noted and considered by us only as our understanding develops.

We conclude that the *possibility* of things, as a mental entity capable of being expressed through a word, is not innate in us, but observed through an act of our mind. *Possibility*, as simple lack of incoherence, tells us only that the *idea of being* contains no contradiction. As a consequence, there is no incoherence in anything we behold in this idea; possibility therefore is not something distinct from *ideal being* itself.

It follows that our only innate element is the idea of being in all its simplicity. Possibility, as a predicate, adds nothing to this idea but excludes something from it (incoherence) and serves to simplify it, allowing it to be recognised in its unity and simplicity.

545. Granted these principles, the proposition 'Any thing can exist' is inexact if used to point to what is innate. The proposition supposes that we have mentally extracted *the idea of possibility*, a purely mental entity, from the simple idea of being and given a positive form, such as a thought or a word, to what is negative by nature. In other words we have changed the idea of possibility into an apparently positive predicate.

If we wish to analyse the proposition 'Any thing can exist' in order to discover its innate elements, we need to strip it of all that has apparently been added to it by the way we conceive and express something. We first need to change the statement 'It is innate that any thing is possible' to 'It is innate (that is, it is naturally present to our spirit) that the idea of being is free of contradiction', or to 'The idea of being is innate; reflecting upon it, we see it is without contradiction.' Because the idea of being, as objective form, constitutes our intelligence, intelligence can be defined as the faculty of seeing being. Further reflection shows that if the vision of being were removed, our intelligence would cease. Being therefore cannot be eliminated or removed from the mind. But removing being and leaving being is a contradiction which our intelligence cannot tolerate. Our intelligence can understand only that which does not involve contradiction; this alone is intelligible and thinkable.

546. It is only *a posteriori* that we observe the many determinations taken by being in the real beings we behold. This leads us to declare that the possibility of things is contained in the essence of being. But this, in turn, simply means 'There is no incoherence between the idea of indetermined being and its determinations and realisations.' The concept of possibility involves a *relationship* with the *determinations* of being, which are unknown to our spirit until we apprehend them through experience.

Summing up, we may say that after observing *being* to be devoid of determinations (this is a negation, not a positive predicate), we conclude (after reflection) that real beings, indetermined in quantity, are possible and thinkable as determinations and realisations of the essence present to our spirit. In other words, these real beings involve no contradiction with the idea itself, while the idea accepts them in itself without incoherence. The concept of mere possibility is, therefore, *acquired* as our faculties develop. There is nothing innate except its foundation, that is, the ideality and indetermination of being.

The idea of being, the innate element devoid of any predicate whatsoever, is itself the universal predicate. Deprived of all determination and real action, it unites and applies itself as predicate to determinations and actions which thus become subject. The idea of being includes no judgment, therefore, but constitutes the *possibility of all judgments* in so far as we can judge anything we feel by means of the idea of being, the common predicate within us.°

§3. Second objection

547. The previous objection was based upon possibility, one of the two primary elements of the idea of being (cf. 423). Its solution depended upon showing that this element is negative when conceived mentally separate from being, and

hence takes nothing from the simplicity of the idea of being which it serves to express.

The second primary element, that is, *any thing* or being, gives rise to another difficulty in understanding how the idea of being can be present to us without the intervention of a judgment. It may be stated as follows: 'Two terms are distinguished in my mental conception when I intuit being: *myself* who intuit, and being as intuited. During this act my consciousness tells me: I perceive being. But this is a judgment, and it would seem therefore that judgment must be present in every objective mental conception that is something more than mere subjective modification.'

Reply to the second objection

548. Our answer lies in an observation that cannot be overlooked, despite its subtlety.[23] The act of intuiting being is entirely different from the act by which I say: 'I intuit being.' Note that I am not asking whether this act follows or must necessarily follow from the other. It is only necessary, at the

---

[23] It would be poor method if I regulated my observation of nature by deciding to record only the most obvious facts. If I were to omit to verify observations requiring repeated, tedious experience and were satisfied with approximate results, I could rightly be accused of wanting to make a fool of nature and of those I am trying to instruct. It would be incredible presumption for me to attempt to construct theories without trying to lay solid foundations for them because facts were too difficult to ascertain or too obscure to clarify. This, however, is the method adopted by the materialist and sensist philosophers who have allied themselves with Locke, and it has even rubbed off on serious students, like Bonnet, who prided himself on rigorous method. Bonnet dismisses feeling of our own existence for the following reason: 'It is not good to admit any feeling of our existence of which we cannot form an idea. There is no doubt that it is better to confine our attention to CLEAR MATTERS we can reason about.' (*Analyse abrégé de l'Essai analytique, II*). But affirming that we want to accept only what is altogether clear in nature is equivalent to admitting very little. Nature, as we know, is full of mystery and obscurity. And if we set out to look for what is *good* rather than what is *true*, who knows what each will take as matter for his philosophy. What is the *good* or the *better* to which we will confine our attention? In fact, it is the philosopher's responsibility to observe nature whole and entire, just as it is. Not only must he admit what is clear, he must accept and clarify, through hard work if necessary, what is *obscure*. The true philosopher, when faced with difficulties and mysteries, increases his efforts to penetrate the secrets of nature. If he still does not succeed in making progress, he admires the wisdom that has made nature so sublime and so profound. Certain questions cannot be neglected, whatever facile philosophy asserts. They must be faced courageously, and modestly. In particular, the fundamental feeling is a matter of such importance that its exclusion from philosophical observation on the grounds of its obscurity destroys any hope of progress in the theory of knowledge.

moment, to know if *intuiting an idea* and *judging that an idea is intuited* are different acts of the spirit.

Intuition is the act by which I fix my attention on an idea. Weak and inconsistent attention, dispersed over many objects, does not change the nature of the act which, it is important to note, is essentially one in so far as its object is one. Wandering attention, although it may associate other unique, entirely different acts with it, does not destroy the uniqueness of the act; each act considered in itself remains unique. Our task is to examine the simple, unique act of attention to an idea, independently of all other acts which may be found mingled with it. Of itself, the act with which I fix my attention on an idea is essentially restricted to the object in which it terminates.

549. First, let us try to find some state in which our spirit concentrates all its force of attention on a single point. This will help us to consider one act of attention separated from every other. Let us imagine that the object of our attention is something we love so much that all our powers of concentration are totally focused on it. As our contemplation grows and reaches a certain point of intensity something strange occurs. Enthralled by the desired object, we have no energy for anything else. Absorbed by this one object, we are in a state of ecstasy where we forget ourselves and everything else; external things no longer exist for us. All our thinking and loving energy is captivated and exhausted by what we behold. Such alienation, experienced probably by all human beings although at different levels of intensity, is a fact, and lesser degrees of alienation in our own lives enable us to form some notion of the total experience.

The question we have to put to ourselves is this: if a person finds himself in such a state, will he pay attention to himself? Will he be capable of reflecting upon his own state? We say that this capacity for reflecting upon himself will be on a par with that of a baby totally absorbed in its feed. He can carry out this kind of reflection on himself and his own state of self-forgetfulness only when he has come to himself and woken, as it were, from his absorption. His energies, previously occupied and almost lost for his own purposes, are now available for self-reflection. However, if his heart and mind are fully and completely immersed in the ecstasy, there is no immediate connection with any following act. All his energies have been exhausted in the ecstasy itself, forcing him to rest before acting once more. There is no connection with his previous intense action, which he cannot even remember. Dante noted this peculiar state when he wrote:

'Its longed-for aim achieved
Our mind, constrained by love,
Unmindful is of love received' (*Par.* 1).

550. What we have said helps us to realise that reflection on the operations of our spirit is an act entirely different from the operations themselves. We can state, therefore, that human beings can think an object, such as being for example, without *reflecting* upon themselves or realising that they are thinking.

Now it is clear that no one can make the judgment 'I intuit being' without reflecting upon himself, paying attention to his state of mind, and making it the object of his attention. *My state*, however, is not the same object as *being*, and I need to perceive my own state by means of an act different from that by which I intuit being. I intuit being through an act of attention directed at being; I perceive myself with an act of attention directed towards myself. When I intuit being, my attention is fixed simply on an *object* very different from *myself*. Perceiving *myself*, my attention is fixed on an object identical with the intuiting *subject*. Again, the first act is an *intuition, the second a perception* relative to myself, a *reflection* relative to being. The act, therefore, by which I intuit being is simple, primary and spontaneous; the act by which I judge myself to be intuiting being is complex (it is a judgment) and derivative. The intuition of being can be innate; the reflexive judgment cannot be innate although the second act may follow more or less closely upon the first. The first is intrinsic and necessary; the second can simply be acquired and voluntary.

551. Distinguishing these two acts, I referred to the state of a person totally occupied by a single object. I did this in order to assist comprehension of the fact at issue, not to prove the distinction made between the two acts. In a state of mental concentration, the energies of our intelligence are all reduced

to a single point of focus,[24] and it is easy to see how one act, normally accompanied by another, can stand on its own. My purpose here, however, does not require me to show one act of attention as temporally distinct from the other. It is enough to indicate that one is not the other in order to prove that one can be innate, and the other not.

My argument would be considerably strengthened were I to insist upon a truth known to classical philosophers, that is, that the understanding can perform only one act at a time, and that *being* (or anything conceived mentally) and *myself* intuiting are two objects requiring two acts of understanding in order to be grasped. In this case, it would be absurd to think they could be grasped simultaneously, or to imagine that in understanding one object I also *know* that I understand it. The argument would be strengthened still further were I to prove the evident truth that the second act, having as object the first act, could not begin to exist without presupposing the first to be already complete. This would clearly indicate the contradiction inherent in claiming as simultaneous the act by which we know something, and know that we know it.

Corollary 1. There is an idea prior to every judgment

552. From what we have said, it follows that a first, natural intuition within us precedes every judgment we can make. This intuition makes us intelligent beings, and forms our faculty of knowledge. The object of the intuition is *ideal being*, the idea.

---

[24] Human absorption in the contemplation of an object gives me an opportunity of commenting on a very common false judgment. When a person has difficulty in remembering something, or experiences a sensation without noticing it, or pays only little attention to it, it is often said that the impression or sensation made upon him must be rather weak. But the explanation could be exactly the opposite. The sensation, and we can say the same about the act of contemplation, could have been intense without its being noticed or reflected upon. It seems to me that when sensation or contemplation is intensified to the maximum, the person experiencing it knows, notices and remembers nothing of his experience: he is no longer present to himself, but constrained by the experience itself. The relevance of this remark for understanding what takes place deep within the human spirit will best be seen by those accustomed to serious reflection in matters of this kind.

Corollary 2. Human beings possess an intellectual sense

553. Being, therefore, is intuited by our spirit without mediation, just as sense receives its impression from what is feelable. The immediate presence of being to the spirit enables us to speak of an *intellectual sense* possessed by human beings.

Our intelligence can be called a *sense* (not a corporeal sense, however) in so far as it intuits being. But in so far as it judges, or notices the relationship between what is felt and being in general it carries out a mental operation very different from that of sense. It no longer receives sensations, but pronouncing and synthesising produces knowledge and persuasion.°

Observation 1. The difference between corporeal and intellectual feeling

554. The difference between *corporeal* and *intellectual feeling* lies in the diversity of their terms. Corporeal feeling has determined and real, corporeal terms; intellectual feeling has a purely spiritual and perfectly indetermined term.

The difference between these terms gives rise to another distinction between the two feelings. Although the nature of *feeling* in general requires an action done in a subject, or a modification undergone by the subject, in corporeal feeling the object is not communicated as object, but as an *acting* force. In intellectual feeling, the *object* is manifested as object, not as agent, because properly speaking an object is characterised by presence and manifestation, not by action. Consequently, intellective feeling does not first sense itself, but immediately understands being. Only then does it experience joy from its understanding of being (intelligence). We can say, therefore, that intellective feeling follows intelligence. Being in general is idea; but the subject intuiting it, *produces for itself* intellectual sensations from this idea [App. no. 9].

Observation 2. The nature of *ideal being*

555. From what we have said, it can easily be seen that besides the form of being possessed by subsisting things (REAL being, as we have called it) there is another, entirely distinct form, constituting the foundation of the possibility of things (the IDEAL form). IDEAL BEING is an entity of such a nature that it cannot be confused with either our spirit, or with bodies, or with anything belonging to REAL BEING.

556. It is a serious error to believe that IDEAL BEING or THE IDEA is nothing because it does not belong to the category of things common to our feelings. On the contrary, *ideal being*, the *idea*, is an authentic, sublime entity, as we saw when we examined the noble characteristics with which it is furnished. It is true that it cannot be defined, but it can be analysed, or rather we can express our experience of it and call it the LIGHT of our spirit. What could be clearer than light? Extinguish it, and only darkness remains.

557. Finally, from what has been said we can form a concept of the manner in which the idea of being adheres to our spirit. We realise that it neither asks nor demands our assent or dissent, but *presents* itself to us as pure fact (cf. 398), because such an idea neither affirms nor denies; it simply constitutes our possibility of affirming and denying (cf. 546).

PART THREE.
ORIGIN OF THE FIRST
PRINCIPLES OF REASONING

558. So far we have seen how the intuition of ideal being is proper to the intelligent spirit and necessary for its existence (Part One). Granted that *ideal being* is present to the spirit, we have shown how the origin of other ideas is explained by means of *sensation* and *reflection*. We have also shown that ideas as a whole originate in this way, and have applied the argument to certain broad, general classes of ideas (Part Two). We must now deduce in another way various ideas and cognitions strengthening our theory and making it easier to use. For the sake of clarity, let us begin with necessary, basic cognitions. They are: 1. the *first principles* of reasoning; and 2. certain *elementary* and very abstract ideas always taken for granted in human reasoning, without which reasoning is impossible. Once possessed, these principles and elementary ideas become instruments enabling our mind to perform its noble operations and produce new ideas and knowledge. We begin therefore with the supreme principles of human reasoning.

1

THE FIRST AND SECOND PRINCIPLES:

COGNITION AND CONTRADICTION

559. Principles are expressed by propositions which, when analysed, must be reduced like mathematical formulae to their simplest expression. When dealing with a formula, mathematicians may reduce it to the expression most suitable for their purposes, provided they do not change the value of the formula or alter the equation.

560. A *proposition* expresses a *judgment*, that is, a relationship between two terms, *predicate* and *subject*. Because the *principles* of reason are judgments, they comprise a predicate and a subject. Therefore the simplest and most natural expression of the principles of reason is that which directly indicates the predicate with one distinct word (or phrase), the subject with another, and the connection between them with a third. Let us take the principle of contradiction as our example.

561. The principle of contradiction, in its simple form, is: 'That which is (being) cannot not be.' 'That which is' is the subject; 'not be' is the predicate; 'cannot' is the copula expressing the relationship between the two terms. In this judgment, the relationship between *being* and *not-being* is *impossibility*. We have seen that logical *impossibility* cannot be thought and is in fact *nothing*. The principle tells us that *being* (that which is) cannot be thought at the same time as *not-being*. When *being* and *not-being* are put together therefore, we have both an affirmation and a negation, that is, nothing; not-being cancels being previously posited and all thought disappears. The principle of contradiction is simply the *possibility of thought*.

562. Without this principle, therefore, investigation of other matters is impossible. We cannot doubt its existence, validity or effectivenes. Like any other thought, a doubt presupposes the principle as already valid and effective; we cannot begin to think, to question or reason without presupposing thought, questioning and reasoning. In this way the principle of contradiction is completely safe from any attack. Attacking it demands thought but, in order to think, thought has to be *possible*, and this is precisely what the principle of contradiction states: we cannot think without thinking! If we think at all (no matter what we think) we admit the principle of contradiction, which states: 'I think or I do not think; there is no middle term, because to think without thinking is impossible.' The principle of contradiction therefore is independent of all human thought and opinion, which is possible only with this principle.

563. Someone might say to me: 'I deny the possibility of thought.' I would reply that to deny the possibility is to think

it! I would ask: 'Do you think at all? Your answer is either
that you think or do not think; whichever it is, you confirm
the principle of contradiction. To invalidate the principle,
you would have to reply: "I am thinking while I am not
thinking", and this would be ridiculous and meaningless.'

564. But let us return to the analysis of the principle of
contradiction which is a proposition expressing the following
fact: 'Being cannot be thought at the same time as not-being';
in other words 'Thought does not exist unless it has being for
its object.'

This fact which I have observed and, it seems to me, proved
beyond doubt, is the idea of being informing and producing
our intelligence (cf. 473-557). Thus we often define
intelligence as 'The faculty of seeing that which is' (being).
The phrase 'being and not-being' expresses *nothing*, and
nothing is the opposite of *some thing*, of *being*. By showing
that our intellect and reason is the faculty for seeing being, I
have also shown conversely that it is not possible to see
nothing, which is all that the principle of contradiction
affirms.

This principle therefore draws its origin from the idea of
being, the form of our reason; it is nothing more than the *idea*
of being considered in its application.

565. As Thomas Aquinas and Bonaventure have said, the
principle of contradiction is in a certain sense innate [App.
no. 10]. According to them the principle reveals itself from
deep in the human spirit at our first use of reason. However it
seems more strictly true to say that while the foundation of
the principle is innate, the principle itself is not.

Principles take the form of *judgments* and are expressed by
propositions. Any principle may presuppose some reasoning
except for the absolutely first principle which is not under
discussion here. In fact the principle of contradiction can be
deduced from a preceding principle, the *principle of cognition*,
which is expressed by the proposition: 'The object of thought
is being or a being' (cf. 535-536). I reason as follows: 'The
object of thought is being; but the phrase "being and not-
being" expresses *nothing*, and *nothing* is not *being*. Therefore
being and not-being is not an object of thought.'

566. Hence, for the *idea* of *being* to have taken the form of

the principle of contradiction, I must have used it, that is, have begun to judge and reason. I must have formed a mental being, *nothing*, and acquired the ideas of *affirmation* and *negation* by thinking, and seen that negation plus affirmation equal nothing.

Judgment and reasoning, although naturally and closely tied to the idea of being and carried out promptly, are only the *idea of being in its application*, disguised and accompanied by relationships. Our reason needs to be released like a spring from its initial state of complete inactivity. But anything in us resulting from such contingently intellectual movement is *acquired*. Such is the principle of contradiction in its explicit form of a judgment.

2

THE THIRD AND FOURTH PRINCIPLES:

SUBSTANCE AND CAUSE

567. The *principle of contradiction* depends on the *principle of cognition* (cf. 565), which is a necessary fact expressed as follows: 'The object of thought is being.' It is the principle of all principles, the law of intelligent nature, and the essence of intelligence.

The second principle is that of *contradiction*, derived directly from the first: 'Being and not-being cannot be thought at one and the same time.'

The third is the principle of *substance*: 'Accidents cannot be thought without substance.'

The fourth principle is *cause*: 'A new entity cannot be thought without a cause.'

568. *Accidents* are perceived through actions on us and can also be called by the general name, *happenings*, which is very appropriate because they are something that happens in substance without being necessary to it. There is no difference between *accidents* and *effects* except that *accidents* are considered as one thing with the substance and terms of it, while *effects* are considered separate from their cause, and

proper to some other being. With that understood, the way we deduce the *principle of cause* will serve as an example for deducing the *principle of substance*,° which the reader can deduce for himself.

569. The principle of cause derives from the *principle of contradiction*, and hence from the *principle of cognition*, in the following way. The principle of cause can be stated as: 'Every happening (anything that begins) has a cause that produces it.' We found this expression elsewhere and analysed it; at this point we must recall the analysis.

'Every happening has a cause that produces it.' This proposition means exactly the same as the following: 'It is impossible for our intelligence to think a happening without thinking a cause that produced it.' To show that 'a happening without a cause cannot be thought', we must show that 'the concept of a happening without a cause involves contradiction.' Once this is demonstrated, we will have deduced the principle of cause from the principle of contradiction.

The demonstration is as follows: to say 'What does not exist, acts' is a contradiction. But a happening without a cause means 'What does not exist, acts.' Therefore a happening without a cause is a contradiction, which was to be proved.

As regards the major: to conceive mentally an action (a change) without a being, is to conceive without conceiving, which is a contradiction. Indeed, the principle of cognition states: 'The object of thought is being'; therefore without a being, we cannot mentally conceive. To conceive an action without conceiving a being that performs the action, is to conceive without conceiving. Therefore to apply the action to something that does not exist is a contradiction in terms, which was to be proved.

As regards the minor: a happening is an action (a change). If this action has no cause, it is conceived by itself, without belonging to a being; there is then an action without a being or, which is the same, what does not exist, acts. Thus the minor is proved.°

The principle of cause therefore derives from the principle of contradiction, and both derive from the principle of cognition, which is only the *idea of being in its application* where it takes the form of a principle and is expressed in a proposition, when considered in relationship with human reasoning of which it is the formal cause.

3

THE NATURE OF SCIENTIFIC PRINCIPLES IN

GENERAL

570. We have seen that the principles of cognition, contradiction, substance and cause are only the *idea of being in its application*, or the law governing its application and expressed in a proposition. This observation opens the way to understanding the nature of all the *principles of reasoning* which in general are only *ideas* used for making judgments. The application of these ideas can always be conceived as a judgment, and expressed in a proposition. The proposition serves as a norm for forming a series of more particular judgments, virtually contained in the first, most general judgment to which they are subordinate. This first judgment is a *principle* relative to others deduced from it. Such deduction is called reasoning.

571. For example, the *idea of justice* becomes the *principle* of ethics when we reason and systematise its applications; the *idea of beauty* becomes the principle of aesthetics when it is considered as directing, regulating and indeed originating all our reasoning about what is beautiful. Hence the *definition of beauty* is only the proposition resulting from an application of the idea of being, and is the first principle of any reasoning about what is beautiful.

572. Generally speaking, then, the *essence* of things is the *principle* of our reasoning about them.

573. The principle of each science therefore is the *definition* that expresses the essential idea of the subject of that science. From this truth comes the *art of classifying* the sciences correctly and reducing them to unity. They are no longer mere collections of disconnected information but well ordered treatises, each regulated by a single principle from

which other truths are clearly seen to originate like rays of light from a common source.

PART FOUR.
ORIGIN OF *PURE* IDEAS,
WHICH DERIVE NOTHING
FROM FEELING

1
ORIGIN OF ELEMENTARY IDEAS OR CONCEPTS
OF BEING PRESUPPOSED IN HUMAN
REASONING

Article 1.
List of elementary ideas of being

575. The elementary concepts conditioning all human reasoning are principally the concepts of: 1. unity; 2. numbers; 3. possibility; 4. universality; 5. necessity; 6. immutability; 7. absoluteness.

Article 2.
Origin of these concepts

576. All these concepts, contained in *ideal being*, are its characteristics and natural qualities. As a result, they are given to our mind together with being itself. We simply have to note them one by one, distinguish them within being, and assign each a name. We do this through various uses of the idea of being, and of reflection.

577. This explains why such concepts, although so far removed by nature from material determinations that their formation would seem to require a long, difficult process of mental operation, are familiar to all human beings and presupposed by them. In fact, they are the most obvious, easily known and available of all human concepts.

Observation

578. Taken individually, these abstract concepts are an element of an idea rather than an idea itself. Of themselves, they provide no content to our knowledge. For this reason, I call them *elementary concepts* of the idea of being. Generally speaking, abstract ideas are said to be *elementary concepts* of the idea from which they are abstracted.

2

ORIGIN OF THE IDEA OF SUBSTANCE

583. So far I have shown that ideas taken as a whole, together with the principles of reason and in particular the ideas which I called *elementary concepts of being* that serve as conditions for the use of reason, have their origin, on the occasion of sensations, in a first idea naturally present to our spirit. As we saw, this theory overcomes the difficulty of the origin of ideas on which so many philosophers, and philosophy itself (cf. 539-551), foundered.

We also noted that the difficulty, set out by us in a general way, presented itself under particular forms to others who attempted to explain the origin of special classes of ideas. It would be helpful, therefore, if I carried on to show how the theory could resolve not only the general difficulty but also its individual manifestations. This implies that all special ideas, which have caused endless trouble to so many philosophers, can be deduced from the supreme idea of being.

We have, however, already dealt with the elementary ideas of being. We can turn, therefore, to the ideas of substance and cause as the closest to the first ideas, and the most difficult and necessary to examine.

Article 1.
The question relative to the origin of the idea of substance

584. The difficulty encountered in indicating the origin of the idea of substance is compounded by the inexact, confused

concept of substance many philosophers have created for themselves. They confuse the idea of substance as a genus with the ideas of specific substances. For example, they maintain that because we cannot know the substance of bodies, we cannot have the idea of substance. This is far from being a rigorous argument.

It is clear that we could have the idea of *substance as a genus* without knowing intimately any *substance* connected with particular things. It is as though we saw a weight suspended from a column without knowing whether its support was a piece of chain or a length of rope. We could be ignorant of the material and shape of what holds the weight and nevertheless realise that there must be some kind of support.

Our own case is somewhat similar. In order to know that a substance must be present, it is not necessary to know that it is the substance we call 'body' nor do we need to understand its nature fully. Conversely, we do not have to conclude that we have no notion of substance as a genus if we do not know what forms substance in bodies. Indeed, we could not know that some substance was necessary to bodies if we had no notion of substance.

585. As someone said not long ago, to demonstrate that we possess the notion of substance is to beg the question.[25] We have to ask those who deny the existence of the notion of substance how they can deny what they admit they do not know.[26] As I have noted many times, the idea of substance is a fact witnessed to by the human race, including those who deny it in words. Even if mankind were deceiving itself, and believed it possessed an idea that it did not in fact have, it would still be necessary for it to think it had it. But thinking it has an idea, and having one, are equivalent because an apparent idea is no less an idea than any other. Further than this one cannot go.

[25] 'I know I am guilty of begging the question when I discuss such a matter. I set out to see if the notions of substance and cause are present to the human spirit while I, a human spirit, put these notions before myself after defining them. It is clear that I am begging my own question, just as it is clear that I am objecting to myself. As Pascal put it so well: "Evidence is not to be proved"' (Cousins, *Fragments philosophiques*, p. 425).

[26] Sceptics create their own difficulty in imagining that *ideas* are external, and mediated. On the contrary, they are totally interior and immediate and, as such, outside controversy. They are facts.

Article 2.

Description and analysis of all that we think about substance

§1. The starting point for the study of ideas of substance

586. First, we must ascertain the facts by verifying our cognitions and thoughts about substance. It is these cognitions or thoughts which must be explained.

One fact is this: the mind thinks of substance. To say: it is an illusion, or it is a false thought, gets us nowhere and is irrelevant to our discussion. Our mind has its thoughts, true or false, illusory or real, and it is our task to explain their origin. The philosopher must indicate the cause of what the mind *thinks* it does, as well as what it does. When we find the origin of the thoughts that we believe we have about substance, we shall be able to weigh their value and decide what legitimate use we can put them to. Their origin determines their authenticity and truth, or shows them to be spurious illusions — at least in their applications (it is impossible for them to be illusions *per se*). Our first step, therefore, is to analyse everything the human mind mentally conceives about substance.

§2. Definition of substance

587. Substance is 'the energy by which a being and all that it possesses actually exists,' or 'the energy in which the actual existence of beings is grounded.' The relationship of *substance* and *accident* is not fully developed in this definition, and will have to be dealt with later.

§3. Analysis of the concept of substance

588. Let us analyse the concept to find how many ways the mind conceives this energy. We note two elements: 1. the act of existence, or that energy by which a being exists[27]; 2. the being itself that exists (the essence).

---

[27] *The energy that constitutes the actual existence of beings* and *the energy by which they exist* is one and the same. The first expression explains the second. In a word, we must not make two things of the *energy* we are speaking about and the *actual existence* of beings. The *actual existence* is the *energy* itself.

The distinction depends upon an abstraction, which is exactly what we need because we are speaking of what exists in the mind, not outside it. What is in the mind is seen separate from other things only by means of abstraction which is incapable of producing division in things subsisting outside our spirit. Abstraction is a fact, an operation of the spirit.

It is also a fact that many thoughts can be abstracted from a single thought. Although our attention is first directed to one entire thought through a single act, attention can then split into as many acts as there are parts of the thought to turn to.

It would be unreasonable to object here, as modern sophists often do, that we are abusing abstraction in order to create imaginary beings. The objection is an attempt to evade the core of the question which requires us to explain the fact of abstraction and its products. We cannot prescind from abstraction, nor avoid noting and describing the different thoughts and concepts it forms and originates in our spirit. Whether ideas respond or not to something outside the mind, they remain ideas, and we have undertaken to explain them all [. . .].

§4. Different modes of the idea of substance

589. What are the different modes that can be taken by our idea of substance?

1. We can think *energy* in general by which beings exist. In this case, we do not think any particular being, but a possible being, without any determination except that necessary for its existence. This is the idea of *substance in general*.

2. We can think the *energy* of a being furnished with some generic determination. This is the idea of *generic substance*.[28]

3. We can think the *energy* predicated of a *specifically* determined being. In this case, we think the actual existence

---

[28] It is necessary to recall what has been said about *genera* and *species* (cf. 499-500), and the way in which we mentally conceive these classifications.

possible to an individual of a determined species furnished with everything necessary to its existence, that is, with what is common and proper. When the mind thinks the possibility of such an individual's actual existence, without knowing whether it exists, it has the idea of *specific substance* which is either an idea-exemplar or can be reduced to the state of idea-exemplar.

590. Before going further, let us examine carefully these three more or less abstract ideas of substance. We have called them: the *idea of substance in general,* the *idea of generic substance,* and the *idea of specific substance.* In all three of these mental conceptions we think of an individual, a single, undivided being, furnished with everything necessary for existence. The difference between them lies in the *mode* according to which each one is thought, that is, with or without its determinations.

A question may help to clarify the matter: when I think substance in general, what am I thinking? What is comprised in this idea of *substance in general*? I think a being (an individual, therefore) that possesses the energy called actual existence. I am not asking to which class, or genus, or species it belongs; I think only its energy or actual existence. Along with this, I think implicitly that the being is determined to everything required for existence, without, however, mentally determining or seeking what these determinations or properties may be.

The idea of *substance in general* contains, therefore: 1. the thought of actual existence; 2. the thought of an individual which exists; 3. the general thought of the determinations it must have in order to exist, that is to say, its thought as a complete being, with everything necessary for existence. But there is no attempt to know what is necessary for determining the being to a complete type.

Similarly, three elementary thoughts can be distinguished in the idea of *generic substance*: 1. the thought of an energy constituting existence; 2. the thought of a being possessing in itself this energy; 3. the thought of the determinations necessary in order that this being exist as an individual.

The third part of these two ideas is variable, and the different modes in which we mentally conceive the third element accounts for their difference. In the idea of *substance in general* we think the being as it is in itself with all the determinations or properties necessary for existence, but without specifying the determinations in any way. In the idea of *generic substance*, however, we think certain generic determinations of the being. For example, we think of a spiritual or corporeal substance. We are not thinking of an individual in general, but of an individual of a determined spiritual or corporeal genus.

Finally, the idea of *specific substance*, if *full*, contains the individual with all its determined generic and proper characteristics. If I think the substance of an individual tree, and not of any tree whatsoever, I must think a tree furnished with all its distinct notes and characteristics.[29]

In all three ideas of substance, therefore, we think some totally determined thing which lacks nothing to its being except subsistence. We call this thing an *individual*. An architect who designs a house with all that it needs for existence thinks a perfect house. Building it, he adds nothing to its idea, which already embraces every part of the house; but he makes the house by giving it existence in itself without losing the ideal existence he has conceived mentally with all its particulars.

Hence, we can think an individual in general when we think all that is necessary for a being to exist without determining any of its characteristics. We can think of a generic individual when, in addition to what is necessary in general for its existence, we begin to think of a being's generic qualities. Finally, when we add specific to generic qualities in addition to what is necessary in general for its existence, we can think of a specific individual. Summing up, we may say that we can think any individual whatsoever, an individual of a determined kind, and a specific individual.

If I think the energy by which an individual can subsist, I think substance in general; thinking the energy by which an

---

[29] We shall see later (cf. 646-659) that it is not necessary for me to offer another class of ideas of substance to accommodate imperfect individuals in a species. Ideas of this kind are ideas of perfect individuals (specific, complete ideas) from which certain valuable characteristics have been removed. Moreover, we are not speaking here of any affirmation of *subsisting* individuals; these fall under our *judgment*, not under our *ideas* alone.

individual of a given genus can exist, I think generic substance; thinking the energy by which an individual of a given species can exist, I think of special substance. The idea of substance in general, of generic and specific substance are always ideas of *energy* constituting actual existence which can only be proper to *individuals*.

§5. Origin of the idea of individual

591. I cannot think the actual existence of a being unless I think simultaneously that this being receives every determination necessary for its existence. The idea of *individual*, therefore, is intimately connected and associated with the idea of substance. Explaining the origin of the idea of substance presents us with the explanation of the origin of the idea of individual. But there can be no other ideas of substance or individual in our mind except the three, general, generic and special, we have listed. Our next task is to describe the origin of each of them.

§6. Ideas of substance differ from judgments on the subsistence of substances

592. Nevertheless, we have not yet explained all our thoughts about substances. Besides *ideas*, we form *judgments* on the real subsistence of substances. Like the architect with a complete idea of the house he is about to construct, we represent an (as yet) non-subsistent being in our idea. As long as we think only of the possible subsistence of the individual, we have not reached out to anything that really subsists.

But let us grant that an individual corresponding to our idea really subsists, and that we can perceive it. How does our perception take place? We have already seen that we affirm, by means of a judgment, the subsistence of the individual we think of in the idea. Let us be quite clear that the act by which we say 'Such a thing subsists' is an operation of the spirit essentially different from simple intuition. It unites to the idea of the thing a *persuasion* or belief in the subsistence of what has previously been thought as possible.[30] It follows that as there are three ideas of substance, so there are three judgments that we can make about the subsistence of these substances in so far as we can judge: 1. that a substance merely subsists; 2. that a substance of a given kind exists; 3. that a substance of a given species exists.

§7. Summing up of all the thoughts the human mind can furnish about substances

593. Our thoughts about substances consist in *ideas* and *judgments*, both of which provide a threefold classification: the idea of substance in general, the idea of generic substance, the idea of special substance; judgment about the subsistence of a substance in general, judgment about the subsistence of a substance of a given kind, judgment on the subsistence of a special substance. We have to describe the origin of all these ideas and judgments, showing how they are possible to the human mind.

Article 3.
The three ideas of substance follow one from the other

594. Let us see if we can facilitate our study by avoiding separate treatment of each of the ideas and judgments we form about substances. First, we can lighten our work by noting the connection which binds the three ideas in such a way that one gives rise to another. If, therefore, we can explain the origin of one of them, we have explained the origin of the other two.

Let us take for granted the idea of special substance. In order to possess the ideas of generic and general substance, it is now sufficient to abstract them from the idea of special substance which provides us with the idea of the actual existence of a being, fully determined in its common and proper characteristics. If we set aside its special characteristics

---

[30] To object that in doing this we acquire a new idea, the idea of subsistence, would be out of place because this was already present; without it, we cannot think 'a being *can* subsist.' The *persuasion* of real existence is something entirely distinct from *mental conception*; its nature is totally different from that of ideas.

we are left with generic subsistence; setting aside generic determinations, we are left with the universalised idea. In a word, the ideas of general and generic substance are only abstractions of the idea of special substance. When we have explained this, we will have explained the other two.

We have already used this method in clarifying the *status quaestionis* (cf. 41-44): explain one idea, and the rest can be explained by means of abstraction. If we restrict the problem to that of substance, it can now be stated as follows: 'We need to explain the idea of specific substance; the explanation of other ideas of substance will then be clear.'

Article 4.
All judgments on the subsistence of substances are explained when one difficulty is overcome

595. What is the origin, therefore, of the idea of special substance? As we search for the origin of this idea, we find it connected with the judgments we make on the subsistence of beings. If we focus our attention on this connection and penetrate its meaning, we notice that a single explanation will satisfy two questions: what is the origin of the idea of special substance? and what is the origin of the judgments we make on the subsistence of substances? We have already pointed out that we make three judgments about the subsistence of substances. If we consider their connection, we shall see how the same difficulty is present in all three.

In judging the subsistence of: 1. any individual being whatsoever; 2. an individual of a certain kind; or 3. a certain species, we have to be prompted by some reason which determines us to affirm the subsistence of individuals. This reason is our perception of the individuals, and once found it explains how these judgments are formed by our spirit. In all three kinds of judgments, therefore, the single difficulty we have to solve consists in showing what prompts us to say, 'Such an individual subsists.'

Article 5.
The explanation of the specific idea of substance depends on the difficulty found in accounting for judgments on the subsistence of substances

596. We must, therefore: 1. indicate the manner in which we form the idea of specific substance; 2. show the reason leading us to judge of the subsistence of these substances. This is our problem, stated simply (cf. 594-595). But granted the connection between the two questions, it can be put even more simply if we take account of the reason prompting us to posit the subsistence of an individual.

We say to ourselves 'Such and such an individual subsists.' Included in the perception of this individual is the idea of substance which, as the energy providing the individual's existence, must be conceived mentally if we wish to conceive a subsistent being. The two questions can, therefore, be reduced to one: how can I judge that a being subsists? If I make such a judgment and perceive the being, I inevitably perceive its substance and easily form or rather have already formed an idea of it.

Article 6.
Explanation of the perception of individuals

597. We have already explained carefully how intellective perception of individuals takes place, and how we form our ideas about them as we make the judgments affirming their subsistence (cf. 528-534). We are now in a position, therefore, to sum up and resolve our present question:

1. We form ideas of individuals by means of the judgment we make about their subsistence;

2. We can draw the abstract idea of special substance from the intellective perception of individuals. From this idea we can draw the more abstract idea of generic substance, from which in turn we can draw the idea of substance in general;

3. The intellective perception of individuals has already been explained.

No difficulty remains, therefore, in explaining both the origin of the three ideas and of the judgments we make about substances.

3

ORIGIN OF THE IDEAS OF CAUSE AND EFFECT

Article 1.
Purpose of this chapter

615. The idea of cause, taken with the idea of substance, forms the basis of human knowledge. We shall not be wasting time, therefore, if we try to clarify its origin and show its validity clearly enough to prevent foolish attempts to overthrow the foundation of knowledge, the source of human dignity.

Common sense asserts: 'That which happens must have a cause.' Our aim is to discover why human beings agree about this; why they accept it as evident; why they use it as a rule from the moment they begin to reason, although forming it much later as an abstract proposition worthy of philosophical attention. The origin assigned to the idea of cause must show how it comes to exist in the mind and explain the facts we have indicated. How is this idea conceived so easily? How can the uneducated, and even children, employ it as soon as they begin to chatter? How can we explain children's fascination with the *why?* of things, and their determination to know the cause of what affects their senses so wonderfully?

To answer these questions, let us: 1. express as clearly as possible the proposition we want to demonstrate; 2. analyse it in order to pinpoint its difficulty; 3. explain the difficulty.

Article 2.
The proposition

616. We have to demonstrate the following proposition: 'Every fact (change) necessarily requires a cause capable of producing it.' By *fact* I mean any *action* whatsoever, whether its effect is found externally or internally, provided it

indicates some change or, in the most general sense, some movement. It is not necessary for me to describe the various kinds of possible *actions* because my intention is to include in this word any type of action whatsoever. The proposition effectively states: every time we perceive an *action*, we perceive an agent or cause of this action. Explaining this fact, describing how it comes about in us, or showing the way in which we come to the idea of cause from the idea of some fact (happening, action), is to indicate the origin of the idea of cause.

Article 3.
The proposition analysed, and the difficulty uncovered

617. The proposition we have undertaken to analyse is a judgment made up of three parts: 1. a fact, a happening or an action that we must have conceived mentally; 2. the connection between this action and the unknown agent or cause; 3. the idea of this agent or cause. To explain how we mentally conceive such a judgment, we have to show how we come to conceive each of the three parts of which it is composed.

618. We first perceive the *action*, or happening, with the help of our internal and external sensibility. Our consciousness assures us of our passivity when real, corporeal things impinge upon the nerves of our body,[31] and of our activity when we will to do something and, through the stimulus of our will, go on to think, move, etc. Through the idea of being we proceed to form the idea of *action*, both that produced by us and that which happens in us without our positive intervention. When we have acquired the concept of action and mentally conceived different kinds of action, we also learn of the existence of other real actions either through what fellow human beings[32] tell us, or by imagining them for ourselves.

[31] I express myself like this to determine the action in some way. In fact, knowledge that our body has been touched by real things comes after awareness of our passivity, and the expression used is posterior to our experience.

[32] Language would be of no use to us unless we already possessed the ideas signified by language, or had the capacity for forming them on the occasion of sounds that we hear. [. . .]

It is not difficult, therefore, to explain how we perceive *action* and form various concepts of it. We know it primarily through what takes place in us (given the idea of being), and through similar things which we can imagine happening to us. Moreover, our consciousness provides awareness of all the actions of which we ourselves are the authors and causes. We realise that it is we ourselves who desire, think, and so on. The cause of all these kinds of actions, therefore, is known to us, by *perception*; we know that we ourselves are doing these things. Analysing them, we distinguish 'myself', as responsible for them (their cause), from the actions caused. In this way, we form the idea of *cause* relative to actions done by us. Once more, there is no difficulty, although here we already have an idea of *cause*.

619. We now have to show that the idea of cause contains something clearly seen as necessary to every happening or action. Our proposition ran as follows: 'Every new fact demands a cause.' In this proposition, one finds a necessary connection between what is produced and what produces, between action and agent. But a necessary connection between two ideas must come from the nature itself of the ideas which, like relative terms, cannot be thought separately. One of them is entailed in the thought and definition of the other in such a way that an analysis of the two concepts inevitably shows their mutual interconnection.

The whole difficulty lies here. We have to submit the two terms of the proposition to a rigorous analysis and show that: 1. *action*, and 2. *cause*, (that which produces action), cannot be thought except together. If we succeed in doing this, we shall also have shown that: 1. a fact or *happening* cannot be thought without a cause; 2. no *cause* can be conceived mentally without thought of at least a possible effect. After this, it will only be necessary to indicate the way in which we acquire one or other of these ideas. Analysis showing them mutually dependent will also demonstrate that the presence of one accounts for the presence of the other.

The idea of action, and the pure and simple idea of a cause presents no difficulty. These ideas are given by experience and interior awareness. We are conscious of our actions, and of being their cause, as we have seen (cf. 618). The difficulty lies in showing that when we think of action, we also think implicitly of cause, and vice-versa. Let us examine the problem.

Article 4.
Explanation of the difficulty in uncovering the origin of the idea of cause

620. All things, including actions, can be objects of the understanding (cf. 603). But according to the principle of cognition (cf. 564-565), every intellectual operation has being or a being as its object. The understanding can think about what belongs to or determines being or a being only in so far as this element is a determination of being or a being. But in order to think what belongs to a being, the understanding must first think the being, and through it mentally conceive and understand these determinations.[33] So much has been seen in the course of our work.

If the matter has been understood carefully it will not raise difficulties, although the rather abstract language employed in the work may be an obstacle to comprehension. We could perhaps make things easier to follow by trying to present the teaching more immediately and directly.

First, it is only possible to think of two kinds of things: 1. a being; 2. some quality or attribute belonging to a being. Readers may assure themselves of this by examining all possible objects of their thought. In the end, they will see everything they understand classed either as a being, or as something belonging or related to a being.

It is important, however, to understand the word *being* correctly, and not to restrict its meaning unduly. By the word *being*, I understand that which *is*. Hence, anything which is not a being, or is not even included in being, is nothing. The word *being* embraces everything; nothing is excluded; outside everything, there is nothing. If we mentally conceive

---

[33] It is easy to see that this necessity arises from the nature of what is thought. It is therefore an *objective* necessity, not a *subjective* law of the intellectual faculty. A being's determinations exist only relative to the being. But because the determinations can be mentally conceived only in so far as they exist, it would be absurd to say that they could be conceived before, or independently of the being to which they belong, and through which they are something.

something, therefore, either we conceive a being, or something contained in a being. The opposite would be a plain contradiction. It would imply saying and denying something simultaneously. We would not be speaking, but 'sounding off' unintelligibly.

It is true, of course, that through abstraction we can consider what belongs to a being as separate from the being. We do not make into an independent being what we have separated. Moreover, we have first had to think of the being as a whole; our abstraction is made from the idea of the being. We cannot abstract or separate something from a whole if we do not first possess the whole from which the required part is detached and separated.

The things that are not beings of themselves, or being, but belong to some being in which they are perceived, are intellectual abstractions presupposing the total idea of the thing of which they are a part. Consequently, 'a being is thought *per se*; through a being, we think the things contained in it, or belonging to it, or in any way related to it, by using our faculty of abstraction.' The truth of this principle can also be understood by considering carefully the nature of abstract ideas. When we separate a quality or relationship, or any of its parts, from a being, we have indeed separated and cut it off mentally from the being as a whole. We are not deceived, however, because we can view the part only as belonging to the being as a whole. It is impossible for the understanding to think of anything belonging to the being without first thinking the being itself. If the understanding then fixes its attention willingly upon a part of the being (which is what abstraction means), it never forgets (unless it deceives itself) that the part is inseparable from the being in which it is seen to exist.

621. If these very simple principles are kept in mind, it is not difficult to see how the understanding forms for itself the idea of cause. In our perceptions, as we have said, we are conscious of an *action* done in us of which we are not the authors. If we did initiate the action, we would perceive it as something belonging to us, that is, we would perceive the action (something appertaining to a being) in our being and thus provide all the conditions necessary for the

implementation of intellective perception. But if our consciousness provides an *action* for our understanding without also proferring an author of the action, could we perceive and understand it? An *action* is not a being, nor does it make a being subsist (substance). It merely belongs to a being.[34] Moreover, we have seen that the understanding cannot conceive anything except through the conception of a being and that which the being contains. In this case, therefore, the intellect conceives *action* only by referring it to a being as yet unknown, but necessarily possessing or producing the action. This being we call *cause*.

These are all undeniable propositions, comprising an irrefutable demonstration that when the understanding thinks the idea of *action* of which we are not the authors, it must think a being different from ourselves as author of an action That is to say, it must think a cause.

We now have to explain how the understanding can think this being (cause) which is presented neither by consciousness nor by internal feeling. Although we have proved that it must do this, we have not shown *how*. Nevertheless, it will become clear if we draw together all that we have said in this section. The idea of a cause is the idea of a being that produces an action. Analysing this idea, we find it is composed of three parts: 1, an action; 2. a being; 3. their connection. *Action* is given by feeling; *being* is innate [App. no. 11]; their connection arises from the *necessity* already indicated as inherent to the nature of the understanding, or more properly of its objects which cannot be conceived mentally without being; being is the first thing conceived by the intellect because it is both the first thing to exist, and that through which everything else is conceived, because everything else exists through it.

Article 5.
Distinction between substance and cause

622. When we, as intelligent natures, supply being to our

---

[34] We prove this proposition from the definition of the action of which we are speaking. We are not considering *first, immanent* act, which is existence itself, but an action following upon first, immanent act.

sense-perception, we form the idea of *substance*, that is, of a being which we conceive as existing in itself, and not in something else. When we supply being in the *intellective perception* of an *action*, we form for ourselves the idea of *cause*, that is, a substance that carries out an action.[35] Our act of understanding is similar in the formation of the idea of substance and of the idea of cause; both operations consist in supplying being[36] to what is provided by feeling or perception. This is possible through the identity of the subject ('myself') which feels, perceives intellectually, and reflects. We enjoy not only external and internal sense, but also possess the idea of being which constitutes our intellect [App. no. 12]. *What is felt* is perceived by the senses, and we refer it to being, considering it as a determination of being. We think a determined being, and hence the idea of substance. When we perceive an action, we refer it to being and consider it as an act of being. In this way, we come to perceive being as operative, and along with it the idea of cause. Substance is a being producing an act we consider as immanent to the substance itself (accident)[37]; cause is a being producing an action outside itself (effect). The idea of substance is generated by need for a being antecedent to accidents; the need for a being antecedent to the existence of a contingent being generates the idea of another being or cause properly so called.

Article 6.
The understanding completes sense-perceptions

623. A *feelable quality* cannot stand without a substance; an *action* cannot stand without a cause. The understanding adds being to the *feelable qualities*, the terms of sensations,

[35] We could imagine something operating differently from substances: one thought, for example, produces another. This takes place, however, through abstraction. The true cause of all our thoughts is the substance of the spirit.

[36] 'Supplying being' does not mean that we create it, or produce it as something immanent to ourselves; it is the object of our intuition from the first moment of our existence.

[37] Although substance is therefore 'cause' relative to accidents, it is not considered such in so far as it produces something, but as an *act of being* relative to its terms which exist through and in this act. We need to remember that all these concepts are abstractions.

and forms a determined being; it adds to the *action* itself the being which produces *action*. In this way the understanding by completing sensation arrives at *substance*; by completing perception, it arrives at *cause*.

From the instant that being is present to the intellect, which it constitutes, the intellect can perceive nothing except beings. In intellective perception, therefore, the intellect can see only beings and, as a result, all it sees must have its explanation in those beings (*de ratione entis*). If it did not see everything in this way, it would not see beings. But to admit that it sees beings, and deny that it sees what has its explanation in being is to affirm and deny the same thing. This is not difficult to understand if we grasp that beings and their explanation are in fact the same thing. All this follows from knowing that the idea of being is the most universal and the simplest of all ideas.

Hence when we perceive with our sense some appurtenance of a being which has its explanation in the being, such as sensations or action towards which we are passive, we immediately perceive *substance* and argue to *cause* because we have a continual, fundamental, natural vision of being. Our perception of a substance and our conception of a cause is simply 'perception of a being possessing feelable qualities, to which we attribute the action that we experience or perceive in ourselves.'

When a philosopher has demonstrated his teaching, he is permitted the use of images. Let us say, therefore, that indetermined being, continually and unmovably present to us, is like a sheet of white paper laid out before us; the determinations of the object are accidental additions, like writing on the sheet of paper. The writing, or determinations of the object to which our intellect continually directs its watchful, interior gaze, are sensations, or feelings referred to being as terms to their principle. Hence with the same act with which we see being, we also see in it, and never without it, its determinations. We are like people gazing at a screen, and beholding all that takes place upon it. [. . .].

624. Our understanding, therefore, is governed by the following law which it receives from the nature of its object: it must complete feeling and perception. The nature of the

understanding consists in a continual gaze focusing on being and beings, which beholds everything as possessing its explanation in beings, such as the determinations and conditions of the beings themselves. When the special power of internal or external sense provides determinations of beings, the understanding naturally integrates and completes them. With our internal vision we inevitably add being to what we sense and form of it a determined being to which we again add all that necessarily belongs to the being. This intellective capacity of ours can be called 'the understanding's integrative faculty.'

Article 7.
Application of the teaching on substance to internal feeling

625. We have shown that the understanding cannot mentally conceive feelable qualities without thinking a substance. This argument is universally applicable, and valid not only for external qualities of bodies but also for facts connected with internal feeling. As we have said, human beings when thinking of feelable qualities, think them in a subject and thus form the idea of substance in the way we have explained. Let us apply the same argument to facts connected with internal sense, that is, to feelings. Human beings have interior feelings; they are aware of possessing ideas, along with spiritual pains and pleasures. Intellectually they conceive these feelings of theirs and refer such modifications to themselves as to existing beings. In this way, they can form the idea of their own substance.

626. But the reality of our own substance is presented to our understanding in another, more immediate way. The feeling of SELF is a substantial feeling. Our understanding, therefore, does not *supply*, but *perceives* our own substance immediately in the feeling providing it. Perception of one's own substance enables the intellect, after abstracting the judgment invariably united to intellective perception, to acquire immediately the positive idea of substance.

627. There is a very noticeable difference, therefore, between perceiving the substance of *external bodies* and that of *our spirit*. In the perception of external bodies, our feeling

receives a force to which we refer sensations as effects, considering them as *feelable qualities* determining that *force*. This force is indeed a substantial *action*, but it is not a being because it lacks *subjective existence*. But because we have to consider that force as a *being* (this is a necessary condition of our perceiving it intellectually), we attribute to it a mode of subjective existence which makes it exist in itself, and not only relative to us. In this way, we assign to the force the support or *substance* without which it would not be a being. However, because we do not experience this substance except in its action upon us, we conceive the being to which this action belongs without giving it further definition; for us, it remains the *proximate cause of that action*.

As a result, some philosophers have considered the substance of bodies untraceable. We are in fact obliged to consider as substance the *agent acting* in us to which we give the substantive name, *body*. This agent is therefore a substance determined by a relationship, although the *relationship* is *real*. We, on the contrary, call this *extrasubjective*; within this field, the idea that we have of the substance of bodies contains nothing positive but only something foreign to ourselves, to our own subject. The understanding does not think positively any other subject whatsoever. But there is a *substantial subject* in the perception of our own substantial feeling. Here we need only apply the idea of being; we do not need to supply substance together with a concept of relationship.

628. Finally, we affirm that we can perceive our own body as we perceive any other foreign body, that is, *extrasubjectively*, and as the term of our internal feeling, *subjectively*. But we shall have to deal with the subjective perception of our body at greater length later.

PART FIVE.
ORIGIN OF *NON-PURE* IDEAS, WHICH DERIVE SOMETHING FROM FEELING

630. So far we have spoken about ideas that come from deep within *being* and are obtained either through analysis of this form-idea or by considering its relationships; no determination of it by feeling has been suggested to our mind. We have called them *pure* ideas because they involve only being in general, the simplest of all principles.

We must now gradually apply this pure part of our knowledge to *feelings*, to explain the origin of non-pure ideas. Non-pure ideas proceed not only from the formal principle but also from a principle of spiritual and animal feeling associated with it in our subjective unity.

631. We will first deal with the pure idea of substance and then see how feeling makes it a *specific* idea, changing it into the idea of the substance of spirit by means of the spiritual feeling, and into the idea of the substance of matter and body by means of the material, corporeal feeling.

1

ORIGIN OF THE DIFFERENCE BETWEEN THE IDEAS OF CORPOREAL SUBSTANCE AND SPIRITUAL SUBSTANCE

Article 1.
The opinion already expressed about substance and cause

632. We have shown how, on the occasion of external and internal sensations, the understanding naturally conceives the ideas of substance and cause. [. . .]

634. [. . .] It is also certain that [. . .] the idea people form of the subject of corporeal, sensible qualities is different from the idea of the subject of their internal feelings. This is a fact to be explained; we must therefore examine the origin of the difference between the idea of corporeal substance and the idea of spiritual substance.

Article 2.
The subject of the following investigation

635. [. . .] Common sense accepts [. . .] that we are subject to sensations and that *sensations* come from an external cause in which there must be different energies corresponding to and producing the different kinds of sensations we experience. We can call these energies *feelable qualities*. Common sense also affirms that this cause is a substance and the necessary subject of these qualities or energies. [. . .] The realism of common sense distinguishes four things in the one fact: 1. sensations; 2. their subject (ourselves); 3. the feelable qualities, what is felt; and 4. the subject of the feelable qualities, *body*: two subjects and their qualities. [. . .]

Article 3.
The difference between the idea of cause and the idea of subject

637. One thing that produces another is its *cause* but not always its subject. The thing produced can have its own existence, that is, an existence seen mentally by us as separate from what produces it. It can also be without an existence of its own so that we can conceive it only as united with the same existence as the cause. In the first case, that which produces is only cause of the thing produced; in the second, it is both cause and subject. Granted that a son is a being with his own separate existence, a father is only the cause of his son.[38] But the intelligent spirit is not only the cause of our thoughts, it is also their subject; our thoughts have the same

---

[38] There is no need to point out that the father is not the full cause of his son, because a human being cannot make matter exist nor create the human spirit. But the example helps.

existence as the spirit and can be conceived only as existing in our spirit that produces and holds them in being. In this case the spirit is at the same time subject.

When a cause therefore produces something remaining with it, it is said to be also subject of the thing produced. This is the case with our thoughts; they all remain within the spirit, of which they are inseparable modifications. On the other hand, a cause can act externally by detaching from itself the thing produced, which then acquires its own existence. That thing is now conceived in itself without need of the cause which, in this case, is only the cause not the subject of the thing produced.

638. This difference is true and important. Only one observation needs to be made: we must not misunderstand the statement 'When the *thing* produced remains within the cause, the cause is also subject.' The word 'thing' in this proposition can give rise to misunderstanding. It is generally used to mean that which exists in itself, while what is produced in a *thing* is a modification or something similar, of a thing, not a thing itself. So we must note that in the proposition the word 'thing' has a very wide meaning; it indicates everything we think in any mental conception, whether such an object has its own existence or not. If what has been produced has no existence of its own, its conception is a pure abstraction which we could not arrive at without first thinking of that which produces it (subject). Only later do we conceive and give it a name as if it were a *thing per se*, thus making it finally a mental object of our exclusive attention (a dialectic being).

Article 4.
A further analysis of sensations

§1. The purpose of this analysis

639. Having distinguished *subject* from *cause* we must now approach step by step the truth we are investigating. To do this accurately, we will first limit ourselves to proving that in both subjects (spirit and body) [. . .] we can and must distinguish by mental abstraction a third thing between

sensations with their feelable qualities and the pure act by which they exist. It is in fact impossible and contradictory to imagine that the act by which sensations with their feelable qualities exist, extends to them only, irrespective of their union with anything else. This implies demonstrating that the subject we have proved to be joined to *sensations* and *feelable qualities* [. . .] cannot be simply and solely the act by which we understand sensations and feelable qualities exist. Such an act presupposes an entity that, in addition to supporting sensations and feelable qualities, is also something in itself, that is, has an absolute property unrelated to things outside it. [. . .]

§2. There is in the subject something other than the act by which sensations exist

640. I have distinguished sensations from that through which they exist, that is, their substance; I will now analyse this idea of substance.

When I analyse the energy by which sensations exist, its concept includes something more than the act of their existence. Careful consideration of the supposition on which the whole argument turns, shows the truth of my affirmation. We have supposed that we are ignorant of the existence of substance; all we know is that sensations exist. Given only this fact, I have demonstrated by analysis that the idea of a *substance* is contained necessarily and implicitly in this fact.

The second step of the argument is this: if we proceed to analyse *substance* found in this way, we encounter in its concept something more than an energy capable of making sensations subsist. The proof is as follows: sensations exist; therefore there is an energy making them exist. But what are these sensations, of colour, sound, taste, smell, etc. and how do they come about?

Observation first shows that sensations happen in me (attention confirms this): colours, sounds, etc. are so much my own sensations that if I did not exist or could not feel, I would not only be deprived of them but they would not even exist. I am speaking about all the sensations I experience, which are quite different from those experienced by someone else. The sensations that I have when smelling an onion, listening to a violin or tasting an orange would not exist at all if I did not feel them. But what I say about my own sensations can be said equally about anyone's sensations: if they are sensations like those from which I draw the concept and understand the word 'sensations', then certainly they would not exist if there were no one to experience them or the person were deprived of feeling or were not actually experiencing them at the present moment. There is no sensation, colour, taste, etc. that is not found in a human being, since every colour, odour, taste etc. is a modification of the feeling of a sensitive being.

Once this nature of sensations has been observed, it is clear that the feeling subject must contain something, in addition to sensations and the act of their existence, which is the foundation of their act of existence. This is so evident that it hardly needs proof.

When I say 'I smell odours, I see colours, etc.', I posit 'myself' as the subject of the sensations perceived. So 'myself' is not simply the act by which they exist, because I do not find 'myself' in the pure idea of existing sensation. On the contrary, without 'myself', I would have to think as many other existences *per se* in the sensations as there are sensations. But as I think of the existence of the sensations in the way I experience them, I am convinced that many of them can be referred equally to just one 'myself'. Hence 'myself' that experiences many sensations is one, while the sensations are many; 'myself' is different from the sensations just as the subject is different from the modifications it undergoes.

641. Furthermore, 'myself' can experience many present sensations, which then give way to others. While this is happening, 'myself,' despite the different sensations, remains itself. Thus it has the power to feel and to be modified, although the power to feel many sensations is totally different from each present sensation.

642. Finally, sensations are felt by 'myself', while 'myself' is that which feels. These two characteristics are not only different but opposite and as such clearly demonstrate that sensations and their act of existence cannot be thought of

without the presence of a subject, that is, without their act of existence first terminating in something other than themselves, from which they receive and have existence.

643. It must be noted in everything said so far that the feeling subject is not deduced by reasoning but by simple analysis of the idea, *existing sensation*. [. . .] To think of a *substance* is to think of something existing different from sensations: this is the result (their subject) of our analysis of the idea of substance. Therefore the subject of sensations is not simply an act involving them but a principle existing of itself that has the power to feel, and continues to exist even without any special, accidental sensation.

§3. The subject of feelable qualities must be an act involving more than these qualities

644. Realists use a similar argument to prove that it is impossible to think of feelable qualities existing through an act that terminates in them alone. Their act enabling them to exist has to make something else exist, different from them. In fact, for realists, feelable qualities are powers producing sensations in a feeling subject (cf. 635). So it is absurd to imagine these powers as existing independently of anything that can be mentally distinguished from them. Let us analyse the idea of *existing feelable qualities*, that is, of powers that excite sensations in us.

As realists understand them, all feelable qualities emanate from a sort of centre called 'body', assumed to be their subject. If these qualities are united in this way and refer to a being from which they originate, this being which potentially unites them, whatever it may be, must be implicit in their idea. In this case, in addition to feelable qualities, the idea includes the existence of some other thing necessary for the existence of the qualities in the way we think of them.

645. It may be argued that this approach is not founded on the pure concept of *feelable qualities* but on the concept obtained from experience, and that the centre, the connection uniting these powers, has nothing to do with the pure concept. But if we examine just one sensible quality, we are still thinking of something in addition to the quality.

I define a sensible quality as a power to produce a certain kind of sensation. If this power really exists, we must think, and do in fact think of it as something in itself, other than in its relationship with us. This subsistence of the quality in itself is different from its relationship with us or its action on us because it is impossible to think of a pure relationship or action of a being without thinking of the being itself. It is impossible to have relationship and action between two beings, unless there are two things.

If, therefore, in conceiving a capacity to modify me, I conceive the real relationship of something with me, we must say that something exists capable of modifying me. This power is: 1. something existing independently of me; 2. a relationship and action that this something exhibits in me. Thus the analysis of the concept 'existing feelable qualities or power to produce sensations in me' results in two ideas: 1. the idea of a being really existing in itself; and 2. the idea of a relationship with us or of an action producing sensations.

However, before continuing the demonstration of the existence of two subjects, one spiritual, the other corporeal, we must say something about essence.

Article 5.
The difference between the ideas of *substance* and of *essence*

§1. Definition of essence

646. I define *essence* as that which is understood in any idea. An idea is the thing thought by me as simply possible. But this possible thing, considered in itself and independently of the mind that thinks it, is the essence. Essence therefore is everything I think in any idea whatsoever.

§2. Specific, generic and universal essence

647. Determined ideas are of two kinds, *specific* and *generic*. To these correspond two kinds of *essences* in our minds: *specific essence*, that is, what I think in the specific idea of a thing, and *generic* essence, that is, what I think in the *generic* idea.

Besides these two classes of more or less determined ideas, there is a *universal idea, being*; what I think in the idea of being can be called *universal essence* or simply *essence* (*essentia* from *esse*), as Plato often calls it.

§3. Specific essence

648. I have already indicated that a thing can be considered in a perfect and complete state, or in more or less imperfect states. Imperfection is only a lack or privation; everybody accepts the truth that evil is simply the lack of good. So the only idea we can have of something complete, free from every defect and imperfection, is the full, positive one. All the other ideas of inferior states of the same thing, are simply the first idea, the real type and exemplar, from which some perfection has been removed; they are modes of the idea (cf. 500-503). *Specific essence*, properly speaking, is what is thought in the complete, perfect idea; to this idea are reduced all other ideas of the thing in its various states of imperfection.

649. But another consideration is necessary to understand clearly what a *specific idea* is. The various *modes* we have mentioned come from defects and imperfections, but in addition to these *modes* there are *modes* of the idea itself which originate, not from its defects, but from its manner of being. These modes are as follows.

The pure object of our mind in any perception is a determined being (the possibility of something real) (cf. 491). The determined being has within itself something by which it is what it is and without which it would not be: this is its *first act* (cf. 587), immutable and immanent. This first act produces other acts which are the *activities* and various *actuations* of the being; these can be called *second acts* because they follow on the first. These activities and actuations together with their effects and terms remaining in the being[39] and following on the first act, are not always joined to the first act necessarily; sometimes they can be absent. If they are necessary, they do not have to be of any particular type. For instance, although a body must have a colour (as a feelable quality), the colour is not necessarily blue or red or yellow.

[39] For example, inclinations, habits, ideas, objects and terms of thought.

Now, as long as I am thinking of the *first act* and all it involves as its term, I am still thinking of the being, because I am thinking of that through which the being is what it is. But the *first act* is not necessarily connected with the many activities and actuations following it, or with their terms, as I have said. Hence, because the act does not involve these, they can be absent or vary, but the being can still be thought. For example, to be able to think of a human being nothing more is required than what is contained in the definition 'rational animal',[40] because the definition involves the first act by which a human being is a human being, without any further determinations being considered. Some determinations, such as a particular amount of knowledge, a body of a particular weight and size, are not necessary at all; but if they are necessary in a general way — for example, in the present order of things a human being has weight or extension — then they are already virtually contained in the definition.

If therefore I am thinking of everything included in the first act, I am thinking of the being; if I am not, then some other being is the object of my thoughts.

These observations suggest the following conclusions: 1. there is something *necessary* in a being for it to be what it is, and therefore thinkable; 2. there is something *not necessary* for it to be thought; and 3. the necessity comes from the *intrinsic order* of the being itself.

Let us imagine a being that has things not necessary for its *constitution* and existence but necessary for its *perfection*. The things necessary for its perfection are not necessary for my *mental conception* of it — for this, it is sufficient to think the act by which it can subsist, since being is the object of knowledge. If, in my idea, I think of the being equipped with everything necessary for its possible subsistence but not for its perfection, I have those *modes* of the idea mentioned above, which derive from its defects. But if I am not thinking that through which the whole being exists, I am not thinking that being.

However, there is another case. I can think of that element in a being by which it exists, without thinking expressly of

---

[40] I am not concerned here with judging the merits of this definition; as the one commonly held it is sufficient to illustrate my concept.

the things necessary for its perfection. I do not deny nor exclude them. On the contrary I consider them virtually included in the thought of the being's existence. In this case, I have *modes* of the *specific idea* not dependent on defects of the thing but on the particular way I have conceived it and on the being itself. The being is such that thinking its root act is sufficient for thinking the being. These *modes* therefore of the *specific* idea are formed by a kind of *abstraction*. I am not thinking of the *defective being*, as in the first *modes*, nor of the *perfect* being, as in the complete idea — I prescind from everything belonging to the being's *perfection* and concentrate solely on what makes or can make it subsist.

650. We must also note that because of the imperfection of understanding, human beings can rarely form that full and complete idea of things of which the *mode*, as we have just described it, is a kind of outline or seed. Thus when they lack the *complete specific* idea (the *type* or rather the *archetype*), they make the *abstract idea* the foundation of species, an idea which, properly speaking, is only a *mode* of the full and absolute idea.[41]

651. It is this *abstract specific* idea that contains what is simply called *essence*, since the *essence* of a thing is only what is thought and presented to our spirit in such an idea.

---

[41] The chronological order in which we receive the *specific ideas* mentioned above, is as follows:

1. First we acquire the *full idea* of a particular imperfect being, which is the state of all beings in nature; in fact they are not only imperfect but sometimes *damaged* — it is rare to find in nature a being without some degree of *damage*.

2. From this full idea of an *imperfect being* we form the *abstract specific idea* by abstracting whatever is damaged and imperfect and without perfections; in short, we abstract everything that is not needed to conceive the being mentally. This abstraction gives us the *specific essence* in outline, so to speak; it gives us the idea commonly used by human beings.

3. Finally we try to ascend from this to the *full specific idea* (the archetype). But we do so with difficulty because it is beyond our ability to know everything composing the ultimate natural and supernatural perfection of a being. However we continually try to come close to this noble idea by using that power of our spirit we have called the *integrating faculty of human intelligence*. Even when we cannot do this, we know it must exist and that we could reach it if we were capable; therefore we direct our thoughts to it as to their possible term at least.

This is the *chronological order* of our specific ideas but the *natural* order of these three kinds of ideas is quite the opposite. First comes the *full specific idea*, then the *specific abstract* idea and finally the *imperfect specific* idea. The last two are only *modes* of the first, not different ideas.

652. We see that, in the formation of this specific idea, we make use of a kind of *abstraction* as well as *universalisation*. However this process does not form *species* strictly speaking, but only *abstract species* because the abstract is already understood in the *full species*. To obtain the *full species*, we need the *integration* as well as the *universalisation* of the imperfect idea we first receive of the thing, although this depends not on the nature of the idea but on the accidental defect of the beings we perceive. This perception gives us our first idea of these beings, an idea obtained by being detached from the judgment on their subsistence.

§4. Generic essences

653. Generic ideas are formed by *abstraction* (cf. 490-503), specific ideas by *universalisation* alone.[42] *Abstraction* is a multiple operation; it takes place in different ways and at different levels, and thus provides different types of genera. We must now list these.

654. There are three forms of *abstraction*, which give us three kinds of generic ideas and generic essences; they can be called *real, mental* and *nominal* genera.

655. The origin and distinction of these three kinds of genera begins with the fact that there are two ways in which I can carry out an *abstraction* on the *abstract specific essence*. I can abstract something from the essence in such a way that, in the resulting abstract idea, I still think a being that can be realised; alternatively I can abstract in such a way that I remove everything that constitutes a being and think only of some *mental* characteristic, like an accident or a quality, or anything at all that, by itself, does not make a being known. If the idea still contains a *being*, then relative to the specific idea on which I carried out the abstraction, it is a *real generic* idea. If the idea contains only a *mental entity*, then it is a *mental generic* idea. It expresses and presents only an abstract that does not exist outside of thought — at least it does not exist as a being in the way our mind conceives it.

---

[42] I have called *specific ideas* (formed only by universalisation), *full* but *imperfect, specific ideas*. From them, we form by *abstraction*, *abstract specific* ideas, and by *integration, complete* or *perfect specific* ideas.

For example take the idea of *human being*. This is an abstract specific idea and I can abstract from it in the two ways indicated. First, when I abstract the specific difference of *reason*, the idea is now one of *animal*. Relative to the species *human being*,[43] this idea of *animal* is a *real generic* idea and includes a *real generic* essence. Secondly, I abstract everything constituting a being and retain only an accident, for example, a colour. Here, the idea of colours is a *mental generic* idea, and, because the abstracted colour is simply an entity of the mind, the *essence of colour* can be called *mental*.

We must also note in this case what I have often pointed out: when I am thinking only of abstract *accidents*, the law of my intelligence, according to which I must think being, makes me consider those accidents as beings, although I know they are not. Because they are not beings but only a form of the mind, I call them *mental* or *dialectical beings*.

656. Finally, in addition to these two ways of abstraction, there is a third way: I can abstract and prescind from both the *being* and the *accidental qualities*, retaining only a *relationship*, for instance, a sign. Consequently I can arbitrarily impose names and consider them as the foundation of genera. For example, if I were speaking about the genus Smith or the genus Brown, I would call them nominal genera, and their corresponding essence, *nominal generic essence*.

§5. A more perfect definition of substance

657. From what has been said, we can gain a more perfect definition of substance in general. Having examined the difference between *abstract specific essence* and *full specific essence*, we said that the first, present to the mind, makes known everything unchangeable in a given *determined being*. Any change would mean the loss of the being's identity; it would either cease to exist, or become another being to the mind.

When, in a *determined being*, we think this unchangeable element that constitutes its abstract specific essence, and consider it in relationship to the changeable element united to

---

[43] Relative to *brute animal*, the same idea is *specific*.

it in the *full specific essence*, the *abstract specific essence* is called substance. It is regarded as the element necessary for the being to exist, the act by which it subsists and which, as a base, supports the changeable element. Substance, then, can be defined as 'That by which a determined being is what it is', or 'Substance is the abstract specific essence considered in a determined being', or 'considered in relationship to the full specific essences of the being'.

658. If a being lacked *abstract specific essence* and had nothing changeable that could be abstracted, any change we might make in it mentally would immediately entail the loss of its identity. If this were the case, the word 'substance' could not be strictly applied to it. We would have to say the whole being was substance or that its substance was everything found in its *full specific essence*. This is the case in the divine Being.

659. To conclude: the variety of *abstract specific essences* is the reason for the variety of substances. Therefore to make the general formula express special substances, we must replace the words 'abstract specific essence in general' with the particular *essence* that represents the desired substance.°

Article 6.
Resumption of the question under discussion

660. Let us return to our argument. So far we have analysed the concept of substance, in order to make it sufficiently clear and distinct, and inconfusible with any other element. We have seen that if a subject of sensations exists (and its existence was proved in the preceding chapter), it cannot have an existence limited to sensations. There has to be something else subsisting beforehand, capable of receiving and supporting external sensations (cf. 639-645).

Likewise, if a subject of feelable qualities exists different from the subject of sensations (as the realists claim), it must be an activity that extends not only to providing subsistence for the feelable qualities but also to being something itself antecedently in order to possess those dispositions called feelable qualities as powers firmly fixed in its being.

After I demonstrated that substance or the subject of the

accidents, is something existing in itself, an act by which a determined being is what it is, I then examined how different substances are *specified* and distinguished, and found that this was due to the different terms in which the act of being constituting a determined being terminates. I was thus able to perfect the definition of substance further, reducing it to the following general formula: 'Substance is the abstract specific essence considered in a determined being.' Then, in order to remove any misunderstanding, I explained what *essence* was and, amongst its various meanings, what *abstract specific essence* was, the foundation of the substance of a being.

With the way now clear, I can return to the argument about special substances [. . .]. The argument is based on the demonstration, already given, that a substance as subject of sensations ('myself') exists. I must show: 1. that the subject of this substance contains nothing found in the concept of corporeal substance; and 2. that a corporeal substance exists. This latter point, however, will be discussed in the following chapter.

Article 7.
A perceiving subject, 'myself', exists

661. There are internal and external sensations. They have a subject, and consciousness tells me that I MYSELF am that subject. We have already seen this in previous discussions.

Article 8.
The concept of 'myself', a perceiving subject, is entirely different from the concept of corporeal substance

§1. There are two series of facts in us, in one of which we are active, in the other passive

662. We can all observe this for ourselves. Some effects take place in us without any effort on our part, others take place because we cause them. When I deliberately want something and use my will to obtain it, I feel I am moving myself by my own energy, part of my internal nature. I am the cause of the

actions; I act, I am not passive. When something happens to me without my willing it and even against my will, then I am passive and do not act.

663. It is not a question of whether it is I who am passive when something happens to me or whether there is any co-operation on my part. What is certain is that, although the action is done in me and I am responsible for the state in which I have to receive it, the activity producing the action is not mine, and I cannot reasonably say that I myself am acting at all. This is not the place to investigate more deeply the nature of passive experience. It is sufficient to indicate the undoubted fact that *passive experience* exists and is different from the *action* of our spontaneous will. What has been said suffices for my purpose, namely, the necessity of recognising in ourselves two series of events, one in which we justifiably say we are active and another in which we are passive.

664. Among passive occurrences we find sensations that come from outside ourselves and it is these that principally concern us at the moment. We have to recognise sensations as facts taking place in our spirit, which is mainly passive in their regard; it suffers but does not produce an action. Thus, with my eyes fixed on the sun, it is impossible for me not to see its dazzling light and feel its rays on my eyes. If I have not stopped my ears, I hear, even unwillingly, the drums and trumpets of a military band. I feel pain when pricked by a needle, although I prefer not to suffer pain — no one likes pain. In short, if I were not passive to sensations aroused in my body, I could get rid of all harmful ones, have only pleasant ones, and never suffer or die.

665. I mention these particular examples, although more general ones would do, to refute the objection that a person could avoid pain and unwanted sensations by concentrating his attention elsewhere. Objectors claim that even unwanted sensations are due to human action in so far as human beings willingly dispose themselves to receive sense-modifications.

I first reply that human beings cannot avoid all pain because, if that were so, they would be capable of making themselves immortal, or at least of dying without the slightest pain even when a bullet had passed through the heart — which is quite contrary to experience! Second, concentrating our thoughts elsewhere requires great effort on our part and is sometimes so demanding that it is impossible to sustain. The only reason for such a great effort is to avoid pain or any unwanted sensation; in our effort we are using our activity to avoid a hostile force that makes us suffer. But if force is needed to prevent an effect, there must also be an opposing force trying to produce the effect: reaction supposes action, and the force that dominates supposes the force that is dominated. Thus the action we sometimes take to avoid being passive is proof of our passivity. Finally, we must see if the effort we make to free ourselves of sense-impressions does in fact prevent sensation. Perhaps all we are doing is simply turning our intellective attention from what we are suffering. We can be suffering in our sense-faculty without being conscious of it (we do not perceive our suffering intellectively) and therefore we cannot speak about it. With our attention thus suspended, we no longer think or pass judgment on what we feel.

§2. We are cause and subject of active facts but only subject of passive facts

666. Every fact taking place in us is a modification of our spirit. Thus our spirit is the *subject* of every fact, as consciousness attests when I say to myself, 'I am the one who feels, thinks, decides, is happy or sad', that is, I affirm that I am the subject of all these facts. However, if we are the *subject* of *passive facts*, we are not their *cause*. As we have said, they do not happen through our action; we suffer and receive them. Anything at all can produce them, against our will or at least without our co-operation. This distinction between two series of facts, of one of which we are cause and subject, of the other only subject, is the same as the distinction made above between the series of active and passive facts. The analysis of what is active and of what is passive in us shows that the idea of activity contains the idea of cause and subject, but the idea of passivity only the idea of subject, not that of cause. Hence the proposition above is contained in the first proposition, which is a fact.

§3. What we call 'body' is the proximate cause of our external sensations

667. At this stage we do not need a complete, final definition of body; it is sufficient to know enough of its essential properties to avoid confusing it with anything else. For this purpose the definition we can obtain from what has already been said will suffice.

I use the word 'body' to mean 'the subject of feelable qualities', that is, the subject of those forces that produce sensations in us. Body therefore is the subject of extension, shape, solidity, colour, taste, etc. in so far as these qualities are forces in bodies producing corresponding sensations in us° [App. no. 13]. These forces or feelable qualities are the proximate cause of our sensations. So we can define body as 'the proximate cause of sensations and the subject of feelable qualities.' Even if bodies did not exist, it is still true that the definition contains the idea people have of body, and this is what we were seeking.

§4. Our spirit is not body

668. This is a corollary of the preceding propositions. If 'body' is the proximate cause of our external sensations (cf. 667), and if these are facts taking place in us and independently of us, then we are only their passive subject (cf. 666). We have to conclude therefore that 'myself' is not a body. The word 'myself' expresses a feeling, thinking subject; hence this subject is a substance entirely different from corporeal substance.

669. This reasoning enables us to form a distinct *idea* of the subject 'myself.' This subject, completely different from body, we call *spirit*.

Article 9.
Simplicity of the spirit

670. By indicating the difference and even the opposition between a being that receives and a being that causes reception, I have shown that spirit is something totally

different from body. To have shown this is to have demonstrated that spirit is incorporeal.

2

ORIGIN OF OUR IDEA OF CORPOREAL SUBSTANCE

Article 1.
Method of demonstrating the existence of bodies

672. Having shown that the feeling subject (the spirit, 'myself') cannot be what is understood in the word 'body' we must now see if what we mean by 'body' really exists, or indicates an imaginary concept without content. Our aim is to discover if there is such a thing as corporeal substance, as common sense affirms, and if so how we attain our idea of it.

When we have found the way in which we form our idea of body and persuade ourselves, as we form this idea, that bodies really exist, we shall also have demonstrated the existence of bodies. Such a demonstration, taking its origin from the persuasion of the existence of bodies, is valid provided that reasoning, dependent upon perception for its first link, is capable of finding or proving the truth. Most people do, in fact, take the existence of bodies as the most certain of all things, but modern sceptics have tried to throw doubt upon ordinary reasoning. In the next section of the work, we shall refute the objections against the validity of reasoning, and thus reinforce what we intend to say here about the existence of bodies.

673. We have said that the concept underlying the word 'body' is that of 'a proximate cause of our sensations' and that 'this cause is the subject of feelable qualities' (cf. 667). We have to show, therefore, how we obtain a reasonable persuasion of the existence of 'a cause of our sensations different from ourselves', and that this cause is 'the subject of feelable qualities'.[44] This will not be difficult if we remember what we have said.

[44] As we said, these definitions depend upon the meaning given to the word 'body' by common usage.

Article 2.
The existence of a proximate cause of our sensations

674. Sensations presuppose a cause different from ourselves. External sensations are facts towards which we are passive (cf. 661-666). Passive facts are actions done in us of which we are not the cause (*ibid.*). Such actions suppose a cause different from ourselves because of the principle of cause (cf. 567-569). Consequently, sensations suppose a cause different from us. And this was what we had to show.

Article 3.
Any cause different from ourselves is a substance

675. We have seen that sensations suppose a cause different from ourselves (cf. 674). It was shown that a cause is always a substance (cf. 620 ss.). The cause of our sensations, therefore, is a substance.

Article 4.
The substance causing our sensations is immediately joined to them

676. Because our sensations are actions done in us of which we are not the cause (cf. 662-666), we experience energy capable of changing us. This energy is a substance working upon us and we call it 'body'. The action of a body upon us is, therefore, the effect not of any particular power of the body, but of the body itself. In our definition of body, we do in fact call it that which modifies us in this way. Moreover, we recognise no other co-ordinated powers in the agent indicated by the word 'body'.

But the action of an operating substance is always intimately joined to the substance itself, because the force or energy of a being is inseparable and indivisible from the being itself. The substance which causes our sensations is therefore joined to them immediately.°

Article 5.
The cause of our sensations is a limited being

677. The energy or force which we experience as producing our sensations is limited because its action within us, of which we are not the cause, is limited. But this is the energy which gives us the idea of substance or, as we could say in equivalent terms, we perceive in that energy or force a being, the cause of our sensations, which is distinct from ourselves. But the being in which we mentally conceive this energy is as limited as the energy we experience because this being is for us only the energy itself considered as existing. Hence the being we think of as the substance and proximate cause of our sensations is limited.

Article 6.
We name things according to our mental conception of them

678. This proposition is evident. We cannot name anything unless we know it and according to the way in which we know it. Hence we cannot name it except in so far as we know it.

Article 7.
How to use words without making mistakes

679. Words express beings in so far as we know them intellectually. The meaning of words is limited, therefore, by our knowledge. It is an abuse of language, leading to equivocation and sophisms in our reasoning, to use a word with a wider sense than the concept of the being it names; we are using it for what it could mean, although we have no idea or perception of what this may be. Words used like this have neither the meaning nor the purpose given them by the human race.

Article 8.
Bodies are limited beings

680. Defining a body is equivalent to stating the use made of the word 'body'. If we wish to define this word, therefore, we can do it either by analysing all the ideas which form its meaning, or by indicating some characteristic idea, wholly proper to the being under review, which will lead us to the being named by the word in question. For the present, we need to clarify the word 'body' only in the second way. Later on, we shall define it more fully and closely.

We have seen that we form the idea of body from that which acts in us, that is, from the force or energy we experience in sensation (cf. 640-643). Because this energy is limited, we can draw from it only the concept of a limited being (cf. 677). All our knowledge of bodies is therefore that of limited beings. But words express beings in the way in which we perceive and know beings (cf. 678). The word 'body' was therefore invented to signify a limited being. Using it in some other sense would be to abuse it (cf. 679).

Article 9.
God is not the proximate cause of our sensations

681. Bodies are the proximate cause of our sensations (cf. 667). Bodies are limited beings (cf. 680). God is not a limited being. Therefore God is not the proximate cause of our sensations.

Article 10.
Bodies exist, and they cannot be confused with God

682. The proximate cause of our sensations is an existing substance. This substance is called 'body'; it is not God (cf. 681). Hence bodies exist, and they cannot be confused with God.

Article 11.
[. . . Résumé of the demonstration of the existence of bodies]

684. [. . .] The demonstration may be expressed and summed up in the following propositions.

1. Everything that occurs in our feeling is a fact.

2. In sensations and *corporeal* feelings (*corporeal* is used to determine the feelings, and may be taken here as an arbitrary sign). we experience in our feeling an action of which we are not the cause; we experience an energy, a force different from ourselves, at work in us.

3. This energy, or felt force, conceived intellectually, is the idea of a being. Our understanding, through the necessary principle of substance (cf. 583 ss.), conceives this energy as really existing.

4. Such energy is real and limited; consequently, because the conceived being is only the same energy considered in the existence it possesses, and as such formed and limited in our conception, it too is real and limited.

5. This limited being, which we call 'body' is not the sentient subject ('myself'), nor can it in any way be God, whose idea embraces that of an infinite being.

6. Body, therefore, a limited substance and proximate cause of our sensations, exists.

As far as I can see, all these propositions are irrefutable and form part of human common sense. [. . .]

Article 12.
Reflections on the demonstration of the existence of bodies

687. In order to know if corporeal substances exist, we must first recall the definition of substance. As we have said, substance is 'Something capable of being conceived intellectually in our first mental conception.'[45] Note that the definition contains the following implications.

---

[45] This characteristic is relative to our mind, but founded in the nature of the thing. The other definition I have given regards the thing itself: 'Substance is that through which a being is what it is', or 'Substance is the abstract, specific essence of a being considered in relationship to its full, specific essence'.

1. In order that something be a substance, it does not have to exist independently of every other thing. If that were the case, there would be no created substances because they exist only in dependence on the first cause. For something to be worthy of the name 'substance', it is sufficient for us to be able to conceive it by itself, separate from its first cause. Although it cannot exist totally of itself, it has its own proper existence which enables it to be thought by us in isolation from everything else; its *first concept* contains no extraneous element.

2. Consequently, a thing can be called 'substance' even if we have to rely on knowledge of something else, such as its cause. in reasoning to its existence or in understanding it completely. As we have said, although nothing can be understood without knowledge of its ultimate cause, this does not prevent us from calling it *substance*. A *first mental conception* can be formed of the thing without need of anything beyond it; it can be seen of itself in our first intuition and thought. In a word, its first concept is independent of every other concept; it presents itself as an incommunicable essence, mentally distinct from other essences.

We have already noted that if we give to the word 'substance' a more extensive meaning than that granted by common usage, we open the way to false reasoning and countless errors.

688. Bodies, therefore, are substances from the moment they can be conceived by us in our first mental conception as separate and isolated beings that cannot be confused with our spirit, with God or with anything else. Accidents, on the other hand, are such that they cannot be conceived as isolated in our first intellectual conception, but only in dependence upon some other being in which they exist or to which they belong. This is not the case with bodies whose perception, as we have seen, terminates in them without need of anything further (cf. 515-516).

689. [. . . We have distinguished] two elements in sensation: 1. the force acting in us (relative to which we are passive), common to all species of sensation; 2. the various

terms and effects of this force, that is, the various sensations. We experience both the *force* and its *different effects*, but while we feel the former equally in all sensations, the effects are felt differently according to the variety of means and bodily organs in and through which the force acts upon us. But if the variety of terms and effects of this force (the sensations in so far as they vary amongst themselves) cannot be conceived mentally without the force that produces them, this in its turn cannot be thought without the being which operates (through the *principle of cognition*) (cf. 536, 483-485). Thus we arrive at substance, at that which constitutes a being.

690. We can now sum up all that we have said about the origin of our ideas of bodies.

1. We attain the perception of bodies with the act by which we judge that bodies exist (cf. 526).

2. Analysing this *perception*, we find it made up of two elements:

a) judgment on the subsistence of a body, and

b) the idea of the same body.

3. Analysing the *idea* of body, we find it made up of three elements:

a) the *idea of existence*—mentally, we can conceive nothing, including bodies, without thinking their existence;

b) the *primary determination* of the idea of existence — this is the *essence* (the abstract, specific essence) of the thing; in the idea of body it is necessary to think, besides the idea of existence, the term in which the act of existence necessarily terminates, that is, the force or energy at work in all our sensations;

c) the *secondary determinations*, or feelable qualities - these are the various capacities the single force possesses for producing different sensations.

4. We conceive the three elements of the idea of body in the following way:

a) the *idea of being* is present naturally in our spirit;

b) when considered in isolation from the variety of sensations we experience, the *energy* at work in us producing sensations is a mental abstraction (an abstract, specific essence); but, in so far as it acts, it is known through our interior consciousness - in this respect, consciousness, because it reveals its own passivity equally in every kind of sensation, could be called a 'common sense';

c) finally, sensations are provided by the exterior sense-organs.

I have within me, therefore, all the faculties necessary to explain the origin of the perception and idea of body. I have: 1. the faculty that continually beholds being (intellect), the first element of the idea of body; 2. the faculty (a 'common sense') that perceives a *force* at work in me which is not myself, and which therefore forms the essence of body, the second element in the idea of body; 3. the five exterior sense-organs that perceive sensations, the third element in the idea of body; and finally, 4. the faculty of *primitive synthesis*, or judgment, with which I judge as subsistent what I think in the idea of body.

691. Having established the faculties enabling us to perceive the individual elements composing our intellectual perception of bodies, we now have to explain how we unite these elements.

First of all, our various sensations and the energy at work in us are bound together naturally in such a way that we have to make use of abstraction if we wish to have and to think this energy separate from its particular term, that is, from one or other of the sensations. Because energy is the sensation itself considered in its general concept of action done in us and not by us, it cannot be perceived without sensation. Sensation itself, taken whole and entire as it exists in our feeling, that is, as the feeling of a *determined action*, is what we have called elsewhere *corporeal sense-perception*.

We now unite corporeal sense-perception with the idea of being in general through the principle of cognition, which includes the principle of substance. We do this for the first time through the act with which we judge that a body subsists, that is, the intellective perception of body. This act may be described briefly as follows: we are intelligent; as such, we perceive all things as they are, as beings, when they act in us; the bodily force corresponding to the essence of bodies acts in us[46] so that we perceive it as subsisting; this is the perception of bodies.

We have given a general description of the formation of ideas of body. We still have to describe how we perceive our own and other bodies.

3

ORIGIN OF THE IDEA OF OUR OWN BODY, AS DISTINCT FROM EXTERIOR BODIES, THROUGH THE FUNDAMENTAL FEELING

692. Bodies exist as substances different from God and ourselves.

As the proximate cause of our sensations their essence consists in a certain *energy* acting upon us, relative to which we are passive. And any activity, different from our own, constitutes a different existence [. . .].

But we do not think of body only as a substance causing corporeal sensations. We bestow upon this substance other qualities such as extension, shape, solidity, mobility and divisibility, and generally speaking all the physical and chemical properties that bodies manifest in their relationship to one another and to us. Above all, body, with its capacity for life when duly united with the spirit (cf. 668-669), also possesses a capacity for change, causing pleasure and pain, sensations of colours, sounds, tastes, and so on, in us. This capacity can even deprive the body of life by separating it from the spirit. We have yet to show how the body is known by us as the *subject* of these properties and capacities. If we succeed in doing this, we shall also be able to explain the ideas of the various qualities attributed to the body.

It is clear that we are about to enter the wide field of physical nature where we have to deal with life, feeling, and

---

[46] As a result, the feeling we experience of bodies is a substantial feeling, an immediate action of bodies upon us, which allows us to use the word *perception* to describe the first knowledge we acquire of bodies.

different kinds of sensations in order to complete our study of
the ideas of matter and of body.

Article 1.
First classification of the qualities observed in bodies

693. Bodies possess a physical relationship amongst
themselves, and a relationship with our spirit. Observation
enables us to know the facts constituting and determining
these two relationships. In the physical relationship among
bodies observation shows that, when bodies are related to one
another locally, various changes take place, according to
stable laws. This capacity for receiving modifications or
alterations corresponding to their respective positions results
in the *mechanical, physical* and *chemical* properties of bodies.

But are these properties, such as propulsion, attraction,
affinity and so on, true powers of the body in such a way that
bodies are the true causes of all the modifications to which
they are subject?

This question has nothing to do with my argument. I
mention it in order that it may not distract the reader if it
should occur to him. We are not asking if propulsion,
attraction, cohesion, and affinity are true forces; we merely
want to know exactly the simple facts presented by
observation.[47]

694. All these facts can be reduced to the following
formula: 'When bodies are placed in certain positions relative
to one another, alterations occur which are constantly the
same, given the same bodies and the same positions.'[48] We
now ask how we form the ideas of these *alterations, ideas*
presented to our spirit by the *alterations.*

We mentally conceive mechanical, physical or chemical
alteration or change in bodies through their presence in
certain positions only in so far as: 1. the modified body
acquires a different capacity for acting upon us by causing

---

[47] Nevertheless what we shall say will throw light on the question.
[48] Any new condition changing the results would be reduced to a *body's*
approaching or distancing itself, which is excluded by the formula. It is understood
that no account is taken of the action of spirits; bodies alone are considered in their
mutual relationships.

internal or external sensations different from those caused previously; 2. the modified body acquires a different capacity for modifying another body — in the last analysis, this modification is reduced to the different capacity that the modified body possesses for acting upon us. When a body changes colour, taste, hardness, extension, force, or any of the feelable qualities resulting from a new state, it has changed only its capacity for producing sensations in us.

Only through our senses can we come to know when a body receives or loses some property or power without changing its feelable qualities. If the change were of such a nature that it presented no direct or indirect sign to our senses, we would not perceive it in our feeling, nor could we think, imagine or assert it.[49] If we adhere to pure observation, we have to say that any change in a body must be feelable by our senses in order to be something for us. It must finally produce some effect or action on our senses. Any difference found through such changes on the part of bodies can be reduced to a change only shown directly or indirectly to our senses. If one body changes colour in the presence of another, as grass and leaves become green on contact with the light, that body has suffered a change shown immediately to our senses.

If I magnetise a needle, the change in the needle is not immediately obvious to my senses. Its new properties are shown only by its power to attract other ferrous metal, or to point towards the pole when set on a balance. But seeing the needle act in this way means that I now receive a certain series of sensations I did not possess while the needle remained unmagnetised. As far as I am concerned, the new power acquired by the needle is reduced to certain new capacities for producing different sensations in me. And this is true whenever we examine the effect of one body's action upon another; any changes mentally conceived in a series of bodies acting upon one another are only capacities for acting upon us.

[49] If we were told about it, we would either have already experienced it with our senses, or not. In the first case, we would have some positive cognition of the fact, together with belief in what we have been told; in the second case, we would only believe in such a *change*, our cognition of which would be merely negative.

Let us imagine that the last of these bodies acts upon us. Through it, and only through it, we know the changes which have taken place in the others. If the series of bodies is called A, B, C, D, E, F, Z, we find that the change suffered by Z, which has affected us, can be defined as follows: 'The change in Z consists in its losing the capacity for producing one series of sensations in us, and acquiring the capacity to produce another series.' I go on to define the change experienced by F as follows: 'The change in F consists in acquiring the capacity for bringing about the change described in Z.' I have experienced the alteration in Z through my senses, but the change in F is known only through that in Z. If I now wish to substitute the known value of Z in the definition of the change in F, I produce an awkward definition, but nevertheless the only one possible: 'The change in F consists in its capacity for producing a change in Z through which Z loses its capacity for producing one series of sensations in me and acquires the capacity for producing another.' In the same way, the change in E can be defined only in relationship to the change in F, and so on, back to A.

Amongst the alterations in all these bodies, only that of Z is known to me of itself. The rest are known as first, second, or third causes of Z, and so on. Everything I know about the possibility of bodies modifying one another is reduced to Z's new power to modify me. Knowing the modification I experience, I know the capacity producing it in me. Knowing this, I know relatively the causes more or less proximate to it.[50]

Our observations show clearly that all mechanical, physical and chemical qualities or properties constituting the relationship of bodies to one another are (when we limit ourselves to observation alone) simply powers capable of modifying us and producing sensations within us.[51] Hence, all the ideas that we have or can have of these properties are

[50] My knowledge of corporeal capacities or forces, derived from their activity upon me, is the *first* cognition I can possess about them. This must not be taken to imply that I cannot deduce other truths about bodies from my *first* cognition. I simply affirm that my *first* experimental cognition is the *basis* of all my other reasoning about corporeal qualities.

[51] This does not remove from sensation the *extrasubjectivity* we have spoken about, and which we intend to explain more fully later in this work.

reduced to the different impressions the bodies make upon us, and to the different feelings they cause in us. We can mentally conceive only those mechanical, physical and chemical powers of bodies that either modify us, or modify and change the powers modifying us.

Our question, therefore, has been reduced to a careful examination of the relationship of bodies to us as we explain the origin of their feelable qualities, to which all other qualities are finally referred.

Article 2.
Classification of the corporeal qualities immediately constituting the relationship of bodies with our spirit

695. In speaking of the mutual connection of bodies, I have kept to pure fact and avoided difficult questions. I intend to follow the same method in indicating the connection of bodies with ourselves, and I ask readers to remember that I am confining myself to the limits placed by observation. I mention this to prevent a fruitless search for something not contained in the work.

Observation does, however, take us further in this field than it did when we examined the connection of bodies amongst themselves. We ourselves are one of the terms of the present relationship, and it is obvious that we can observe ourselves more intimately because our consciousness shows us the facts taking place in our spirit. While observation cannot tell us if bodies are the true causes of the modifications discerned in them, we can, given certain relative positions of the bodies in question, distinguish our own from other actions by simple observation on ourselves.

696. Observation of the connection of bodies with ourselves offers three distinct relationships which can usefully be indicated here.

The first relationship: an intimate bond between our sense-principle and a body that becomes its term (matter). This I call *life*.[52]

---

[52] That is, *animal life*.

The second relationship: a *fundamental feeling*[53] proceeding from life, that is, from the first bond. Through this feeling, we habitually feel all the material, sensitive parts of our body.°

The third relationship: the capacity possessed by the sensitive parts of our body for being modified in certain ways. Various species of external sensations correspond in us to these modifications, and in them the perception of bodies external to our body.

697. The connecting bond between external bodies and ourselves consists, according to the idea we have formed of it, in considering these external bodies as capable of modifying the sensitive parts of our body and providing our spirit with varied sensations.

Article 3.
The distinction between life and the fundamental feeling

698. First, we have to clarify the opinions proposed, then prove them. To clarify them, we begin by establishing clearly the distinction between *life* and the habitual, fundamental *feeling* caused by life.

We said that life was a certain intimate, unique bond of spirit with matter. In this bond, matter becomes the constant term of the sense-principle in such a way that the two things form a single underlying factor.[54]

Life is not feeling, or at least not feeling as observable by us; feeling is an effect of life. We can see this if we realise that all the parts of our body, provided we are alive and healthy, enjoy a life of their own and are joined to us according to their condition in such a way that this bond is called *life*. Thus animated parts in us carry out the vital acts proper to them, the principal of which are nutrition, heat, and vital movement, which result in incorruption and the capacity of each of the various parts of the body for different functions. But the seat of feeling, as we have seen, is not every part of the body, but only those parts we call *nerves*. We say this

---

[53] Proofs of these assertions will be given later.

[54] We do not want to describe the union here, but simply indicate it under its own name to avoid confusion with any other kind of union.

without wishing to enter the physiological field, foreign to our argument.[55]

699. We can usefully employ our imagination to form a clear concept of the sensitive body. Let us picture the human body present to us simply as a network of nerves and bereft of all parts that have no feeling. This is the sensitive body which, when joined to us vitally, enables us to feel. In my opinion, we perceive this body habitually and uniformly with an innate, fundamental feeling which, however, we do not advert to easily because of its continual sameness, although we are aware of the changes that take place as o   or other of our nerves is touched. Stimulation of the nerves produces a more marked sensation, easily adverted to because it is unusual, temporary and incomplete, not universal and constant like the first, stable feeling which, diffused throughout the nervous system, often goes unobserved, even by philosophers, because it is connatural and permanent.

700. We now have to examine in detail: 1. how we feel our sensitive body in which the fundamental feeling is present; and 2. how we perceive external bodies which only touch and stimulate our sensitive body.

Because bodies, as we have said, are perceived by us as substances causing sensations, and as subjects of corporeal qualities, it will help us if we apply what we have noted about the perception of bodies in general, first in a special way to bodies that feel, and then to feelable, non-sensitive bodies. We can then discuss both kinds considered as subjects of the qualities indicated in them, qualities which are either feelable or reduced to feelable qualities (cf. 693-694).

Article 4.
Two ways, subjective and extrasubjective, of perceiving our body

701. First, I note that our body (and when I speak of our body I always mean the part where we are sensitive) is perceived in two ways.

---

[55] Some physiologists have pointed to apparent anomalies in this law. For our purposes, it is sufficient that sensitive and non-sensitive parts are present in the human body, given certain cirumstances and moments.

1. Like every other external body it is perceived by touch and sight or, in a word, by all five sense-organs. When I perceive my sensitive body as *acting* on my five organs, I do not perceive it as sharing in sensitivity (this must be clearly understood because of its supreme importance), but as any other external body which, falling under my senses, produces sensations. In this case, one organ of my body perceives another. It is as if someone were to anatomise and perceive the nerves of another living, sensitive being whose nerves are not sentient to the person anatomising them, but only to the person to whom they belong.

2. We also perceive our body through the universal, *fundamental feeling* by which we feel life in us (a feeling witnessed by our consciousness, as we shall see later), and through the modifications experienced by the fundamental feeling itself in its adventitious, particular sensations.

These two ways of perceiving our sensitive body can be distinguished appropriately enough by the words 'extrasubjective' and 'subjective.' When we perceive our body subjectively, through the fundamental feeling given to us with life itself, we perceive our body as one thing with us. Hence, through its individual union with our spirit, it too becomes part of the sentient subject, and we can truly say that it is *felt* as *co-sentient* by us. On the contrary, when we feel our body extrasubjectively, in the way we feel external bodies through our five senses, it is outside the subject, like other bodies, and different from our sensitive powers. We do not feel it as co-sentient, but merely in its external data, in so far as it is capable of being felt. We must take great care to distinguish the *subjective* from the *extrasubjective* way of perceiving our body. A great part of what we have to say depends upon this distinction.

Article 5.
The SUBJECTIVE way of perceiving our body is twofold: the
FUNDAMENTAL FEELING and MODIFICATIONS of this FEELING

702. The *subjective* way of perceiving our body is twofold.
We perceive the sensitive parts of our body subjectively with
both the *fundamental feeling*, of which we have spoken, and
the *modifications* experienced by this feeling when impressions are made on the nerves.

703. The *second, subjective mode* of perceiving our body is
shown by an accurate analysis of external sensations which
reveals two things in every sensation:

1. the change arising in the sensitive, bodily organ
which, as a result of the change, is felt differently, that is, the
fundamental feeling suffers modification;

2. the sense-perception of the external body that has
acted upon us.

Let us take the sense of touch as our example. When we rub
some rough surface against the back of our hand, we feel two
things: the hand and the surface rubbing against the hand.
The first is what I have called a *modification of the feeling* of
our body; the second is the *sense-perception* of the rough
surface.

704. This *twofold quality of sensation* must be noted with
extreme care. But here it is sufficient to indicate the
connection between these inseparable, simultaneous feelings
included in the single fact of sensation. What I am saying is
this: on the one hand, the feeling that we experience through
the simple change[56] occurring in our bodily organ is a
modification of our fundamental feeling; on the other, we
have a sense-perception of an external body accompanying
this modification, but altogether different from it. This fact
occurs in us on the occasion of the first change and feeling,
although we are unable to find a necessary connection of
cause and effect between these two things. Nevertheless, as
we shall see, we can note the presence of a single cause of both

[56] The change in our sensitive organ is still not feeling. Nevertheless, given that
change, we feel because of our habitual feeling of the organ, whatever its state. Hence
its changes are also felt. But we must not confuse: 1. the physical impression on the
organ, with: 2. our first feeling of the same impression.

the *subjective feeling* and the *extra-subjective perception* experienced in the senses.

Article 6.
Explanation of sensation in so far as it is a modification of the fundamental feeling of our body

705. What do we mean when we say that our first feeling of change in a bodily organ is simply a mode of the fundamental feeling of life through which we feel all the sensitive parts of our body? This feeling begins when life begins and ends with life itself, but what does it enable us to feel? As we have said, the *matter* of this feeling are the sensitive parts of our body. But when we feel them, it is natural for us to feel them *as they are*; and if we feel these parts *as they are*, it follows that we feel them differently when they change their state. The matter of feeling has changed because the state of these sensitive parts has changed.

706. The activity of the fundamental feeling, therefore, is always the same in so far as it is alert to feel the *state*, whatever it may be, of our sensitive body. Consequently all the changes taking place in our bodily organs must be perceived by us through the act of the primitive, fundamental feeling. The act by which the feeling is modified as changes take place in the body constitutes the first of the two elements forming our adventitious sensations which arise when foreign bodies influence our body (here I follow common opinion).

Our body is perceived by one and the same act in two ways, substantially and accidently. The primary feeling and the change it suffers are two facts from which I conclude that the spirit, on first uniting itself individually with an animal body, must direct its activity in such a way that it mingles, as it were, with the body which it embraces and unceasingly perceives. As long as this vital union endures, the spirit perceives the body *in the act and state* in which it finds itself. When the body changes through external influence, the sense-activity of the spirit united with the body also undergoes a change of form. The spirit's activity experiences inevitable modification because its matter changes, although without deliberate intervention on its part. It is as though a person finds a scene changing before his eyes not because his glance varies, but because the object of his vision changes. In our case, the act of feeling is the same whether we are dealing with the body's first state, or with all the other acts and states and partial modifications of the sensory powers that follow the first state.

Article 7.
Explanation of sensation in so far as it perceives external bodies

707. If the nerves possess all the necessary conditions[57] for sensitivity, they feel when suitably touched and affected by external bodies. If we then go on to say that the sense-faculty of the soul is spread throughout the sensitive body, and that the soul with its power of feeling is therefore present to every part of the body, we are not offering a theory° but merely affirming what observation tells us. Because our power of feeling possesses a primary, essential act (the fundamental feeling), extending to all sensitive parts of our body, it is inevitable that this power, or rather the ever-present soul, experiences a disturbance (I mean, undergoes some passive experience) when the sensitive parts of the body are changed through the action of some external body. Perception of this passivity, experienced in a determined way according to the quality of the sensation, is what we call *sense-perception* of bodies, as I said above (cf. 674).

Article 8.
The difference between our own and external bodies

708. If our previous observations are correct, they show that two different forces affect our spirit. One causes our vital, fundamental feeling; the other modifies and changes the matter of this feeling, producing simultaneously both subjective sensation and bodily perception. According to our definition, the essence of body consists of an action done in us *in such a way* that we feel ourselves passive relative to the energy perceived intellectually as a being at work in us but different from us (cf. 674, 684). Experiencing two species of

---

[57] For example, communication with the brain. Without this, the organ feels nothing.

feeling, undergoing two kinds of action, and feeling two sorts of energy, we realise that there are two species of body, our own and external bodies.

The existence of these two kinds of body is proved by the fact of our consciousness, and is as certain as that fact [App. no. 14]. Not even sceptics deny conscious facts. The existence of these two bodies, therefore, is proved by observation, not by reasoning. In the same way, their definition does not exceed the limits of observation because we make it consist in a *certain* energy which we feel working in us without our being its authors.

709. But because it is difficult to reflect upon the fundamental feeling of our sensitive body, we need some suggestions to help us observe what takes place within us and become aware of this feeling which has escaped observation by so many thinkers. What follows, therefore, is not a proof from principle, but an attempt to make observation easier.

Article 9.
Description of the fundamental feeling

710. First, it is necessary (and we cannot insist sufficiently on this) to distinguish the existence of a feeling within us from our awareness of it. We can indeed experience a sensation or a feeling without reflecting upon it, or being conscious of it, although without reflection and the consciousness resulting from it, we could not affirm, even to ourselves, that we have and experience such a feeling. Indeed, if we did not know how to advert to it, we could happily deny its existence. [. . .] In order to conclude that a feeling was not present in the first moments of my existence it is not sufficient therefore to say: 'I did not notice then and do not notice now the universal feeling of my body that you posit.' You could have experienced it, and could be experiencing it now, without paying sufficient attention to advert to it.

Thinkers accustomed to concentrating on what takes place in their consciousness notice matters connected with the human soul that totally escape ordinary, unreflective people. 'Know yourself' is a much-needed reminder of where we normally stand with regard to self-knowledge. It is extremely difficult to discern what really takes place at the source of our passions, where our affections, habitual tendencies, and intentions are rooted. Only those generous enough to pursue virtue with all their mind and heart attain to adequate self-knowledge.

We must insist, therefore, that those who have not yet recognised in themselves the feeling of which we are speaking should focus their attention more carefully and delicately upon themselves rather than reject blindly any notion of the feeling. But if people have not been able to distinguish between *feeling* and *noticing feeling*, they are certainly ignorant of the essential difference between *sensation* and *idea*. Sensation can never be aware of itself; the understanding alone is aware of sensation because such awareness is either intellective perception of sensation, or reflection upon intellective perception. The act by which we understand sensation is altogether different from the act of sensation itself, that is, from the act with which we feel. If a being undergoing sensations does not perceive them intellectively, and remains unaware of possessing them, it can never indicate them to others or to itself. This explains why beasts lack the power of speech: they lack reason.

711. On the other hand, it may appear easy to advert to the existence of the fundamental feeling. In this case, there could be danger of mistaking the nature of the feeling. We need to remember that it always remains in us, even after the elimination of all acquired, external sensations. If I sit in a totally dark room, and stay perfectly still for some time while trying to disengage my phantasy from every image I have ever received, I will eventually arrive at a point where I seem to have lost all knowledge of the limits of my body. My hands and feet, and other parts of my body, will no longer be located in any discernible place. When I carry out this experiment as perfectly as possible, or try to arrive by abstraction at a moment anterior to all acquired sensations, I find that I still have a vital feeling of the whole of my body. It is easy to see, therefore, that if this feeling exists it must be very difficult to recognise and indicate because we do not normally pay attention to what is in us unless we experience change, without which we lack awareness, reflection and a

means of comparison. Change is necessary for awareness; it is not necessary in order to have *feeling*.

Let us imagine that we move from a cold to an oppressively warm room. Obviously we notice the higher temperature immediately. But this is not the case with people who are accustomed to such warmth. For them it is tolerable and perhaps natural. Because they are used to it and experience it stably; they feel the warmth of the room without adverting to it. Hence, if we are going to believe we feel something, it must be enough simply to know that it acts upon our senses. We have to reason in this way: because the heat acts upon my senses, it is felt, although it may not be adverted to.

712. It may be objected that the feeling of life, or of being alive, which only death can obliterate, extends to all the sensitive parts of my body. In that case, it would seem that my feeling necessarily puts me in touch with the size and shape of my body without the intervention of sight and the other senses.

The objection is based upon a misunderstanding of the point at issue. The size and shape of our body are not comprised in the vital feeling of which we are speaking. This feeling alone would never enable us to form visible or tactile images of our body which depend upon the use of sight and touch. The phantasy simply imitates what our eyes and hands have presented to us. But the primary, primitive feeling contains nothing like this. What we see and what we touch is only the matter of this fundamental feeling; and we have already noted the difference between perceiving bodies through the (supposed) *representations* coming from our external senses, and perceiving our own body through the *fundamental feeling*. The two, or rather three kinds of perception of our own body, are to be kept separate and distinct (cf. 701-707). I cannot say: 'Perceiving my body in the first way (with the fundamental feeling), I do not perceive it in the third way (through sense-presentations); therefore I do not perceive it at all.' This kind of argument is mistaken because it implies that the first kind of perception has to possess the characteristics of the third.

The real difficulty consists in forming a precise, well-defined concept of the fundamental feeling. If more is

demanded of the fundamental feeling than it actually
possesses, it immediately appears absurd and pointless. But
its denial in these circumstances is nevertheless unreasonable.

713. There is another difficulty to overcome. Attention is
normally given to *feelable representation* of bodies, the third
kind of perception which naturally holds our attention for
several reasons. First, because exterior sensations are more
vivid and impressionable than the other two kinds of bodily
perception. Second, because sensations continually change
and, as we have said, *change* draws the attention to
differences and comparisons in such a way that we think we
understand things only through this attention. Third, the
direct act of understanding, through which our intelligence
perceives exterior bodies, is our first, easiest and most *natural*
intellection. On the other hand, in order to perceive
intellectually our *subjective* body, we have to turn back and
reflect upon ourselves. This is not easy. Drawn outside
ourselves almost naturally, reflection is our last act and seems
to lack light when compared with our vision of exterior
things[58] [App. no. 15].

714. Our primitive feeling, therefore, does not make us
know the shape or the visible size of our body; it makes us
perceive our body as quite different from external sensations,
and can be grasped only by intense concentration upon
ourselves and the vital feeling quickening us. As we turn our
attention and observation to this feeling, we must be careful
to become aware of it as it is, without speculating about its
nature or adding to it products of our imagination and reason.

---

[58] The *chronological* order of feelings, therefore, is the inverse of the order of
advertence to them. First, we have our interior and fundamental feeling; second, our
exterior sensations. But we advert to our exterior sensations first, and then to our
feeling. Moreover, in order to advert to our feeling, we need to have acquired control
over our will so that we may freely reflect on and advert to our internal feeling. I
have already shown, however, that we acquire this control over our thoughts only
after having formulated abstract ideas (cf. 525-526). In order to advert to our interior
feeling, therefore, we must have: 1. *adverted* with our understanding to external
sensation, and *perceived* bodies; 2. obtained *ideas* from these *perceptions*; 3. obtained
(generic) *abstract concepts* from these ideas. When our spirit has developed to these
three levels, and by means of the last of them, acquired dominion over our thought
(which is done only with the help of language) (cf. 521-522), we are in a position
finally to direct our thought to our interior, fundamental *feeling*.

Article 10.

The existence of the fundamental feeling

715. This feeling must also extend to all the sensitive parts of our body. To recognise this, it is sufficient to note the movements continually occurring inside the body, such as the circulation of the blood, the constant movement of liquid substances, the various kinds of assimilation, and general vegetable life, which inevitably act on the sensitive parts of the body through the pressure they exercise. These facts also help to remove vestiges of doubt about the existence of the great number of small, habitual, unadverted sensations which take place in us without ceasing. It is clear that when a nerve is touched and modified some sensation must be present, even though our capacity for adverting distinctly to it has been obliterated by its constant recurrence.

I have no wish to investigate here the mysteries of the origin and continuity of life, but I must note that our habitual, fundamental sensation would be easier to understand if some interior movement amongst the components of the body were considered essential to life (and certainly here on earth such movement is a necessary condition for life). It is not difficult to conceive the existence of sensation where the sensitive parts of the body undergo change.

716. Some detailed observations may help us to understand that we feel our body continually.

1. Atmospheric pressure on all parts of the human body is constant [. . .]. Changes in this pressure, which may be felt when climbing a mountain, produce nausea, vomiting and dizziness, forcing us to admit what we can so easily deny: that we feel habitually.

2. Circulation of the blood must also cause some sensation, although we appear to feel it only minimally. But if some change takes place, through anger or fright for example, we feel our heart thump and our pulse race, or we faint. Previously we had felt our circulation, but had been unable to advert to it because there was nothing new to attract our attention.

3. Our body has a certain temperature which we feel because we feel heat. Nevertheless, we scarcely notice it unless some change takes place. Let us imagine that different degrees of temperature, from freezing to very hot, are applied successively to a part of our body. We feel them all, and we notice that we feel them. Amongst these changes in temperature is the degree of heat normally experienced by our body which, however, we do *not* normally notice. We do notice it, however, amongst other variations in temperature because we compare various feelings produced by the different temperatures. The comparisons we make do not produce sensations and are not felt because we make the comparison. Comparisons are possible because we feel each sensation independently of any other, and independently of any comparison. However, comparisons are necessary if we are to advert to the sensations which exist even when no comparison has been made. We have to say, therefore, that we feel habitually the natural temperature of our body, although we do not notice this habitual sensation.

4. All the particles forming our body are attracted to the earth by the force of gravity. There is continual action on every molecule of our body and although we do not advert to it, some sensation must result from it. This is more noticeable in overweight people, but it also causes tiredness when people walk a lot. Nevertheless, we are naturally accustomed to a uniform feeling from the first moments of our existence, and normally are unaware of it. If, however, the attraction of gravity were to cease, or fall appreciably, we would experience a new kind of general sensation which would attract our attention by its novelty. We would notice in ourselves a sense of lightness, agility and mobility never before experienced. If the attraction increased suddenly, we would be overburdened by the weight of our body and immediately notice the change even in the shape of our body. On the other hand, without gravity our body would at least lengthen (there may be other difficulties as well) because all its particles, instead of pressing on one another, would tend to expand rather than move downwards. If these changes in the force of gravity caused the feeling in our body, this would take place because the attraction does indeed exercise an effect

on our sensitive body which excites the feeling. This would also happen relative to the force actually exercised in normal circumstances, although the evenness of such a force would provide no stimulus for attention.

The same argument could be used about the cohesion present in the body, about the continual movements and alterations caused by breathing, digestion, growth and the infinite chemical changes taking place in us. Everything leads us to think that our body must be felt by us with a feeling of its own, made up of many tiny, particular feelings habitual in us from the first moments in which we are joined to our body.

But besides this complex of innumerable, particular feelings which fuse into a universal, constant feeling in the human being (as I have said, I do not wish to say whether they form part of life, although they are certainly necessary conditions for it in our present state), I believe that there is in the spirit itself, joined to matter and to being, a single, fundamental feeling that embraces and mingles with all other feelings, forming them into an undelineated, undefined feeling through which we feel our spirit and its body. It is a pure, very simple feeling, not an idea, from which it differs according to the distinction already established by which feelings actualise ideas.

Article 11.
The origin of sensations confirms the existence of the fundamental feeling

717. Feeling, therefore, is an original datum. Consequently, we are not investigating its origin, but discussing its modifications and the genesis of sensations.

718. Those philosophers who imagine that human beings began to exist without feeling make their fellows statues, and then go on to claim that sensations arise in these statues when they are touched by external bodies. Such a sequence of events, however, only creates inexplicable difficulties at odds with nature's normal way of acting. That feeling should

suddenly arise where no feeling had previously existed would be as difficult to understand as creation from nothing. According to this hypothesis, sensation comes about in the statue when exterior bodies act upon it, and provide it with a sense of its own existence. In this case, we feel something different from ourselves without being able to feel ourselves!

But the hypothesis (and it is nothing more than an hypothesis) is not only impossible to understand; it is also contrary to the constant order of nature which never works by leaps. There certainly would be a leap if we passed, when touched by an external body, from not feeling ourselves to feeling both ourselves and something outside. The external movement, which has nothing in common with sensation, would be accompanied by the creation of a spirit within us. How could we form the idea of a spirit totally devoid of any feeling and thought? Spirit has no extension, nor any other bodily qualities. Deprived of spiritual qualities such as feeling and understanding, it is annihilated or rather its idea is abolished from the mind even though imagination may pretend to fill its place with a spirit not attested by observation and consciousness.

719. All these reflections confirm the existence within us of a fundamental feeling. Serious attention to the nature of 'myself' would indicate the existence of this feeling because 'myself', reflecting upon itself, in the last analysis discovers itself to be a feeling constituting a sentient and intelligent subject.

Article 12.
Explanation of St. Thomas' teaching that the body is in the soul

720. What we have said explains the classical teaching, repeated by St. Thomas, that 'the soul is in the body by containing it rather than by being contained' (*S.T.* I, q. 52, art. 1).

The word 'body' indicates something known, as we noted earlier; we give names only to what we know (cf. 678). In order to know the meaning of body, therefore, we have to rely on experience (cf. 672-673), not on speculative reasoning or *a priori* deduction. Experience indicates as fact a certain action done in us of which we are not the cause. The essence of body was found consequently to be a certain[59] force modifying us (cf. 676). We feel this force from the first moments of our existence, although we do not advert to it; we feel it (cf. 715-716) in a constant, uniform way in a determined mode; and this is what we call 'our body'. This force, although essentially different from 'myself' (cf. 668-669), nevertheless acts in 'myself', in our spirit. We can rightly say, therefore, 'Our body is in our spirit' rather than 'Our spirit is in our body'. Later, we shall explain why common usage prefers the second to the first way of speaking.

Article 13.
The physical relationship between soul and body

721. This also explains why long arguments about the question of harmony between soul and body are unnecessary. We have to find the answer to this celebrated question in the fact provided by consciousness. Examining this fact, I find that which is passive to action and that which acts, that is, spirit and body. My body, therefore, is in *fact* and by *definition* a substance acting in a special way in my spirit. The physical influence needs no proof because it is already contained in the notion of body.

---

[59] Later, when we perfect the definition of body, we shall specify the precise meaning of 'certain'.

4

ORIGIN OF THE IDEA OF OUR BODY BY MEANS OF MODIFICATIONS OF THE FUNDAMENTAL FEELING

Article 1.
The analysis of sensation (contd.)

722. To form an exact idea of sensation,[60] we must set aside completely the idea of external bodies, which we always imagine as something striking our organs and producing sensations. Sensation is the only fact provided by consciousness and we must confine ourselves strictly to it.

723. The analysis of a particular sensation results in two elements: 1. a feeling; this, as we have seen, is a modification of the fundamental feeling (cf. 705-706) and its matter is the modified organ; and 2. a supposed representation or, as we call it, a *perception* of something different from us and our body (cf. 708-709). The first of these elements is *subjective*, a modification of the subject; the second, which I call *extrasubjective*, is a perception of something different from the subject.

A correct understanding about the nature of bodies and the way we perceive them depends on distinguishing accurately these two elements, which are never found separated; time spent on the distinction will not be time lost. We should also note that the first of these elements, the partial modification of our feeling, is the weaker of the two and therefore usually escapes our observation, which generally notes only the second to the exclusion of everything else.

Article 2.
Definition of the fundamental feeling, and how it is distinguished from the sense-perception of bodies

724. In every corporeal sensation, we perceive our sense-organ in a new way. Moreover, in a modification experienced

[60] The word 'sensation' is generally taken to mean an *acquired, particular* sensation.

by our sensitive organ there arises a perception of an agent different from us. The particular perception we have of our organ as *perceiving* is the modification of the fundamental feeling. As we have said, the fundamental feeling is a constant perception of the sensitive parts of our body in their first, natural state. The modified fundamental feeling is the perception of some part of our body modified and noticeably changed from its first, uniform, natural state.[61]

In order, therefore, to distinguish a particular perception of our modified organ from the perception of an agent that accompanies the perception but is different from it, we must consider the nature of the fundamental feeling, of which the particular perception is only a mode.

725. The fundamental feeling that comes from life is a feeling of *pleasure*, granted life in its natural, unspoilt state. It is uniformly and pleasantly diffused in all the sensitive parts of the body, without distinctive features. Thus, it would be impossible for anyone who has experienced only the fundamental feeling without ever experiencing particular sensations, to form the image or represenatation of our body (shape, size, etc.) which our sight and external senses offer. The fundamental feeling, then, is only pleasure diffused in a determined way,[62] and its modifications are only a particular *kind* of *sensible pleasure* and *pain*.

726. These considerations give us a more complete definition of the fundamental feeling as 'a fundamental action that we feel done directly and necessarily in us by an energy that is not ours; the action is naturally pleasant but can vary

[61] When I describe a particular perception of our sense-organs in this way, I am not taking anything for granted. Certainly *modification of the organ* is part of the definition; but the modification is not gratuitous from the moment the organ itself is a body and therefore part of the energy acting in us and simultaneously producing the fundamental feeling.

[62] Although the pleasure of life is diffused throughout all the parts of our body that have feeling, we cannot use the expression 'We refer the primitive feeling to different points of our body's *extension*' with the same meaning without putting the reader on his guard. This way of speaking could be confusing because it is not the way we know the body in the primitive feeling, nor therefore see or touch its *extra-subjective* extension or, *a fortiori*, its parts. When we speak about the feeling of the whole of our sensitive body, we should always remember it means nothing more than a *mode* of that pleasure. This mode becomes clothed, so to speak, with external, figured extension at the time we obtain the perception of our body with our external senses. But more of this in a later chapter.

according to certain laws, being in turn more or less pleasant, or even unpleasant.'

Article 3.
The origin and nature of corporeal pleasure and pain

727. The action we experience of the fundamental feeling is the very essence of corporeal pleasure and pain. The particular modifications the action undergoes (according to a law we need not investigate at the moment) are particular perceptions of our organs felt more pleasantly or painfully. Pleasure and pain are thus feelings which must be distinguished from what, in a sensation, is external and has shape. We shall go on to describe this second element of sensations when our idea of the first is so accurate (if that is possible) that we can no longer confuse it with any other.

Corporeal pleasure and pain are simply a change experienced in our spirit; they represent nothing and have no shape. They are a fact; they are what they are, and anyone who has no experience of them cannot understand them. Because such a change has nothing in common with anything outside it, it is undefinable and unintelligible to anyone who has not experienced it.

728. However, *corporeal*[63] pleasure and pain: 1. terminate in the subjective extension of the body (I call this extension therefore *matter* of the corporeal feeling); and 2. have different levels of intensity.

Article 4.
The relationship of corporeal pleasure and pain with extension

729. There is no difficulty in proving that corporeal pleasure and pain terminate in corporeal *subjective extension*.[64] For example, a square piece of metal placed on

[63] I use the word 'corporeal' as a simple sign to indicate the difference from any other feeling, without going more deeply into the difference and discovering a third element of sensation.

[64] Corporeal pleasure and pain are *experienced* passively in the spirit but at the same time they are accompanied by some *activity* of the spirit. I cannot stop at this

the hand is felt at every point it touches the skin; if the metal were a disc or any other shape, the points of contact with the skin would correspond to the changed shape.

730. In the same way, the fundamental feeling is present in all the sensitive parts of the body and therefore must extend and be referred to them; this is its *mode* of being. However this does not mean that just by looking we know the shape and size of the parts occupied by our pleasure or pain. The imagination is no suitable guide in these matters. Pure feeling, not the images seen by our eyes, makes us perceive the extension. Thus I call this extension *subjective*[65] to distinguish it from the extension presented by our sight or other senses relative to external bodies.

731. This should cause no difficulty if we reflect that this extension can be understood only as a *mode* of the feeling, as I have already said; the extension can change but never be separated from the mode of feeling.

We must not think that the feeling and the subjective extension are two entirely separate things, nor that the feeling is first centralised and then spreads through the extension already felt as through something different from itself. This imaginary explanation contains images taken from the sense of sight, but all such images must be excluded while we restrict ourselves to the pure subjective feeling we are discussing. If we concentrate carefully on ourselves, refusing to be distracted by these images, we will easily recognise in our own subjective feeling that it is impossible for the soul to perceive an extension different from the feeling with which it perceives that extension.[66]

point to describe how these two conditions are united — I have touched on this elsewhere. It is enough to note that in so far as pleasure and pain are acts of the spirit, it can be said they terminate in extension; but in so far as they are *experienced*, it is more accurate to say that corporeal extension terminates in them with its *action*. The reason for the truth of these two seemingly contradictory ways of speaking must be found in that strange but true and perfect *unity* between what is *subjective* and what is *extrasubjective*, between what is active and what is passive at the time of the action.

[65] This name does not indicate its nature because all extension is *extrasubjective*; it indicates its close union with sensation which is itself subjective and takes its mode from this extension.

[66] Extension is therefore the *matter* of the feeling, since matter and form together make one thing.

Anyone wishing to observe the nature and modifications of the fundamental feeling we are discussing, must set aside every *shape* presented by sense; he must get rid of the idea of external extension given by the sense of sight or any other sense. He must turn in on himself attentively and reflect on the pains and pleasures he may be experiencing uniformly or variably in the different parts of his body. He will then find that these feelings have no *figured* extension comparable to the extension we perceive with our eyes and other external senses in external bodies. However, he will find that they have a certain limitation, a *mode*. Now if we abstract this mode from the sensations and compare it with the extension perceived through our eyes or other external senses, we find that it harmonises with *extension*, and we call it *extension*.

Article 5.
Confutation of the opinion that 'We feel everything in our brain and then refer the sensation to the relevant parts of our body'

732. The following argument will be enough to show that the feeling of our own body must extend to all its sensitive parts. I agree with the those who say: 'It is by touch that you project outside yourself the objects you see; otherwise they would be attached to your eye like a veil.'°

733. But they go on to say: 'In the same way sensation takes place in the brain. If communication between an organ and the brain is interrupted, you feel nothing; you locate the sensations at the affected organ by means of habitual judgments.' Here I part company with them. In my opinion it would be impossible for us to touch bodies with our hand and move them externally, if we did not locate the sensation at the extremity of our hand, rather than just at some centre of our brain.

734. If it is by touching the object I see that I locate it outside myself, how do I locate my hand outside myself? For example, if I believe that the response of the sensitive nerve is in my head, why do I not feel in my head the sensation I feel in the touch of my finger-tips? Why do I not feel the response in my spirit or along my arm or in some other part

of my hand instead of only at my fingers-tips? In my opinion, this cannot be explained by acquired habit. If it could, we would have to demonstrate that there was first a time in our life when all sensations were not located at different points of our body, and later some *means* by which we learnt to locate them at the outside points; but no one has ever indicated this *means* nor can they.

If our eyes need touch to move things seen externally through a certain distance, and we conclude that the same must be true for the parts of our body felt by touch, then we must invent another sense of touch in the soul that would move the parts of the body outside the brain. This is absurd and denied by experience. There is therefore in the soul a power that immediately, and not by acquired habit, locates sensations at various parts of the body and feels them there.

Article 6.

Comparison of the two subjective modes in which we feel and perceive the extension[67] of our own body

735. The extension of our own body is a *mode* of the fundamental feeling. This *mode* is always present whether the *fundamental* feeling is in its *first*, natural state or in a state of accidental, adventitious modification. Hence we feel our body's extension *subjectively* in two modes: 1. by means of the fundamental feeling; and 2. by means of the modifications of this feeling, or the partial sensations, we receive through our organs.

736. The difference between these two ways of feeling our body subjectively must be noted:

1. The *whole* extension of our sensitive body is perceived by the fundamental feeling. But when the fundamental feeling is modified by some external sensation, only the *part* of the extension affected by the sensation is felt.

2. The extension of the body is felt in a *constant* mode by the fundamental feeling. The part affected by a sensation is felt in a *new* mode, more vividly than the other parts, or at

---

[67] We should not forget that this *subjective extension* is known to us only as a *mode* of the fundamental feeling without any *configuration*, unlike the extension of external bodies.

least in a different mode; it stands out from the other parts, as it were, in the feeling experienced by our spirit.

3. If life is present, the fundamental feeling produces a *necessary* mode of feeling. The affected organ in a sensation is felt in an *accidental* and adventitious mode.

4. The extension is felt *equally* with almost no variation by the fundamental feeling; at least we are certainly not conscious of any inequalities. In a sensation the organ is felt in many *different* modes, according to the different levels of pleasure or pain and the phenomena of colours, sounds, tastes, smells.

737. These four differences are sufficient to show clearly how unsuitable the fundamental feeling is for attracting our attention and being noticed. It is connatural to us, one with and part of our nature. On the other hand, no sensation of our own organ is essential. It is *partial, new* and *vivid, accidental* and *changeable*; it is equipped in every way for exciting our curiosity and attention; it attracts us to itself and makes us aware of perceiving the individual parts of our body with a subjective perception.

We can therefore conclude that, as regards the two subjective ways of feeling our body and its extension, the first (the fundamental feeling) easily escapes our observation, whilst the second makes itself known without any difficulty. No wonder that few people know they have this fundamental feeling, when the sensation of our own organs is so blatantly evident to all.

Article 7.
Further proof of the existence of the fundamental feeling

738. When one of our sense organs is stimulated, the sensation we experience is a fresh confirmation of the existence of the fundamental feeling, which precedes the sensation. For how could we locate the sensation at a certain part of our body if we had no feeling in it? We must note carefully: to say we feel the part at precisely the same time as we have the sensation is not sufficient. To feel the part means to locate the sensation at the part; this would mean we locate

the sensation at the part without having any feeling there. Such a fact would be inexplicable.

739. The same can be said about the capacity for moving the limbs of our body. If these were not naturally felt by us, they would be extraneous to us, and our will would not be able to move the limbs it wished with its internal act.

Without the fundamental feeling, therefore, two kinds of acts of our spirit would remain inexplicable and even absurd: the act by which our spirit locates a sensation it experiences at different parts of the body; and the act that imparts movement to them as it pleases. We must understand that it is "MYSELF" who locates sensation and produces movement as an effect of my very own activity.

Article 8.
All our sensations are simultaneously subjective and extrasubjective

740. I call sensation *subjective* in so far as I feel my co-sentient organ in it; I call it *extrasubjective* in so far as I simultaneously feel an *agent* outside my organ. If we observe the fact of sensation attentively, we find there is no sensation in which we do not feel our sentient organ. Likewise, when we feel a modification of our organ, a perception of something outside the organ takes place in our spirit. We call this *corporeal sense-perception*; it is very often so strong and vivid that it engages all our attention, so that we forget the organ completely and are unaware of the sensation.

741. The difference between the *corporeal sense-perception* and the *sensation* in the sentient organ is so important that we cannot be too careful in identifying it. The solution of a great number of psychological problems depends on the clear recognition and demonstration of this difference.

To indicate the co-existence of these two perceptions, I will begin with the sense of sight. We all accept that feeling our own eye, the organ of vision, is different from seeing bodies with our eyes. Anything perceived by our eyes has such a vivid, attractive presence that it draws all our interest, especially when our eyes have been conditioned and taught, so to speak, by touch. When our gaze is captured by a panorama or a beautiful work of art, we pay no attention to our eyes themselves where we are experiencing a weak sensation caused by the light striking them and passing through unnoticed. But this sensation, although unnoticed, is very real. Imagine a beam of strong light suddenly striking our eyes so that it is too intense for the pupils. At once we will feel and will be conscious of an unpleasant sensation in our eyes, smarting from a light too strong for them. In situations like this, we fix our attention on the organ affected by pain. We may conclude that, to be aware of feeling our perceiving organ, there must be a level of unusual, vivid pleasure or pain drawing our attention away from the exterior agent perceived by the organ.

What I have said about the eyes clearly demonstrates the elusive but true fact that granted a suitable modification of a sense-organ, we experience the two things I have mentioned, that is: 1. we feel the modified sense-organ; and 2. we perceive the exterior *agent* in a way compatible with our feeling. This *perception* has nothing to do with the *sensation* of the organ; but the perception is so indivisibly joined to the sensation that it forms one thing with it so that one cannot exist without the other.

742. The same can be said of hearing, smell and taste. Hearing gives us sound, but sound is not the sensation we have of the acoustic organ with which we perceive sound, nor is it the exterior body. Sound, which arises when our organ is modified, has no similarity with the feeling we have of our organ; the stimulating action we feel is different from the action produced in us by our modified organ. The stimulating action accompanied by the phenomenon of sound is more assertive than the feeling we have of our organ and is able to attract our attention, especially when the action has special qualities. Thus, if I hear a flute or harp, I am attracted by the pleasant sounds and pay no attention to my ear, which would need to be modified in a painful way, for example, by a deafening explosion, to turn my attention from the sounds to the feeling of my ear. When such a thing happens, we usually cover our ears to protect them, which is a clear sign that we perceive the organ.

743. The same is also true for the senses of smell and taste: these are the phenomenal part of the sensation experienced when the organs are modified by their corresponding agents. For example, when we smell a carnation or taste honey, we can note the same two things. In the first place, my olfactory nerves are stimulated by particles from the carnation; it does not matter whether the stimulation is a slight vibration of the nerves, or a small mark or impression made on them. The question is: what do we perceive by smell? We certainly do not perceive the vibration or impression to which smell bears no resemblance. Nor does smell suggest any movement of, or form received by the olfactory nerves. Smell is a particular feeling arising in our spirit on the occasion of those minute and perhaps imperceptible movements of our nostrils. It is this feeling I call the phenomenon of smell. On the other hand the odorous particles striking our nostrils could be of sufficient force and intensity to cause us pain, and make us aware of the feeling of our nose, as happens when an offensive smell makes us wrinkle it with displeasure. Although the weakness of the impression may prevent this, we cannot say that the phenomenon of smell (in which we have the term of an external action) is not completely different from the feeling we have of the organ itself.

The same can be said about taste. The different form that our taste buds assume on contact with honey is not what we feel in the taste. The *taste* is the phenomenal part of the sensation and is completely independent of the perception of our palate.

Article 9.
Touch as a general sense

744. Touch is a general sense; it is equally present in all the sensitive parts of our body.°

745. The other four senses are themselves touch, from which they are distinguished only by the phenomenal part of sensation. When they are stimulated, these senses are subject to touch-perception and to this extent are the same as touch.[68]

---

[68] We have seen that *touch* has a *double* nature: it is simultaneously *subjective* and *extrasubjective* in so far as we perceive the sentient organ (the subjective part) and the

But certain kinds of touch affect our spirit with four kinds of phenomena: colour, sound, smell and taste. These phenomena distinguish the organs and, as a group, are different from touch which is common to them all and diffused through the rest of the body.

Article 10.
The origin of touch

746. The sense of touch in its *subjective* element is only the capacity for modifying the fundamental feeling. Extension is only the *mode of being* of the fundamental feeling, which extends to every sensitive part of our body. If therefore the mode of being changes, so does the fundamental feeling. This is why we experience sensations of touch when some suitable motion takes place in our body.

Article 11.
The relationship between the two subjective ways of
perceiving our body

747. Because the sense of touch is the foundation of all the different kinds of sensations, we also feel a modification of the sentient organ although we do not always advert to it. In fact we rarely advert to a modification of those senses in which the four sensible phenomena are found. The intensity and singularity of these phenomena, like their usefulness and necessity, attract all our attention away from the unassertive sensation of the organ itself. But this does not happen so noticeably in the sense of touch which, phenomenally weaker, concentrates our attention more on the organ itself.

The second way of perceiving our body (by means of particular sensations) is not essentially different from the first. It is *subjective* in so far as, together with it, we sense our organs as *co-feeling*, not just as *felt*; in short, we feel them as forming one thing with the feeling subject, 'myself'.

---

touching, external agent (extrasubjective part). From what I will say later, it will be more evident how the *twofold sensation* and the four *phenomena* are present in the particular senses we are discussing.

748. But in these two ways of feeling and perceiving our body, the matter of feeling and sensation (the body itself) is always the same. Hence there can be no contradiction between them. What makes them coherent and equal is the fact that we locate feeling and sensation at the same points in space.

5

CRITERION FOR THE EXISTENCE OF BODIES

Article 1.
A more perfect definition of bodies

749. After our analysis of the fundamental feeling and acquired sensations (in their subjective part), we can offer a more perfect definition of bodies. [. . .]

752. As usual we start from observation because our description must depend on this. Whether bodies have something that is outside our experience or intellective conception of them is irrelevant.

Observation confirms that we are passive in sensations, that is, we experience an action of which we are not the authors. Consciousness of such an action is consciousness of a certain energy acting in us; and knowledge of such energy is knowledge of a being, a substance. Hence the first but imperfect definition we gave of body: 'a substance acting in us in a *certain mode.*' To perfect this definition, we had to discover the meaning of 'in a certain mode', which we then inserted into the definition. We went onto analyse sensation because sensation or corporeal feeling is how this kind of substance acts. The analysis showed a constant, uniform feeling[69] and an action partially modifying this fundamental feeling, that is, two actions, two energies, two substances, two bodies. Our own body produces the fundamental feeling and an external body modifies our body; we experience a body that is co-feeling as well as felt, and a body that is only felt. The fundamental feeling, the action of our body, is not

---

[69] Growth of the human body modifies the fundamental feeling.

only a pleasant feeling, but is a pleasure with its own mode and limitation called *extension*, which does not derive from the simple notion of pleasure.

All acquired sensations are a species of touch. *Touch* is both a *subjective* and an *extrasubjective* sensation because in it two things are felt: the feeling *organ* (the *subjective* part) and the *external agent* touching us and producing a sensation of touch (the *extrasubjective* part). The *subjective* part is a modification of the fundamental feeling and makes us feel in a new, more intense way whatever part of our body is affected, while locating it at the same points as the fundamental feeling. Furthermore, there are four classes or species of sensation particular to four organs of our body. They have four kinds of phenomena attached to them, *colours, sounds, tastes and smells*.

This analysis of the action of the corporeal substance in us indicates that the essence of bodies must consist in: 1. pleasure and pain; and 2. extension, in which pleasure and pain are experienced. These are the two common, variable elements in the action. We can therefore improve our definition by saying: 'Body is a substance producing an action in us, felt by us as pleasure or pain and having a constant mode called *extension*.' To which we may now add 'It can be accompanied by four kinds of phenomena called colour, sound, smell and taste'; but we should note that this addition does not mean these phenomena must be present. They are only an *aptitude* of a body to arouse them, given the necessary conditions.

753. Thus, if such a substance is firmly joined to us in the bond we call *life* (I am not investigating this here, whatever it may be), it is a subjective body, exercising in our spirit a constant, uniform action called the *fundamental feeling*. If this bond is absent, the substance is a foreign body, able to produce only partial, transient sensations.

Article 2.
The general criterion for judgments on the existence of bodies

754. With the establishment of the definition of body (cf. 752), we have also established the criterion for judging about

its existence: 'I can say I am certain of the existence of a body when I am certain of the existence of that which, forming its *essence*, is expressed in its definition.'

Article 3.
Application of the general criterion

755. In the first perception of our body we experience the feeling of life as pleasure or as the pleasant, individual union of a body with us. This feeling, endowed with extension as one of its modes, is located at different points of space.[70] Thus by means of extension we perceive a body.

756. The existence of external bodies is proved in the same way. We perceive the two elements found in the definition of body. The primitive extension in which we locate our feeling undergoes some modifications from a cause different from us. In this modification we find: 1. a partial, adventitious sensation of pain or pleasure which, 2. is diffused in an extension more limited than, but not exceeding, the first extension. Sometimes the phenomena of the four organs, eyes, nose, ears and palate are also present, if the organs are stimulated. These conditions confirm our perceptions of an external body.

757. A sensation of pleasure or pain by itself does not indicate the presence of a body. It tells us that an action is being done in us and that the action must have a cause different from us, but of itself it would never tell us that this cause is a body, because the essential element of extension would be missing. The sensation must be capable of making us perceive an extension if we are to have a corporeal sensation. The extension determines our sensation, making it a *corporeal* or *material* sensation. And viceversa: extension by itself is not body, since the first essential element of body is the *energy* for producing a feeling in us.

---

[70] To say the feeling is located at different points of space is the simple way of indicating space perceived in a *figured* way. But calling extension simply a *mode* of feeling keeps us within the subjective sensation of extension.

To avoid making a mistake about the existence of a body, we must verify for ourselves the following conditions or elements that form its essence: 1. a feeling (our passivity, external action); 2. an extension to which the feeling is referred (*mode* of the feeling).

758. There is an *action* done in us that constitutes the fundamental feeling; joined to this feeling is the *mode of extension*. Thus a body exists permanently united to us. Its existence is no longer subject to doubt because we cannot be deceived as to whether we are alive or dead; the two elements constituting our body in this case are two facts of consciousness.

In adventitious sensations we distinguish: 1. a modification of the fundamental feeling, that is, a new, more intense sensation of some part of our body; and 2. a perception of an agent outside the extension in which our fundamental feeling is diffused. The modification is the second *subjective* way of perceiving our body; the perception is the *extrasubjective* perception of external bodies. The existence of our body therefore is always founded on the evidence of the fundamental feeling.

759. The certainty of the existence of external bodies is also founded on the fundamental feeling, because their action on us is indivisibly joined to the modifications of the feeling, while their extension is measured by the extension first occupied by the fundamental feeling.

Article 4.
The certainty of our own body is the criterion for the existence of other bodies

760. Our body, perceived in the first mode, becomes a *criterion* for the existence of all other bodies. The other modes of perceiving a body must be reduced to this first mode, that is, perception by the fundamental feeling. Thus, the second *subjective* mode is reduced to the first because it is a modification of the fundamental feeling, and the third *extrasubjective* mode (for external bodies) is reduced to the first because the extrasubjective extension becomes known through a comparison with the subjective extension.

Article 5.
Application of the criterion to possible errors about the
existence of some part of our body

761. We cannot err about the existence of our own body
perceived in the first mode, that is, with the fundamental
feeling (cf. 755-759). We can be misled about the existence of
some part of our body when it is perceived by acquired
sensations. A perception of this kind includes the other two
modes, the *subjective* and the *extrasubjective* (cf. 760).

762. For the moment I am not concerned with possible
error in the third mode, that is, in perceiving our body as an
external force rather than as subject. This error, common to
the perception of all external bodies, will be dealt with later.
For the moment I want to examine possible error concerning
the existence of some part of our body perceived in the
second subjective mode. For example, an amputee acutely
feels the pain of a lost hand or foot, not in the stump but in
the limb that still seems to be there. In this case the person
locates the pain deceptively and wrongly at the extension.
The error can be discovered by applying the criterion.[71]

The amputated limb is not felt by the fundamental feeling
but by the adventitious sensation of the pain. To know
whether such a sensation is misleading, it must be reduced, as
we have said, to the fundamental feeling as its criterion and
proof. This is done when we verify that the acquired
sensation is a modification of the fundamental feeling. In the
case of the amputee, the sensation of pain in the arm or leg is
certainly a modification of the fundamental feeling but this
fact does not prove the existence of our body (cf. 757); the
extension felt by the sensation must be capable of being
reduced to the extension of the fundamental feeling. Now we
have noted that there are two characteristics of the
fundamental feeling: 1. its constant, uniform existence; and 2.

---

[71] The cause of this error lies not in the sensation but in an *habitual judgment*.
When we still had our hand or foot, the pain we felt was referred to them by a
necessity of nature because that was where we felt the pain. This necessity then
became a *habit* which remained even when the necessity had disappeared. And
because we now feel a pain that is no different from the previous pain in our hand or
foot, we think it is the same and assign it to the same place without adverting to the
real place.

its ability to be modified. By applying this second characteristic, let us see if the extension of the amputated limb is felt in reality.

If the limb we perceive is the same limb felt by the fundamental feeling, it must be subject to modifications, because the fundamental extension (our hand perceived by the fundamental feeling) is essentially modifiable. If then the hand exists, it can be touched, seen, moved, etc. because these are modifications of the fundamental extension. But this cannot happen with the amputated hand — it is felt, but not by the fundamental feeling. It is a misleading phenomenon since it cannot be reduced to the fundamental extension nor shown to be a modification of it. Indeed when I feel my hand through the pain I experience in it, the mode of this sensation, that is, extension, must be identical with the extension of the fundamental feeling; the only other possible difference is that the sensation in the fundamental feeling endures but not so strongly, while the acquired or adventitious sensation, although more intense, is partial and transient.

Article 6.
Response to the idealists' argument based on dreams

763. The idealists' argument, drawn from what we see in dreams, is clearly without foundation. They ask: could life not be one long dream? They do not observe that the images in dreams may mislead us about the existence of external bodies but not about the existence of our own body; in fact, they argue against this.

The illusions of dreams are the result of the body's being stimulated in a certain way and would therefore be impossible if we did not have a body. They do not cast doubt on the existence of bodies in general; on the contrary, they prove and confirm their existence. Later we will see how to distinguish between what is false and true in external phenomena.

6

ORIGIN OF THE IDEA OF TIME

Article 1.
The connection between what has already been said and what follows

764. We have seen how we perceive our body in the first two *subjective* ways. We must now speak about the third, the *extrasubjective* way, which is valid for all bodies as external agents applied to our corporeal sense-organs. Even our own body can be perceived, not as ours, but as any external body. However, before examining this third way, we must mention some *abstract ideas* that can be obtained, at least in part, from the body perceived subjectively.[72] They are the ideas of *time*, *movement* and *space*.

765. In fact, *time* is connected with all the actions and experiences we are aware of; *movement* does not require our exterior senses for its perception, because *our locomotive faculty* is an *internal*, subjective faculty whose existence is confirmed by our consciousness; lastly *space* or *extension* is also a mode of our corporeal, subjective feeling[73] from which it cannot be separated, although we can distinguish it mentally in our own feeling just as we can note its *mode* of being in any other thing, even if the mode is *per se* inseparably united to *being*.

The starting point for these three ideas of *time*, *movement* and *space* is found in the ideas we have so far discussed. However it will help if we make use of our exterior senses and *extrasubjective* perception of bodies, so as not to separate what our mind customarily sees as united.

---

[72] Our mind makes this abstraction only when it is sufficiently developed, through the use of our exterior senses. But this does not prevent the body, subjectively perceived, from being the foundation of the abstractions we are discussing.

[73] This is all we have discovered so far about extension; later we shall understand its nature better and see that it exists not only in the subject but also in the agent.

Article 2.
The idea of time derived from consciousness of our own actions

766. When we perform an action we are limited in two ways.[74] The immediate, interior feeling by which we are conscious of performing the action informs us of this double limitation. The first limitation is the *level of intensity* in the action; the second is its *duration*. The words 'intensity' and 'duration' indicate the *limitations* in their abstract state, after the separation from the internal and external actions they are limiting has made them two mental beings.

767. We can increase the *intensity* and *duration* of our actions up to a certain point, and we can imagine them increasing indefinitely. *Successive duration* is the idea of *time*.

768. Just as my present action has *successive duration*, so has every other action done by myself or others. Comparison of the duration of one action with that of other actions gives a certain relationship, called the *measure of time*.

769. The measure of time is generally based on an important, uniform, constant and easily noticed action, such as the movement of the earth on its axis around the sun. The parts of this movement form the parts of common measures of time: years, months, days, etc.. Any action at all could have been chosen, provided the duration of all other actions was related to it.

770. I can increase or decrease the duration of my own actions. But if I want to retain the same *quantity* of action in a shortened duration, I must compensate with greater intensity; and if I increase the duration, I must reduce the intensity. There is therefore an invariable relationship between the *duration* and *intensity* of the action.

In motion, the *intensity* is the *velocity*, which is greater in direct proportion to the distance covered and in indirect proportion to the time taken to cover the distance; hence we have the formula $v = \frac{s}{T}$ or $T = \frac{s}{v}$.

---

[74] Life, which is also limited in *duration*, is the first action we feel ourselves doing. Hence the feeling of *time* is included in the *fundamental feeling*. But the analysis of this feeling is difficult, and here I need only mention what is necessary for my purpose.

771. The constancy of this relationship is founded on two constant data: 1. the constant quantity of the desired effect or action; and 2. the limited quantity of forces involved, which is also constant and given. Thus, a law founded in the nature of things establishes that within a certain duration, only a particular, fixed *intensity* can produce a determined *quantity of action.*

772. Let us now suppose that the duration of a desired action is fixed but not its quantity and intensity. By applying various levels of intensity to the duration, we have various quantities of actions or effects proportionate to the levels of intensity. The general result is that for any duration, the quantity of action will be exactly proportionate to the intensity of the action; this gives us the idea of the *uniformity of time.* No matter what is done within a fixed duration, there is a constant relationship between the intensity of the action and its quantity; where little has been done, more can be achieved, provided the intensity is heightened. In short, I can think the possibility of doing something within a certain duration by means of a determined intensity of action; the same applies to any similar duration.

773. We can express the relationship between quantity, intensity and duration of action by the formula: $T = \frac{Q}{S}$, where T = duration, S intensity, and Q quantity. This is valid where there is only one agent; if there are several agents, then the formula is $T = \frac{Q}{SM}$, where M is the number of agents.

Article 3.
The idea of time indicated by the actions of others

774. What has been said about actions attested as our own by consciousness can also be said about actions we perceive, but of which we are not the authors. In this case, time is a *limitation* not only of actions but also of passive experiences. *Passive experience* and *action* are very often the same fact considered from opposite points of view.

Article 4.
The pure idea of time

775. The limitation we have called 'successive duration' can be abstracted from all the actions and passive experiences of finite beings. We can also add the *idea of possibility* (of a possible action, that is) which, as we have said, is innate in us. This gives us the pure idea of time, that is, of time in a possible, but not real action.

Article 5.
The idea of pure, indefinite long time

776. We perceive successive duration as 'a possibility that a certain quantity of action can be obtained by means of a certain level of intensity.' This is the idea of time in general, the pure idea, given by observation.

777. Granted constant intensity, *quantity of action* is the *measure of time*, while *uniformity of time* means simply 'the same quantity obtained by a constant level of intensity.'

778. This quantity of action, obtained by a fixed, constant level of intensity, can be conceived as repeated an indefinite number of times, if we use the idea of *possibility*. Hence the idea of *pure, indefinitely long time* composed of: 1. the idea of *possibility*, which is *per se* indefinite; and 2. the (abstract) idea of one of the two limitations to which successive actions are subject.

Article 6.
The continuity of time

§1. Everything happens by instants

779. Anything subject to succession begins, grows, comes to perfection and then deteriorates and perishes. But at whatever moment we observe this process, we find a determined state. Indeed, according to the principle of contradiction, there cannot be a part or perfection that is and is not at the same time. Let us take for example a baby cutting a tooth, or an adolescent's facial hair changing into a beard. In

answer to the question 'Has the tooth come or the beard grown?' we can indeed reply 'Not yet, but it is *beginning*.' Nevertheless, although the word 'beginning' involves a mental relationship with the future state of the thing, that is, when the tooth is formed or the beard grown, the early form of the tooth and the first growth of hair already exist as such. Their state is not something between being and not-being.

780. This simple observation of fact leads us to the remarkable but true conclusion that all that happens, happens in an instant provided we understand the words 'all that happens' to mean whatever exists (a part of nature or an element) at each instant. It does not mean a composite thing, or something with a fully formed nature (which is what usually attracts our attention). At any given moment the thing, whatever it might be, is perfect relative to itself and its existence, but imperfect when considered as part of a greater thing, of which it is an element or outline or principle.

781. However a serious difficulty now presents itself. If all that happens, happens in an instant, what is the origin of continuous time? The idea of time is obtained by abstraction from what happens, from actions. Therefore when we think a series of things happening, each one of which happens in an instant, we perceive a series of points, a succession of instants, but never continuous time.

§2. The difficulty is not solved by the idea of time obtained by observation alone

782. Let us return to the example of the growth of hair and see whether observation alone offers us an idea of time containing the characteristic of true continuity. Suppose one hair has taken two months to grow ten centimetres. This growth is an *action* which we call *complex* because it consists of many little actions of shorter duration. The same would be true for the production of any other kind of thing: the unfolding of a flower, the sculpting of a bas-relief; any event whatever that gave or changed the being of anything, would be called a *complex action* because it could always be mentally subdivided into many parts which would still be actions or events.

We must note carefully that the time taken by the hair to grow maintains a constant proportion to all the actions done within the two months, as we mentioned above (cf. 764-765), that is, in proportion to the intensity of the action. With the intensity of the action fixed for two months, any entity acting within this period can give only one *quantity of action* or determined effect. Let us see how this complex, successive action, or total effect, can be thought as divided into instants during the two months period.

Suppose we distribute the instants in such a way that the hair has grown 10 cm. in 5,184,000 instants. In each of these instants it will have acquired its corresponding tiny increase. Now, if at the end of two months the hair's length must not exceed 10 cm., the interval between the instants of its growth must be determined. If we presume the interval is uniform, it will be exactly one second. Intervals as small as these (or smaller) would completely escape our observation and could not be measured. They can be measured only by reasoning, that is, by knowledge of the total effect or quantity of action taking place in a fixed, observable length of time, like the two months. The measure of the quantity of action is the comparison with the other quantities of action within the same length of time.

Let us return to the little intervals we suppose exist. In themselves they are not observable, because as such they are a negation, a cessation of action. They are observable only through the relationship between the different frequency of instants in different actions. If we could observe the successive, instantaneous growth we have supposed takes place every second in the hair, we would not be able to measure each of the seconds by observation of the action alone, unless we compared them with the intervals of something happening in us, like our heart beat or a degree of tiredness. On the other hand, if we compared different actions, like the growth of an old man's hair and a young boy's, we would notice that while the old man's grows a certain amount, the boy's grows two or three times that amount. This would give us a measure of the interval: it would be the quantity of action (the intensity being uniform) taking place in the course of two instants. The measure of the intervals, granted it is observable, would simply be the relationship between the quantity or total effect of different causes acting within two instants. It would not differ in any way, therefore, from the measure of a noticeable duration or series of instants, at the end of which we compare greater quantities of actions or total effects large enough to be observed.

So far we have shown: 1. everything happens by instants; 2. the idea of time given by observation is an interconnection of these events, that is, of the quantities of actions within the instants. We can therefore conclude that 'any observation, even an observation so acute and penetrating as to be beyond our capabilities, could never directly offer our mind the idea of a *continuous* time, that is, of a continuous succession. It would supply only the idea of a series of instants of greater or less proximity to each other and their relationship.' Nevertheless, we do have the idea of a *continuous* time and *observation* has not explained it. We must therefore look elsewhere.

§3. We need to consider the simple *possibilities* of things, which must not be confused with real things

783. We now separate our mental conceptions of time given directly by observation from those we form by abstract reasoning, which itself starts from observation. Observation presents *matters of fact* to our understanding, that is, to our faculty of judgment. *Ideas* express *pure possibilities*, not matters of fact. We must not disdain pure ideas that express simple possibilities [. . .], although *possibilities* must be kept distinct from cognitions of *real* things and facts.

Ideas or possibilities are important for two reasons: 1. we cannot reason without them, even about things of fact, as we learn from the theory of the origin of ideas, which shows how possibility is necessarily mingled in every idea (cf. 470); 2. reason can sometimes establish which element in possible contradictions is true. A major mistake, however, is to combine what is possible in a thing with what is fact; this falsifies the method itself or means of finding the truth. In our case, therefore, we must carefully distinguish ideas of time obtained directly by observation and presenting us with facts,[75] from ideas that express only simple *possibilities*.

§4. Granted the same intensity of action, observation presents time simply as a relationship of the quantity of different actions.

784. Only *large actions* are observable because any action, divided and reduced below a certain minimum, escapes observation. The relationship of the quantity of these large actions (with due regard for the intensity involved) can be observed.[76] Granted the same intensity, the different quantity is followed by a circumstance enabling observation to provide us with the idea of time. An action of smaller size (the intensity still being uniform) is terminated and observable at an instant in which we cannot observe the action of larger size, that is, the total effect, because it is not yet finished. This explains the aptitude of the smaller action, part of the large action, to be observed at the time when the large action, composed of a more or less long succession, is not yet fully present to us. We call this aptitude the *successive duration of the action*. It is the same as the idea of time offered by observation.

§5. The idea of pure time and of its indefinite length and divisibility are mere possibilities or concepts of the mind

785. Up till now we have dealt only with the *fact*. So, granted the fact, what are the *possibilities* that present themselves to our mind? We must remember that, in deducing *possibilities*, our mind goes as far as it can, right to the point where it sees contradiction.

1. First, our mind observes many real actions happening within any two given instants. These actions differ in quantity but maintain a certain relationship. By abstraction

---

[75] These cognitions are perceptions of things composed of *ideas* and *judgments*. *Ideas* separated from *judgments*, and not subject to any other action, express *possibilities* some of which have been actuated in reality.

[76] Previously conceived of course by our intelligence because only intelligence observes *relationships* [. . .].

the mind thinks these real actions as simply possible and thus forms the *pure idea of time* (cf. 775); it thinks that between two given instants[77] certain quantities of action can take place having a certain relationship with their respective intensities and amongst themselves.

786. 2. Next, the mind considers that the various large actions it observes are longer and shorter, that is, within two given instants, an action is sometimes repeated twice, three times or even a thousand times. Mentally therefore, we think the *possibility* of *indefinite* repetition of the action, even beyond the two instants, and see the action no longer as real but as a never-ending posssibility. Hence we have the *indefinite length of pure time,* which is only a mental *possibility.* The mind sees no contradiction in the indefinite repetition of any action no matter how many times it has been performed in the past.

787. 3. Noticing longer and shorter actions amongst those we can observe, we realise that while one action is being done, another is repeated many times. Our mind then reasons as follows: the shorter is repeated twice, three times, a thousand times, while the longer action is performed only once, but at the moment when the shorter action is completed for the first time, only a part of the longer action is done. Hence our mind thinks an action to be the result of many parts or else a complex of many smaller actions. It is true that a very short action escapes our observation but we then think of the *possibility* of a powerful observation, beyond human capacity. Such a thought, which contains no contradiction, enables us to see the possibility of an action shorter than the minimum we can observe. We recognise the *possibility* of indefinitely shorter actions because our mind finds no contradiction in any action, however short. This is the source of our idea of the *indefinite divisibility of time.*

788. 4. The *indefinite divisibility of time* is only the mental possibility of identifying a series of ever-closer instants and thinking of ever-shorter actions, whose beginning and end are precisely the instants of the sequence, just as the ends of a line are its points. But we are still without the idea of *continuity*

---

[77] These instants are only the *principle* and *term* of a possible complex action taken as a norm.

we are seeking. We must therefore consider how this idea also is a mental possibility to be identified carefully because of its importance and difficulty.

§6. The phenomenal idea of the continuity of time is misleading

789. We have seen that *large actions* producing something have to be subdivided into smaller actions, and that the minute intervals separating these little actions from each other completely escape our observation. Thus new existences, that is, the total effect of countless tiny actions, are presented to us as a product of a single, truly *continuous* action (cf. 784-788). But this is only what appears, and consequently observation offers us a *phenomenal* idea *of the continuity of time*. That the idea is purely phenomenal and apparent is shown by our proof that everything necessarily happens by instants (cf. 779-781). A series of instants can never be identified in a continuous time, no matter how close to each other they are.

790. Because this truth is so important, I want to reinforce it with another proof which leads us to the principle of contradiction by showing that the idea of a perfect *continuity* of time or the continuous production of a large observable effect, contains an immanent contradiction. As we said, the mind moves freely in its world of possibility until it encounters something contradictory, about which it cannot think because a contradiction is impossibility itself. I now add that *continuity in succession* is a contradiction, and therefore impossible to be thought. The proof is as follows.

First proposition: 'To think the existence of an indetermined number is a contradiction.' An idea of an existing number means the number must be determined. The fact that I think of a number means the number itself is determined; if it were not determined I could not think of it as a number. It would no longer be a particular number but number in general, a purely mental being. For instance, if I write the series of cardinal numbers 1, 2, 3, 4, 5, etc. and suppose it continued, this series is the formula expressing and including all possible particular numbers. If I then think of a particular number, I must necessarily think a number contained in the formula.

But all the numbers of the series are determined; each number is itself: 3 is 3, not 2 or 4. The specific essence of the number is such that the number must be determined, and therefore an indetermined number does not and cannot exist.

Second proposition: 'For a number of things to exist, the number has to be *determined*. Therefore it must be *finite*.' If a number is *determined*, it must include the idea of *finite* being, because to be determined, as I have said, means that the number is itself, neither more nor less; its existence must not be confused with the number preceding or following it in the series. No number can be chosen outside the series, since the series contains all particular numbers, and any number chosen from the series will always be the preceding number increased by one unit. But the preceding number is also finite, which is true for all the preceding numbers right back to the beginning: every number equals its preceding number plus one, and the whole series is a sum of finite numbers. Thus every particular number must be finite in such a way that the idea of particular number includes the idea of finite number. The existence therefore of an infinite number of things is an absurdity.

Third proposition: 'A succession of things infinite in number is a contradiction.' The explanation of this proposition is found in the two preceding propositions. A succession of things infinite in number cannot be thought because to think an infinite number involves contradiction. What cannot be thought because of the contradiction involved is not possible. Therefore a succession of things infinite in number is impossible, that is, it involves contradiction.

Fourth proposition: 'The production of a being by means of a continuous, successive action gives a succession of things infinite in number.' I can assign an indefinite number of instants in a continuous succession but I fully understand that this number of instants, no matter how large, can never form or diminish a continuum in any way. An instant has no length; it is a perfect point without any continuous length whatsoever. Mentally I can assign and abstract any number of instants in a continuous time but I do not diminish the length of time by the smallest fraction; I have not abstracted any length from it but assigned a number of points in it that have no length at all. Thinking like this, I conclude that, although the same continuous length still remains (divided into parts maybe, but with each part continuous), I could never finally exhaust this length even if I multiplied the instants to infinity: an infinite number of non-lengths can never make a length. However, this nature of the *continuum* does not involve contradiction because it does not contain an infinite number of points which I only imagine or make myself imagine in it.[78] The continuum may in this respect be mysterious but it contains no intrinsic repugnance or contradiction. On the other hand, I maintain that, granted a *continuous succession* (which is our case), there would be no question of being able to note mentally an indefinite number of instants but of having to distinguish in reality a *truly infinite number* of instants in this succession. In fact, the instant in which a thing exists is distinguished in reality from the preceding instant when the thing does not yet exist.

Let us suppose that the hair in our previous example has grown 10 cm. with a continuous movement. The time required to do this can be divided by me into any number of instants. No matter how many points I freely imagine present in a continuum, there is also a corresponding real division in fact. Let us take the second, third and fourth instants of the series I have imagined; the hair is longer in the fourth than it is in the third, and longer in the third than in the second, if the growth is continuous. No matter how small, this difference is real, so that the growth in the third instant did not exist in the second instant, and the growth in the fourth did not exist in the third. So these little growths or differences exist at different instants and are therefore really distinct from each other. Now if the growth is continuous I can not only increase the number of instants indefinitely but also see that they would not exhaust the continuum even when increased ad infinitum.

But what proves my thesis is this: granted a *continuous, successive increase*, the division into an infinite number of

---

[78] Later, when I speak about the *continuum* in space, it will be more clearly seen that the concept of a *continuum* is not repugnant in itself.

instants, which I am not able to make, would be made by nature herself, which would be absurd. In fact, we have seen that, when I assign a large number of instants in the continuous growth of the hair, they presuppose a real division in nature and an equal number of differences in the hair, and therefore a real number of different states and lengths. It is not I who have divided the hair into a fixed number of instants and created the differences; the differences exist independently of my mind. I see I can multiply the number of instants at will and find differences really distinct from each other. The number of instants, even if infinite, does not equal the continuum; for this reason I also see that an infinite number of really distinct differences should correspond to this infinite number, and each of these would have its own continuous length. If then a successive, continuous growth takes place, an infinite number of differences or lengths have to be distinguished in time in an infinite number of instants through which the hair has successively passed. We note that, if this result involves contradiction, the contradiction comes only from the *infinite number*, such that, granted the premises, the infinite number is necessary; and if the *infinite number* is absurd, as it in fact is, we must say that the premises contain absurdity.

Fifth proposition: 'The production of a being with continuous succession is absurd.' This is a corollary of the third and fourth propositions and is therefore demonstrated.

Our final conclusion, then, is that the continuity of time as given by observation is purely *phenomenal* and illusory because reason proves it to be impossible.

§7. The continuity of time is a mere possibility or concept of the mind

791. If we have no idea of the real continuity of time by observation, we do have an idea of its abstract continuity; but it is a confused idea, obtained by considering the *possibilities* of things.

While one observable action is taking place within any two instants we can also see a large number of other shorter or longer actions, happening or at least beginning. The instant these actions begin is not determined by their nature. We think of the *possibility* of their commencement at any instant within the two given instants. Thus their commencement cannot be assigned to any interval or to any part different from another in that space of time; we can fix a point anywhere we like for the action to start. This capacity of this space of time, its perfect equality and indifference to any starting point within it, its absence of interval and exclusion at any instant, is precisely what gives us the abstract idea we have of the continuity of time. In effect, the idea is the *possibility* of assigning the beginning or end of an action indifferently to all the thinkable points in a certain space of time.

792. But we said that this *abstract* idea of continuity is *confused* because, although we find on analysis that an action can begin at any instant we choose, the instants cannot be totalled together or result in any continuity of time.

§8. Distinction between what is absurd and what is mysterious

793. Absurdity involves contradiction; mystery is inexplicable. No matter how often sophists confuse the two concepts, they remain distinct. What is absurd must be rejected as false; what is mysterious, far from having to be rejected, frequently cannot be rejected at all. Very often, what is mysterious is a fact, and facts cannot be denied. If physical nature is full of mysterious facts, how can anyone claim there is no mystery in spiritual nature, which is far more sublime, active, immense, and profound?

794. Although I have shown that a *continuum in succession* is absurd, I believe that the concept of a *simple continuum*, which is mysterious but not absurd, definitely exists in reality. So, while I have rejected a *continuum in succession*, I have neither the right nor power to reject the *continuum* in nature, because its concept implies no evident contradiction. And just as I have proved that a continuum in *time* is absurd, I shall also prove the non-absurdity of a continuum in *space* and of *duration* without succession.

§9. There is no succession in the duration of complete actions
and therefore no idea of time, only of continuum

795. An action, a being, the essence of a being endures, and
sometimes changelessly. In the existence of such an essence
there is *duration*, but not the *succession* assignable to actions
and beings produced and generated imperfectly. Although
there is no succession in the duration of a complete being,
there can still be a *continuum*. The possibility of a continuum
in a succession is excluded in only one case, that is, when its
presence would mean, as we have seen, an infinite number of
things really distinct from each other, which implies an
absurdity.

796. The existence of God, of our soul, and of all things
that endure, is *continuous*. On the other hand succession, as
found in what is generated, is not continuous, and it is this
that gives the idea and measure of time. However it is difficult
for us to think *duration* without *succession* because, as I have
said so often, we are accustomed to seeking enlightenment
from change and limitation.

§10. The idea of being constituting our intellect is unaffected
by time

797. The idea of time is the idea of a succession related to
duration. *Succession* is found only in passing, transient
actions, that is, in the production, generation and change in
things. The idea of being that constitutes our intellect, is
unchangeable, simple, and always the same. It is therefore
totally unaffected by time.

798. Consequently the idea of time is not obtained *a priori*
[. . .] but *only a posteriori* from finite things perceived as
changeable, that is, by the use of reason.

799. This clarifies even more the ancient truth that the
intellect in its superior part is outside time[79] and, when
reasoning *a priori*, abstracts from time, which it does not find
within itself. I mean it does not find time in its first

---

[79] Properly speaking the intellect is the superior part. St.Thomas says: 'Intellect is
the highest part in our knowledge, not reasoning; the intellect is the origin of
reasoning' (*C. Gent*. 1, 57).

constitutive idea, in the analysis of which alone consists the matter of its *a priori* reasoning.[80]

7

ORIGIN OF THE IDEA OF MOVEMENT

Article 1.
We perceive movement in three ways

800. One of the great actions carried out successively that form and measure time[81] is movement, which we now have to examine.

Related to us, movement is *active* and *passive*. I call it *active* when we ourselves cause it by using in any way the locomotive faculty with which we are endowed. Thus we may walk or otherwise dispose the position of our body. Movement is *passive* when it is produced by an exterior force causing our body to change place.

801. Besides our own movement, there is also movement in bodies surrounding us, which however we experience neither actively nor passively.

802. Because movement is something affecting both our own and external bodies, we perceive it along with our perception of bodies in a kind of *co-perception*. Hence, we apprehend it in as many ways as there are perceptions of bodies. As we have seen, we perceive bodies in three ways:

1. *subjectively*, through the fundamental feeling. This applies to *active movement*, where consciousness indicates that we are its cause;

---

[80] St. Thomas also deduces the idea of time *a posteriori*, from the phantasms: 'By turning to the phantasms the intellect adds time to its composition and division.' This explains why the Fathers of the Church speak so eloquently about the noblest part of the human mind; century by century they all repeat those expressions, consecrated by a constant tradition, which assert that our mind is *joined to eternal and immutable things* and enjoys the vision of an *unexchangeable truth*. As St. Bonaventure says, it sees *eternal things eternally* (*Itin. mentis*, etc.).

[81] In general, *succession* forms time, but each particular *succession* is called a measure of time when it is taken as a norm with which to compare other successions.

2. *subjectively* once more, through acquired sensations which cause us to feel movement in the parts of our affected sense-organs; in this way we perceive subjectively some kind of *passive* movement;

3. *extrasubjectively*, through the senses which, in enabling us to perceive our own and external bodies, also make us perceive all the movements, active or passive relative to us, taking place in bodies. These variations of *activity* or *passivity* can be distinguished and perceived only *subjectively*, not *extrasubjectively*.

Strictly speaking, I should confine my attention to the *subjective* ways of perceiving movement because so far I have only dealt with subjective, not extrasubjective ways of perceiving bodies. This, however, would leave our work very lop-sided, and I think it better consequently not to separate totally the *extrasubjective* from the *subjective* way of perceiving bodily movement.

Article 2.
Active movement described

803. I have no wish to go too deeply into an examination of the nature of movement. My sole aim is to indicate the origin of the ideas of movement. Here, too, observation and especially the facts presented to us by consciousness must be our guide. I shall speak first about active then about passive movement.

We have the capacity to move our body.[82] What is this capacity? What does observation tells us about it?

The fundamental feeling causing us to perceive the body directly is furnished with a *mode* we call extension. The faculty for moving our body as presented to us directly through observation is a power of our soul over the fundamental feeling consisting in a faculty for changing the *mode* of the feeling in a given way. The new *mode* taken by the feeling is a new space in which it is diffused, enabling us to

---

[82] We could not begin to move any part of our body spontaneously if we lacked the feeling that we could do so. The power that we have over our body, therefore, must be included in the fundamental feeling.

say that changing the mode of the fundamental feeling indicates a change of *space* or *place*. Because the soul has the power to change the mode of the fundamental feeling, it is also said to have power of movement over its own body. In fact, if the body is the agent producing in the soul the fundamental feeling which has extension as its term, the soul must be acting on the agent if facts show that it can change its action in a given way.

Article 3.
Passive movement described

804. Not only do we possess the energy to move ourselves; we can also be moved. When we move ourselves, the *quantity of effort* we make gives us perception of movement and a way of measuring it. When we are moved by some external force, we do not always perceive our movement. If the force moving us produces change in our sense-organs — for example, when we are pushed or dragged from one place to another — we experience an action upon us and perceive our movement. This movement, however, is not seconded by the other inert parts of our body outside the immediate effect of the moving force. If we are moved by an external force making us change the position of the whole of our body simultaneously, the force changes nothing because it does not disturb any individual particle relative to the whole body. In this case, our interior feeling provides no perception of the quantity of movement, nor of the movement itself.

This explains why we have no perception of the movement with which we are involved by living on a planet revolving on its axis at a speed of thousands of miles an hour. We are not aware of being moved because we do not move ourselves, but depend upon a uniform force without experiencing any internal or external sensation in our vision or touch, or in any other senses indicating movement.

805. While our active movement is perceived in two ways, through the interior feeling of consciousness and our external sensations, our passive movement is perceived through external sensations alone.

Article 4.
Of itself, our movement is not feelable

806. A corollary of this observation is that our movement is not *per se* feelable. Observation shows that we can be moved, and not feel movement in any way. As we have said, we know movement subjectively through its *cause*, and extrasubjectively through its *effects*, but if our position is changed not by ourselves but through an external force producing no change in our sense-organs we cannot know this *movement* because there is no change in our feeling [App. no. 16].

Article 5.
Movement in our sense-organs is feelable

807. It is true that when a movement of any sort is produced in our sense-organs, we feel the particles composing those organs in a shape different from that to which we previously referred the fundamental feeling. Consequently, the feeling itself is moved and heightened in such a way that, along with its modification, we perceive movement in so far as *matter* which is felt stimulates our fundamental feeling by changing its own form. Nevertheless, movement is not felt through itself but through the particular circumstance by which it changes the *state* of the sense-organ that is always felt by us in *its actual state*.

Such movement, therefore, is change of the respective position of the molecules composing the sense-organ that is felt by us according to a law determining the position of the molecules making up the organ. If the position required for one *state* of the organ (relative to feeling) is altered, the organ takes on another *sensible state*, and is felt in a new mode and place according to the nature of the change it has experienced. The sense-organ could, therefore, be transported vast distances (and this actually happens relative to the daily motion of the earth) without our feeling movement in any way. We have to conclude that we feel not the movement of the organ, properly speaking, but its *feelable state*.

We affirm that the feeling and feelable particles making up

the organ give the whole organ another form when compressed or separated in different ways, proportions and relative positions. In this new form the organ is felt in another way, with varying pleasure or pain, while the change itself is also felt. The new pleasure or pain, that is, the new sensation, is referred to all the feelable points within the new form where the force has acted. Because the previous form was different, the pleasure or pain appropriate to it was referred to different points. We do not feel the change of place undergone by each individual sensitive molecule (the absolute movement of the molecules), but only the change in the total form of the organ, that is, the change of place of several molecules at a time (the relative movement of the molecules), which causes the various parts of the organ to be felt in different places.

808. If we analyse this subjective feeling with which we perceive the sensitive parts of our body when a feelable movement takes place, we see:

1. that this feeling is of variable, corporeal pleasure or pain diffused in an extension of given limits and shape;

2. that the *shape* of this felt extension can change through relative movement of its parts, and that the feeling is, nevertheless, always diffused, in the extension of all the shapes it assumes;

3. that consequently our *subjective feeling* perceives the particular *movement* taking place when the *shape* of the organ changes, but only in that part where the force applied operates in the way necessary to produce a sensation.

Our subjective feeling perceives movement, therefore, in so far as it is a change undergone by its matter.

Article 6.
Relationship between movement and sensation

809. Absolute, general movement is therefore altogether different from sensation. Relative movement, which takes place in parts of the sensory organ as it changes shape is 'an occurrence in the matter of sensation', and is felt as a happening in this matter.

Article 7.
Movement relative to touch-perception[83]

810. Touch perceives the hardness and surface of bodies. But do we feel movement with touch when the tip of a body, a pencil, for example, is drawn along the length of our stationary arm? At first sight, it seems we do; certainly we perceive something similar to movement.

Nevertheless, we are faced with a difficulty. Although we feel a sensation moving, as it were, along our arm, and through the sensation perceive the body producing it, it would seem that we cannot be sure of the identity of the body producing the sensations. Instead of a single body running along the arm, we could posit a multiplicity of bodies substituting one another in rapid succession.[84]

---

[83] We have distinguished in external sensations: 1. the *sensation in the organ*; 2. the *perception* of something different from the organ. We have dealt with movement relative to sensation (cf. 806); we are now speaking about movement relative to corporeal perception.

[84] Generally speaking, we can show that in touching bodies with different parts of our own body we do not perceive their identity. Different perceptions of external things correspond to different affected parts of our body, and the bodies (agents acting on us) seem as many as the perceptions we have in different parts of our body, especially if the perceptions take place simultaneously. Nevertheless, when we are touched in (phenomenally) continuous space, touch gives notice of several bodies forming a continuity amongst themselves, as happens with solids. On the other hand, if we have non-continuous sensations, for instance, when we are touched by a body on our hand and again on our foot, we can only think that two bodies have touched us. Only the use of sight, or the continuity of touch, as I said, and habit, enables us to judge the unity of a body.

The judgment that we make about the identity of a body touching us simultaneously on several parts of our body is an *habitual* judgment, dependent upon experience, and as such can sometimes deceive us. For example, if I touch a button with two fingers crossed one over the other, I feel two buttons because I feel two sensations in different parts of my fingers where I am not accustomed to be touched simultaneously by a single body. The natural position of my fingers, when I touch a body, is straight out and flat so that the sensations produced by an external body are close together. In this case, the sensations are different from those present when two fingers are in the other, unusual position, and take place in a part of the finger-tip not normally employed.

In our case of the pencil tip running along the arm, we have the (phenomenal) continuity of a sliding sensation which makes us believe the body to be the same although different parts of the arm are touched. Nevertheless, pure touch tells us that only similar sensations succeed one another without notable interruption. This is certainly not sufficient to prove the movement of the external body. On the contrary, when I take a body in my hand and carry it from one place to another, the

Article 8.
Movement relative to sight-perception

811. When we move, what we see changes around us. The changes themselves become signs by which we learn about our own movement and that of others. How this comes about, I shall explain when we deal with the third way of perceiving bodies.

In the meantime, we ask whether we can perceive movement through vision when with motionless eyes we see something which itself moves. A black dot moving across a white surface gives us the concept of movement, and although we cannot be sure about the movement of the external thing because of the existence of apparent, illusory movements, the concept itself is present to us.

But while the difficulty about the identity of a body relative to sight-sensation is similar to that caused by touch-sensation, it is also less than it. The characteristics of bodies we see are greater in number than those of bodies we touch, and are shared with greater difficulty with other bodies than in the case of touch where the same sensation can easily be produced by various bodies.

Article 9.
Movement relative to aural-, smell- and taste-perceptions

812. In so far as these senses have something in common with touch, perception of movement is the same for them as it is for touch (cf. 810); in so far as they are distinguished from touch by their own special phenomena they do not perceive movement although they can, with the other senses, measure it by means of time. The time needed for a body to come within range of our touch, sight, smell, taste or hearing is an indication of the length of its movement towards us or our movement towards it. This measure of movement is possible for those born blind, and for those lacking some, but not all senses.

---

identity of the body is proved by the continuity of its perception, unmoved relative to my hand grasping the body. In this case, I would perceive the movement not with pure touch, but with touch assisted by interior awareness of my arm which I move.

Article 10.
The continuity of movement

§1. Observation cannot perceive minute extensions

813. It is a fact that minute extensions escape our observation. Although the invention of the microscope has revealed a world hidden to observation, nature will always provide subtleties beyond the range of the most developed instruments. The intimate texture of bodies is such as to make me believe that it will always remain veiled to our senses under ever smaller extensions which, although they lessen constantly, still fall entirely outside any possible advertence on our part.

§2. Observation provides only phenomenal continuity of movement

814. Whatever observation tells us about the continuity of movement, therefore, can only witness to an *apparent or phenomenal continuity*. Unable to tell us anything about the minute, possible intervals that escape our observation, it cannot provide any certain proof about the real continuity of movement.

§3. Real continuity of movement is absurd

815. Although observation fails to provide us with anything certain about the real continuity of movement, we can try to reason about it. It is true, of course, that reason cannot provide us with facts, but because possibility is the object of the mind, it can as such allow us to say something about their possibility or impossibility.

We have already shown that *continuity of succession* is absurd (cf. 779-799). But succession is present in movement, as in every action subject to increase and decease. In movement, therefore, true, real continuity is absurd.

In this way, reason is sometimes able to pass from an argument about mere *possibility* to conclusions about facts through denial of their possibility by means of the initial fact of intrinsic repugnance. If this repugnance is absent, however, it cannot affirm their existence; it can only declare them *possible*.

§4. Solution to the objection drawn from leaps in nature

816. If no true continuity is possible in movement, movement must come about by leaps. But in human thought, leaps have always been excluded from nature. And indeed a *leap* in nature is absurd.

817. However, lack of true continuity in movement does not imply the introduction of *leaps* in nature. The idea of a *leap* is not and cannot be present in what occurs in an instant. A *leap* supposes two points, and a *passage* from one to the other without touching what is in between. When we think of *passage*, on the other hand, we have to include the notion of *touching* what is between the two points; passing from one place to another without touching what is in between means passing without passing. In this sense, the concept of a leap in nature is absurd because it implies putting links in the middle (the necessary steps) and at the same time mentally eliminating them, an obvious contradiction.

Real movement on the other hand only offers successive existence of a body in several places without our having to think of it as leaping from one to another, provided our imagination does not add anything to the concept of real movement. Such a concept does not imply a leap because it does not entail a necessary passage from one place to the nearest place. Our imagination renders this passage necessary because we are accustomed to the presence of phenomenal continuity of movement in which we think we observe continual passage. But what we see is the simple, successive existence of a body in several places so close together that it is impossible to advert to the distance between them.

We will understand this better if we remember that extension is simply the term of a force, according to our explanation of the concept of force. Force, however, can vary its term and extend itself in one space rather than another without our needing to suppose a true continuous passage between the spaces. It can withdraw itself at immense speed from one place while simultaneously diffusing itself in another. Certainly there is no contradiction in such a concept.

818. I realise that this will be difficult to grasp; our understanding is constantly complicated and confused by the use of our imagination. And it has to be admitted that we have no experience of the fact. The different spaces in which corporeal force gradually diffuses itself are (according to a law established by the author of nature) so close that separation between them is imperceptible. Hence, our apparent vision of continuity, and our difficulty in thinking that movement could come about in some other way. But let us consider carefully the reasoning which leads me to deny perfect, true continuity in local movement.

§5. Mental continuity of movement

819. The difficulty present in understanding the truth of what we have said is aggravated by the presence in our mind of the idea of a certain *mental continuity* of movement, corresponding to that of *time*. This abstract, *mental continuity* consists in the possibility (which we conceive as equal and indifferent) that movement may begin or end in any point whatsoever of time and space. Because no point of time or space is more apt than another for receiving the principle or the term of movement, the equal *possibility* of all points produces, or rather is, the confused idea of *abstract continuity* in movement of a body between any two moments or points whatever. I call this a 'confused' idea because analysis immediately shows that no continuity can ever be formed by a number of neighbouring points.

8

ORIGIN OF THE IDEA OF SPACE

Article 1.
Distinction between the ideas of space and of body

820. I have defined body as 'a substance capable of producing in us an action which is a feeling of pleasure or pain

having a constant mode we call extension' (cf. 749-753). Extension, therefore, when derived from body, is a mental abstraction, like *time* and pure *movement*. It is a particular mode of the feeling caused by the body in our spirit. Once this abstraction has been formed, it can exist independently of bodies, like all abstract ideas.

Article 2.
Extension, or space, is limitless

821. Extension, or space, taken in this abstract way, or in any other way, is *limitless, immeasurable* and *continuous*. We must now examine how our concept of space, taken only from bodies, acquires these undeniable characteristics. We shall begin with limitlessness and immeasurability.

The power of moving our body (cf. 672-692) is simply a capacity for changing or reproducing the *mode* of feeling of our body. In other words, we can reproduce the extension our body occupies. But we can reproduce acts of our faculties indefinitely; and even when our limited energies prevent our reproducing them any further, we can still imagine ourselves reproducing them indefinitely. This capacity is given us by the idea of possibility, continually present to our mind, which we can join to anything we mentally conceive (cf. 403). We have already explained, through the idea of being, how our spirit can add the idea of what is possible to any event or object it conceives and, with the help of this idea, imagine the indefinite reproduction of the event or object (cf. 469 ss.).

Thus our capacity for imagining or thinking of the indefinite reproduction of our body's extension enables us to acquire the idea of limitless extension. This idea is, in fact, only 'the possibility of reproducing indefinitely, the mode of feeling that we call our body's extension by abstracting in thought and imagination from the body itself.'

822. In this way we draw the idea of limitlessness of extension from extension perceived subjectively.[85] At the

---

[85] Extension is something in exterior objects. It is also something in the *fundamental feeling* in which, and related to which, it has the nature of *matter* and term. Moreover, extension is common to our sensations and to external bodies. In our sensations we call it their *matter*; in external bodies we call it the *external term*.

same time, extension perceived subjectively can also be perceived extrasubjectively, that is to say, in external bodies, because the exteriority of a body is only the extrasubjective mode with which we perceive bodies.

Granted this perception of bodies, we have by abstraction the perception of their bodily extension. Hence the limitlessness and immeasurability of extension conceived in this way, which can in general be defined as 'the possibility of thinking the indefinite reproduction of the extension of bodies.'

Article 3.
Space or extension is continuous

823. As we have seen, the idea of unending space which first lends itself to analysis is an abstract idea, expressing the possibility of limitless change to the extension of a body. It is true that in dealing with this we have been paying more attention to our own body than to that of external bodies, because until now we have spoken intentionally only of subjective perception. However, what we shall say about space perceived subjectively, the reader will be able to apply for himself to external bodies, that is, to bodies which we perceive extrasubjectively.

Dealing with our present question 'Does the concept of space contain perfect *continuity*?', we must be careful not to confuse feeling as it actually exists with the possibility of its other states. We could indeed raise an extremely difficult problem connected with the fact of feeling: does the actual feeling of our body include the feeling of the perfect continuity belonging to our body? To answer this question through experience would not only require very accurate and extremely shrewd observation and insight; it would in the end be impossible. Only conjecture or very acute philosophical reasoning would perhaps provide a solution. What we are asking is whether sensation could be stimulated along the nerves in such a way that sensitive parts are posited according to mathematical contiguity. Now observation can tell us nothing about such a problem because it cannot attain such penetration.[86] However, this kind of research is not necessary for our present question.

An explanation of the *continuity* of extension is not furthered by knowing whether all the mathematical points encountered in a nerve passage are truly sensitive. We are not dealing with a factual truth, but with an abstraction or idea resulting from the clear possibility of locating the sensation we experience at any of the points along the nerve. If the nerve we feel has pores and gaps in its delicate texture, it is entirely accidental whether these gaps come in one place rather than another. We can think of a nerve full of them, although it may in fact be devoid of them; mentally we can change the place of any of the sensitive particles of the nerve, just as we can for the empty spaces found along it. This power of the *intellective imagination* is sufficient to explain how we can fully conceive 'the possibility of locating a feeling at any assignable point whatsoever', that is, how we are able to conceive the idea of continuity.

Our *capacity* for locating a feeling at any assignable point in a space arises from the neutral disposition of the nature of space which receives feeling indifferently at any point. Because of this indifference, a sensation may terminate in any point within the confines of the body. The possibility of indifferently locating the feeling at any point or place includes, and is, the idea of the continuous in abstract space.

Our power of movement facilitates the attainment of this idea because it indicates in fact the indifference of every part of space relative to the diffusion of our feeling. Let us imagine that we have a microscope powerful enough to show us the the nerves in our hand. Such an instrument would reveal how the molecules composing them cling together, and how there are tiny spaces between the molecules where the nerve lacks feeling because it is insensitive. But now we move our hand slightly, and find that the spaces previously occupied by the molecules have been left empty while empty spaces have been filled. In the new position of the hand, feeling is now located at places which were empty. Movement, therefore, enables us to dispose our feeling in any mathematical point of space, and

[86] However, there is no absolute repugnance, rationally speaking, in the thought of such observation.

such a possibility makes us conceive space as an absolute and perfect *continuity*.

It is true, of course, that the feeling of the organ acquired through movement remains unchanged (granted that movement is per se unfeelable, cf. 806). This, however, does not prevent the mind, assisted especially by the external sensation of bodies, from arriving at the idea of the continuity of extension in the way described.

Article 4.
Do really continuous things exist?

824. So far, by mentally drawing together various possibilities we have arrived at the idea of a continuum. But does the continuum really exist in corporeal extension? We shall have to answer this question later, when we deal with the extrasubjective perception of bodies. This provides an easier approach to the problem and throws greater light on it. In the meantime, it is enough to know that continuity of bodies and of space is not repugnant.

Article 5.
What is continuous has no parts

825. *Continuous* means that which has no gap or division or split. What is continuous, therefore, cannot have parts, because parts presuppose separation amongst themselves.

Article 6.
What is continuous can have limits

826. So far, we have defined the *continuum* as 'the possibility of a body's terminating simultaneously in any assignable point of a given extension.' The idea of *limitless continuous space* has been defined as 'the possibility of a body's reproducing indefinitely its continuous extension.' But we can also restrict our thought to the possibility of some, rather than all, possible changes. In this way, there arises within us the idea of something *continuous, yet limited*, for example, an area measuring a thousand square metres, or

something similar. Because it has no parts, this area although limited is also continuous. While I can imagine as many of these areas as I please, each of them, whatever its size, remains continuous, that is, without parts.

827. All these ideas of continuous limitations are, therefore, potentially comprised in the idea of what is unlimitedly continuous, that is, unending space.[87] Each one, moreover, has a relationship of size with every other (one may be twice, or three times the size of another, and so on). In other words, it has another characteristic beyond those assigned it by mathematicians, whether this characteristic is actually measurable or not.

828. In this way, we come to consider lesser continuous things as parts of those which are greater, although this depends on various acts of our mind and its capacity for limiting in different ways its conception of the continuum. Lesser things, as parts of larger, are only mental, not actual things.

829. Consequently, these mental parts do not form one continuous thing while they are conceived as parts; they are lesser continuous things and nothing more. When we want to consider them altogether as a single continuous thing, we have to remove the idea of parts and division completely, running them together with our imagination so as to eliminate even mental confines. The concept of continuum is clean contrary to the concept of part.

Article 7.
Can what is continuous be said to be infinitely divisible?

830. The continuum can be said to be infinitely divisible only in the sense that we can limit it indefinitely.[88] This

---

[87] That which is in potency cannot truly be said to be. In what is continuous, therefore, we find only the limitations we ourselves put there, and nothing more. The infinite number of ideas imagined by Malebranche as possessed by our mind in the conception of space and shapes — his infinite number of infinites (book 3) — is fallacious. The idea of the continuum is a single idea which, when limited by us, produces other ideas but always in a limited number because our mental effort finally comes to an end without ever arriving at an infinite number of limitations.

[88] What is continuous is improperly said to be *divisible* because what is *divided* is no longer *continuous*.

indefinite reduction arises from the nature both of the continuum and of our faculties which can always repeat what they have done previously. This is especially the case with our power of thought which, by means of the concept of possibility, can imagine and think as possible all that is not contradictory. Infinite divisibility, therefore, is only the possibility of repeating indefinitely the limitation of the space we think of. Hence St. Thomas' teaching: 'The continuum has infinite possible parts (in potency), but none in reality.'

9

ORIGIN OF THE IDEA OF BODIES BY MEANS OF THE EXTRASUBJECTIVE PERCEPTION OF TOUCH

Article 1.
Analysis of the extrasubjective perception of bodies in general

831. We have indicated two elements in acquired sensations: 1. a modification of the fundamental feeling, by which the affected part of our sense-organ is felt in a new way; 2. a sense-perception of an external body. Subsequent analysis of this extrasubjective perception also results in two elements: 1. a feeling of the action done in us; 2. extension in which we locate this feeling and which includes some extended thing outside us.

832. We can therefore conclude that when we have perceived something different from us, something extended, we have the perception of a body through acquired sensations. I must now explain how our exterior senses furnish us with a subject of these three qualities. I shall begin with touch.

Article 2.
All our senses give us a perception of something different from us

833. Each of our senses receives an action. An action done in us, of which we are not the author, indicates something

different from us.° Therefore each sense perceives something different from ourselves.

Article 3.
All our senses give us a perception of something outside us

834. In order to ensure clarity in our ideas, we must first note the distinction between what is *different* from us and what is *outside* us. Something *different* from us means simply something different from 'myself'. Difference as a concept does not include any idea of extension nor any relationship with extension. On the other hand, the word 'outside' in its proper sense has a relationship with extension: one thing outside another does not occupy the *place* of the other. Thus, outside 'ME' means outside the parts and sentient organs of my body,[89] and only by transference is applied to our spirit. While therefore 'different from me' indicates a relationship of difference from my spirit, 'outside me' correctly indicates a difference from my *body* in so far as it is co-sentient through its intimate union with my spirit. In order, then, to show that each of our senses perceives what is outside us, we must demonstrate that each sense perceives something different from our body perceived subjectively.

835. That this is the case results from what was said, when we showed that the fundamental feeling is produced by an activity different from the activity that changes it. Hence two kinds of activity: 1. my body which acts directly in my spirit; 2. external bodies which act on my body. Thus in every sensation we perceive an active principle or body different from our body; every sensation is an experience we receive from something other than our body. Therefore each sense gives us something outside us.

836. The following observation will help to remove all doubt on the matter. My body is felt in the fundamental feeling; what is felt outside this feeling is not my body. Let us fix our attention on the four phenomena, colours, sounds,

---

[89] Every part of my body, whether sentient or not, can be said to be *outside me* in so far as it is perceived *extrasubjectively*. In such a perception we consider what the part has in common with all external bodies; as such, it is outside the *subject*, that is, the *perceived part* is perceived as outside the *perceiving part*.

smells and tastes, and also on the various qualities of touch, like hardness. If we ask ourselves whether all these things are perhaps nothing more than our sense-organs, we will see that the term of these sensations possesses something different from our organs. Smell, for example, does not have the slightest similarity to our nose, nor taste to the tongue or palate, nor sound to our ears, and so on for all other qualities. The sensations, therefore, cannot have only our body as their matter. Even if the *sensation* of our own body is included in them, our body is certainly not everything we perceive with them. They therefore indicate a principle external to our body, a term different from the term of the fundamental feeling.

Article 4.
Touch perceives only corporeal surfaces

837. When we are touched on a sensitive part of our body, we feel our body, that is, a certain pleasure or pain.[90] We also feel an action done in us by something foreign, that is, we perceive an agent outside us (cf. 834-836). The action, different from a sensation in an affected part, is a feeling with an extended *term* and is diffused in a surface extension. For instance, if a sharp point touches us we locate the discomfort at a point, at a very small surface; but if we are touched by a bigger surface, a coin for example, we locate the discomfort at points enclosed within that surface and feel nothing outside it. Suppose a piece of metal in a form of a cross is pressed to our arm. The sensation we have terminates in that particular shape, and is diffused throughout the whole area covered by the metal, to which it corresponds exactly.[91]

---

[90] There are feelings essentially different from pleasure and pain. For example, the sensation of tickling seems to be wholly *sui generis*, and the same can be said of many other feelings. It is not my intention to investigate this matter but it seems to me beyond doubt that all the feelings we experience are accompanied by some level of pleasure or pain, or are themselves *modes* of pleasure or pain. So I say 'a certain pleasure and pain' or else 'corporeal pleasure and pain' where 'corporeal' indicates the differences not investigated in this work.

[91] It is really the ends of the nerves that are touched and hence the contact takes place at the surface, which is true for external touch.

Article 5.
Touch together with movement gives the idea of three dimensional space

838. When we are touched on the surface of our body, we receive a sensation confined within a surface space.[92] If we add the faculty of movement, we have the power to repeat at will the space in which the fundamental feeling terminates (cf. 803). The same faculty enables us to repeat at will the surface felt by touch. Thus, a surface moved by a motion outside the plane of the surface itself traces a solid space having three dimensions, length, height and depth.

The power to move ourselves, and other things with us, makes touch-sensation possible at any surface of solid space;[93] hence the idea we have of this possibility. The idea of the possibility of indefinitely changing and repeating the surfaces which are terms of our sensations of touch is the idea of solid, indefinite space acquired by means of the sense of touch joined to movement.[94]

Article 6.
A review of the ways we perceive solid space

839. What we have said shows that the idea of extension or space is formed in two ways: 1. by means of the fundamental feeling accompanied by the faculty of spontaneous movement of our body; 2. by means of the sensations of touch aided by the same faculty. The indefinite space of the first way is produced by a movement in all directions of a solid space felt

---

[92] I am speaking of adventitious sensations, not the fundamental feeling of which, I am convinced, there is a continuum in the parts where it terminates.

[93] This solidity need not be known to our senses. Of itself, motion is not feelable, as we have observed, but is a means for us to form the *thought* of feelable solidity.

[94] Spontaneous movement is the principal cause of the information we acquire about distances and measured spaces. Touch (by means of time) and sight do nothing more than make us perceive exactly the *term* of the distance. A delicate sense of touch, therefore, is not necessary for measuring great distances. Birds are an example: they fly and measure immense distances, having only the weak sense of touch of their claws. The vulture, for instance, measures the *space, time* and the *speed* necessary to catch its prey. But all it needs for this is its weak sense of touch and its powerful eye-sight together with its great power of movement.

by us, that is, of our body; this movement is mentally conceived as indefinitely possible. The indefinite space of the second way is produced by the possible movement of a surface that is felt — a movement in all directions outside the plane of the surface itself. This explains how people born blind perceive indefinite space and are able to understand mathematics.

Article 7.
It is easier for us to think about the idea of space acquired by touch and movement than by the fundamental feeling and movement

840. We have seen, on the one hand, how hard it is to think about and be aware of the fundamental feeling, and on the other, how easy to be aware of acquired sensations (cf. 710-721). For the same reason, indefinite space perceived by the possibility of the movements of our body easily escapes our reflexion. Hence, because sensations of touch are acquired, they and their movement attract our attention more easily.

Article 8.
Space perceived by the movement of touch-sensation is identical with space perceived by the movement of the fundamental feeling

841. The term of the external sensation of touch is a more or less extended surface (cf. 837). This surface is identical with the external surface of our body because the sensation is felt only in the nerve endings where we are touched.[95] The same surface[96] is also the term of both the *subjective sensation* we feel in our organ and the action done in us from outside. Consciousness of this action constitutes what we have called

---

[95] The sensation of our body must always be distinguished from the perception of an external thing in the same surface. Although we feel the same surface, we feel two things: 1. our body, a subject that feels and is felt; 2. an external agent that is felt but does not feel.

[96] The unity of this surface determines the nature of the touch, and of the mysterious unity of agent and recipient in every kind of action, as we have already pointed out. [Cf. App. no. 14]

the *extrasubjective perception* of the senses. Because the external agent is called an external body, the surface, when touched, is not only the term of our body but also of the external body. Now if we think of this surface, felt and perceived by us and common both to our body and the external body, as being moved in all directions (cf. 839), we arrive at the origin of the concept of indefinite space.

Indefinite space is therefore perceived by us in two ways: either by moving the organ that we have felt through a modification of the fundamental feeling or by moving the surface perceived in the external agent. In both cases it is always one and the same surface.

Space, therefore, whether perceived in the two *subjective* ways or the *extrasubjective* way, is one and the same, because any modification of the fundamental feeling (an acquired sensation of our organ) has the same extension as the fundamental feeling.

Article 9.
The identity of the extension of our body and of an external body is the basis of the communication between the idea we have of each of them

842. Our body, when considered in association with its feeling *subject*, shares the same extension with the external body, which is simply the agent we feel. The communication of these two bodies in the same extension provides the step from the idea of one to the idea of the other; it is the *communicating bridge* we were looking for. The very act by which we perceive the mode of our body's existence is the same act by which we perceive the mode of existence of an external body.

Article 10.
Continuation

843. This fact (cf. 842) is of the greatest importance. We have established two elements necessary for the essence of a

body: 1. an action done on us; 2. an extension in which that action is diffused and terminates. Our own body exercises a continual, internal action on us, occasioning the fundamental feeling, and this effect of the agent spreads throughout an extension. Here we have therefore the two elements forming the essence of body. Hence the perception of our body is undeniable, and its essence is as certain as the fact of consciousness.

844. The perception of an external body is brought about when we first feel an action done on us, although the immediate effect of this action is simply a modification of our fundamental feeling. This effect alone does not draw us out of ourselves. We still feel our body as we did before, but in a new way (with an accidental sensation). We are then easily led to argue to a cause, which is unknown because the action is still indetermined. This alone would not suffice to make us perceive a *body* outside us. For this the action has also to be *extended*, and then we would perceive an *agent in extension*, which is the notion of a body.

But how are we able to perceive the extension of an agent? The author of nature, in his wisdom, provides the answer: we feel extension habitually, that is, the diffusion of the fundamental feeling. Consequently, we are able to feel the extension of the external agent when it diffuses its action in the *same extension* as our fundamental feeling.

This explains why the surface of the extension of our fundamental feeling and the surface of the extension of an external body should unite to form a single surface in which we experience two feelings. Hence the action of an external body takes place in and extends over the very same surface in which the fundamental feeling is diffused and terminates. Consciousness itself tells us that the action comes from outside and takes place in an extension already felt by us naturally.

We perceive: 1. an external action; and 2. the surface in which this external action functions or terminates. Thus we perceive the two essential properties of our own and external bodies, and confirm for ourselves the existence of two types of body, each having the same corporeal nature, although their effects upon us are quite different.

Article 11.
The subjective sensation of our body is the means of corporeal, extrasubjective perception

845. What we have said explains how the extrasubjective perception of bodies is founded on the subjective perception. The first element in extrasubjective perception is a force modifying us. We perceive this force in its action according to the kind of impact it has on us, and with it perceive a subjective modification of our fundamental feeling. The second element is extension, and in particular the extension of the fundamental feeling, which we feel naturally. But because the fundamental feeling is changed in extension by an external force applied to each part of the extension, we perceive this force as extended in its term. This explains why the criterion for the perception of an exterior body is ultimately the perception of our own body (cf. 845-844).

Article 12.
The extension of bodies

846. Before continuing, I must give some attention to the real extension I have sometimes attributed to a body; it is a very important matter, discussed by others at various times. I will show that the *extension* we perceive in a body is real, not apparent and illusory.°

§1. Multiplicity is not essential to corporeal nature

847. Many thinkers have considered multiplicity essential to corporeal nature. But it is easy to see, as Leibniz pointed out, that the concept of multiplicity cannot be the concept of an individual nature but of the coexistence of several natures. It is a relative concept, presupposing and based on an absolute concept. In short, where there are the many, there must be the one; multiplicity is merely the aggregate of many unities. Thus the nature of things must be sought in unity[97] and not in a multitude, which is only several natures joined together.

[97] If corporeal nature is to be found in the elements from which composite bodies result, such elements cannot be thought of as unextended. Continuous extension is sufficient because the continuum is one, as we saw (cf. 825).

848. The essence, therefore, of a body or of anything else will never be *multiplicity*, which is purely a mental entity. Only idealists, especially transcendentalists, who suppose that bodies are an emanation of our mind,[98] are content to posit corporeal nature in multiplicity.

§2. The complex unity of our sensitive body

849. Certain conditions are required for our organs to feel, one of which is communication with the brain. We may conclude from this that the sensitivity of each part of our sensitive organ depends on the form of the whole sentient system, that is, on a division and organisation of parts whose harmonious result is a single whole, sensitive in all its parts. Thus the parts composing the organ are sensitive because of this single whole, or rather because of a unity rooted in the whole. We can say that our body, in so far as it is sensitive, enjoys a certain complex unity which makes it one because it has in itself an order or harmony of parts.

850. This truth remains valid even if we cannot say whether there is a centre in the brain, and if there is, whether it consists of a single particle or several in which all the nerves end. For even independently of the intelligent spirit, the unity of the human body is sufficiently established by its need of a certain disposition if it is to be vivified and inhabited by the spirit, and its different powers be, as Dante says, '*organised.*'

§3. We cannot err about the unicity of our body

851. Let us imagine we possess two bodies. In this case we would then have two fundamental feelings and extensions, because these are the two essential elements of our body. Our consciousness, therefore, which indicates one fundamental feeling only, diffused in a definite extension, indicates the unicity of our body.

Let us imagine that we feel we have two bodies. In this case we could not have one only because in our sensation the two constitutive elements of our body would be perceived as

---

[98] I mean *actual multiplicity*, although the nature of what is extended always involves the idea of a *potential multiplicity*, which however is not yet multiplicity.

doubled. Thus we still could not err in judging whether our body is one or two.°

§4. The multiplicity of the feeling of our body

852. Because our body is *one* through the harmony of its parts, we perceive its *unicity*. Anything outside this harmony and foreign to us is not felt. However such unity and unicity does not exclude multiplicity from the being, as I must now explain.

Through the organisation of the body, my spirit feels all its sensitive parts by means of the fundamental feeling and of the adventitious sensations in its sensitive parts. This makes possible at least a mental multiplicity of bodily feeling.

853. If we keep to sensation, because the same reasoning can easily be applied to the fundamental feeling, we have to ask what can and cannot be affirmed about the multiplicity of sensation?

If the impression given when we are touched has a certain extension and sufficient intensity, we can say that we feel a sensation of touch to which we generally advert. But if the extension is small, it escapes our attention. The smallest extension we can be aware of may be called *minimum* extension. Now if this *minimum* is regarded as the basic element of extended sensation, it is certain that one element is not identical with any other because in each we find two separate things: 1. sensation; and 2. extension, which are the two constitutives of body. Thus we can consider these *elements* as tiny bodies, subsisting separately and outside each other, which cannot be confused or take one another's place. In our body therefore we perceive with equal certainty both *multiplicity* and *unity*.

§5. Our perception of multiplicity in external bodies

854. A similar argument can be applied to external bodies. When an external body is so minute that its extension is less than a certain limit, it entirely escapes our attention. If we take this *minimum* (that is, the smallest noticeable body) as the basic element, it can safely be said that in the perception

of a larger body we can mentally distinguish and separate *minimum* perceptions as possible, and even as really distinct existences, if considered individually.

Furthermore, because two constitutive elements of body are present in each of these *minimum perceptions*, we can mentally distinguish minute *bodies*, whether they are divided or not. They can also have an independent subsistence because they have separate and incommunicable action. As we have seen, in each of these minimum spaces that we have distinguished, there is an extension outside every other extension. Thus each agent is outside every other agent and is a substance that, while it can be contiguous with another substance, appears separate and alone in its own existence. In this way we perceive *multiplicity* in external bodies.

§6. The difference between a *body* and a *corporeal principle*

855. We 'name things according to the way we intellectually perceive them' (cf. 647). To investigate what a *body* is, is to investigate the notion given by the human race to the word 'body' (cf. 653-656). We found this notion was the result of two elements, an *agent* acting on us and an *extension* in which this action and our own experience of it were diffused.

However if the *agent* effected nothing in us, we could neither know it nor name it, since we know it and name it in so far as it acts on us. So the word 'body' is determined by the *immediate effects* of the agent on us and by the laws governing its action.

But the *agent* could have powers and laws unknown to us, different from but not contrary to those we experience. If all possible or unknown effects and their laws were like this, they would be neither known nor named by us. The name 'body' therefore cannot be applied to these qualities as long as they remain unknown: 'Words may not be used with a sense wider than that for which they were devised' (cf. 648-652). Suppose however that the order of things were changed. We might discover new effects with new laws dependent on the same principle as the effects now determining the meaning of the word 'body'. In this case the common use of the word would change. But while we continue to use the *word* in the present condition of things, it has a meaning limited by its immediate effects or actions and by the laws according to which bodies present themselves to us.

856. For this reason I prefer to distinguish *corporeal principle* from *body*, including the former in the definition of body only in so far as body is accompanied by effects and laws enabling us to know it. But I would also let the corporeal principle, considered in itself, retain its capacity for whatever is still unknown to us.

857. Speaking therefore about *body* in this sense, I have no hesitation in affirming that we know with certainty the *multiplicity of bodies.*[99]

§7. Granted that corporeal sensation terminates in a continuous extension, a continuous real extension must also be present in the bodies producing it

858. Let us suppose that the surface of our body where sensations take place is continuous, or at least that there is in it some continuous space. It seems to me that a body producing an extended, continuous sensation must also be extended and continuous.[100] This is a corollary of what has already been said.

I have said that 'bodies are the *proximate* cause of our sensations' (cf. 639-645). I have explained that 'proximate cause' means a being receiving its name only from the immediate effect it constantly produces. I concluded that the constant sensations (the fundamental feeling and its modifications) are not produced by a *power* of a body but by a body's *substance*, by a body itself; the word 'body' indicates only those immediate effects contained in its total meaning.

The result of these findings was the recognition that in each space where we experience a sensation diffused in extension, we must acknowledge an agent possessing all the

[99] No new properties would falsify former properties, whatever might be discovered in bodies or whatever change they might undergo from a force outside nature. Hence the extrasubjective qualities we now perceive in bodies are not deceptive; they are true even if they were to be changed.

[100] The same would be true if the fundamental feeling were diffused in a surface or solid continuum, that is, without any interruption.

characteristics required for what we call 'body'. Hence we must acknowledge a *multiplicity* of bodies obtained from a multiplicity of sensations in a multiplicity of spaces. I can always imagine a sensation ending in one space while another continues in another space, or one sensation beginning here and another ending there, so that all I know about sensations in different spaces indicates their mutual independence.

This essential difference of effects compels the acceptance of a substantial difference, and therefore multiplicity of causes. This in turn shows that, granted a continuous sensation, there must be a continuity of extension in the body producing it.

859. We have imagined various small spaces as divisions of a larger space in which sensation is diffused. We saw how a force or a minute body is present, producing a sensation in each small space. Now if we fuse all these small spaces together, they become one large, continuous space. But this fusion does not affect our argument; nothing is altered. Provided the spaces are distinct, a corresponding minute body is necessary for each of them whether they are distant, near or even contiguous with one another. However, their continuous contiguity, resulting in one large, continuous sensation, must also give one continuous body.

The whole force of the argument lies in this one principle: wherever there is sensation, there is also an acting energy. So if a sensation is continuous and equal in every assignable point of a space, an acting cause, the body, is present throughout the same space. Hence if there is no interval in the sensation, there is no interval in the body. Granted a continuous sensation, the body producing it is continuous.

The need for such a conclusion is found in the wonderful, mysterious but undeniable nature of continuous extension. No space, however small or wherever present, can be assigned in continuous extension unless it has its own entity outside and fully independent of other spaces. Every smaller space can be at least mentally separated from the whole, giving us the *indefinite limitability* of the continuum we have noted. The fact that each space is outside every other means that the action confined to one space cannot operate within any other; the smallest space presupposes an agent outside the

agent acting in the next space. In an external body therefore
we must be able to identify as many contiguous parts acting
on our body as there are contiguous spaces identifiable in our
body felt by us.

860. Someone might object: when an external body
wounds some part of our feeling faculty, it produces pain
more extensive than itself, as the pain spreads, by sympathy,
to other parts. There is no necessity therefore for the
extension of a sensation to correspond exactly to the
sensation of a body causing the sensation. But:

1. I note that in all the places where the pain extends
by consent there must be sensitive parts. The argument given
above must be applied to these parts; if the pain extends in a
continuous space, the injured parts producing it must be
continuous.[101] Now if the parts of our body are continuous,
there is a continuum in bodies, which was to be proved.

2. diffused sensation, propagated sympathetically,
follows the same law as all other sensations: 'A force is felt at
the spot where it is applied.' A sensation spreads precisely
because the force changing the state of the parts in the
sensitive organ spreads. Let us suppose the movement of the
organ which gives rise to the pain (it does not matter whether
the pain is produced by a mechanical, physical or chemical
force) spreads from one part to another part of the limb, let us
say from one layer to another. The third layer receives the
movement from the second. It feels only the pressure or
action of the second layer, not the external body. The pain
present by sympathy or communication in the sensitive
material does not indicate an *external body*. Only the limb is
perceived more acutely, that is, those parts of it causing the
pain actively and immediately. But in this case, the sensation
produced directly by the external body is indeed detected and
indicates the existence of the body; we are aware of feeling a
disturbance at the place where the body is acting. Thus the
principle I began with, to demonstrate the continuity of
bodies, is valid also for sensations diffused sympathetically. It
is always true that 'in every place where we feel a sensation,
there is a force in act, a body acting.'

---

[101] We can sometimes wrongly locate a sensation, as in the pain of an amputated
limb; but here our *judgment* is deceived, not our feeling.

§8. The sensitive parts of our body do not produce a feeling extending beyond themselves

861. This truth has just been demonstrated. It is also proved by the definition of the sensitive parts of our body. Because we feel a sensitive part only where we feel and confirm a sensation, sensations therefore do not extend outside the sensitive parts and vice versa.

§9. The extension of external bodies is neither greater nor less than the sensations they produce

862. This follows from the preceding proposition. The size of an external body is measured by sensations, especially touch. We have already seen that the extension of our body, perceived subjectively, is the measure of the extrasubjective extension of external bodies. Therefore the extension of external bodies is neither greater nor less than the extension of the sensations produced by the contact of external bodies.

§10. Phenomenal continuity is present in our touch-sensations

863. When we touch a very smooth surface with a part of our body, we are unable to notice any break in the sensation we experience. The sensation, spread throughout the surface, seems to be continuous, that is, the continuity is phenomenal.

However if we look at the surface through a microscope, it is seen to be uneven and rutted. This would seem to contradict what we have just established, that a sensation of touch produced by an external body does not extend outside the size of the body itself. But we must always bear in mind the real, necessary distinction between a *sensation* and our *awareness* of that sensation.[102] We must convince ourselves by observation that there are very minute sensations which

---

[102] On many occasions I have distinguished between *feeling* and *awareness* of feeling. I am certain and will show, that, although a corporeal stimulus acting on our spirit may produce a sensation, the stimulus needs to be quite intense for it to produce a sensation capable of drawing our attention with relative ease. The weaker the sensation, the more difficult is it to advert to it, even if it exists. Hence, a very weak sensation must be totally unsuited to making us aware of it or of its extension.

entirely escape our awareness. This explains why we think a surface is even and smooth, because in the sensation of the surface we do not advert to the tiny corruscations and intervals. Hence a large sensation is not in fact continuous; we think it is because we do not advert to its very minute intervals.

§11. Elementary sensations are continuous

864. There is no perfect continuity, therefore, in a notably extended sensation (like the surface we have discussed); there are intervals and irregularities in its parts. The large sensation is broken up by intervals, so to speak, into small, elementary sensations, next to each other but not contiguous on every side. It is my opinion that these tiny, elementary sensations are diffused in a truly continuous extension, as I will now show. We begin by supposing the opposite, that is, they have no continuity and are merely mathematical points.

865. Mathematical points would necessarily have between them spaces of various minute sizes which would always be continuous, and also contiguous because a mathematical point does not prevent contiguity. But here we must note a law governing sensations: 'If our body has two or more sensations located in quite different places, we notice the space separating them', because we refer the sensations to different points. When these spaces are noticeably extended, we feel them, especially by comparing the places affected and unaffected by sensation. Now if we were to feel the sensation only in many unextended points, would it be possible for such a sensation to be phenomenally continuous, as it is in fact? It would not, as the following reasons will show:

1. If we are capable of adverting to sensations that have no extension, we would be much more capable of adverting to the tiny spaces separating them, for these have an extension infinitely greater than mathematical points. Thus the total sensation could never seem continuous. If it were continuous, we would have to advert to it as something composed of unextended points, distantly separated from each other. In such a case it would be impossible to explain the phenomenon of continuity in sensations.

866.   2.   An infinite number of mathematical points placed together could not cover a surface or even a line. They cannot give the extension they do not possess. Thus, if we were to join together all the supposed unextended points we feel, the size of the surface in which they are spread would not be covered in any way. We would have to feel on the one hand the sensation of the unextended points and, on the other, the surface exactly as it was previously felt by our fundamental feeling, or indeed feel no continuum at all. All the tiny spaces that as a result had no sensation would, taken together, form an extension as large as the extension existing prior to the sensation of the points. If therefore the whole extension we felt in the points were non-existent, we would have to be aware of the extension remaining between the points. This extension would be exactly the same as it was before we received the impression that has only unextended points but no extension. In this case we could never have a perception or idea of any continuum.

867.   3.   Again, if we felt simple points, we would feel a complex of non-corporeal sensations because such sensations would not terminate in extension (cf. 754), which is of the essence of corporeal sensations; nor would sensation of this kind supply matter for the idea of a body.

868.   4.   Finally, let us suppose we feel only unextended points. It would be possible to locate them at different places in the body's periphery. This can be done only by measuring in some way the distance between one point and another. Now either we feel these distances, or we do not. If we do, we will feel a *continuum*; if we do not, we will have no means of locating the points at the places we do locate them. In this case, they would be sensations, foreign to every place, located perhaps in the simplicity of our spirit but nowhere else. There is no doubt that only the *continuum* can be a measure of distance; a simple point is no measure because entirely devoid of extension. But granted we perceive a *continuum*, we can measure the interval between one point and another. The size of these intervals is only a projection we make of their ability to repeat a certain number of times the *continuum* we use as a unit of measure.

We have to recognise therefore that small, elementary sensations, whether acquired or forming the fundamental feeling, are extended, that is, terminate in a continuous extension.

§12. Elementary bodies have a continuous extension

869. We cannot affirm or deny the simplicity of the *corporeal principle* because we can be ignorant of it (cf. 855-857) to some extent. But it is clearly false that *bodies* can be a complex of simple points [. . .].° We have seen: 1. that elementary sensations are extended and continuous; 2. that the size of bodies, which are the *proximate causes* of sensations, is equal to the size of the sensations. We therefore conclude that elementary bodies have a continuous extension.[103]

§13. Argument against simple points

870. Points escape our senses. We can never perceive unextended points which, therefore, cannot be bodies. We cannot give a name to what we do not know; names indicate things only in so far as things are known.[104] Thus the word 'body' must indicate things known, things falling under our senses that we touch, see and perceive with our other organs. The word does not mean unextended points, of which we have no experience at all.

Wherever there is a sensation, there is an experience relative to ourselves, and an action relative to the agent, an *acting force* that we call body. Now if there are continuous sensations in some of the little spaces, the force must be diffused in the whole space, be present in every point, and be extended and continuous. Hence elementary bodies must possess real continuity and cannot be simple points, if we use reason, not imagination, as our guide for the data provided by observation.°

[103] Besides having a certain continuous extension, elementary bodies must have certain regular forms, like crystals, and must be perfectly hard and unchangeable.

[104] Cf. 647-652. However we must always remember that words indicate the *real thing*, although only in the limited way we know it.

Article 13.
The definition of bodies completed

871. Having established that continuous extension is real in bodies, we can now perfect the definition of body[105] by adding to it this quality of extension: 'A body is a single substance[106] endowed with extension, and producing in us a pleasant or painful feeling termininating in the same extension.'[107]

Article 14.
We perceive external bodies by touch and movement

872. If a body is a force whose act terminates in a solid, continuous extension, we must investigate how we perceive it by touch.

Extension has three dimensions, length, breadth and height, which we first perceive in our body through the fundamental feeling (cf. 692 ss.). In the action of external bodies on the surface of our body, we cannot feel and perceive more than a surface, that is, two dimensions, length and breadth. Our body alone does not allow us to perceive the dimension of depth in an external body.[108] But if we consider the external surface, perceived by our touch, in relationship with the faculty we have of moving the surface,

---

[105] I first defined bodies imperfectly, basing the definition on common sense (cf. 635). I say 'imperfectly' not 'falsely' because it contained the entire essence of bodies without analysis of their elements. Analysis of the definition has allowed me to perfect it (cf. 749-753), especially here. The progress of knowledge, I believe, must be something like this, and begin with natural, composite ideas (popular understanding), which are analysed and then scientifically synthesised to form knowledge. Hence those who deny the necessity of starting from definitions, fall into the opposite error. If anyone wishes to be understood, he has to begin with definitions; but there are scientific definitions and popular definitions, and both are true. We must begin with the popular to finish with the scientific.

[106] It is *single* because it is *continuous*, nothing more.

[107] This was demonstrated earlier.

[108] Sometimes an external body seems to act simultaneously in all the points of a solid space of our body, for example, a penetrating, acidic substance. Granted this, we would indeed perceive our body's solidity but not the solidity of the external body. This observation can help us to distinguish our body's extension from the extension of the external body; the two bodies can easily be confused because we perceive them united in our sensation of their touching. A relationship that distinguishes two agents is different for each of the agents.

we obtain the idea of a solid body. Just as we obtain the idea of solid space by conceiving a body movable in all directions outside its plane, so the idea of a solid body comes from the movement we partly experience and partly expect or think as possible, of a corporeal surface moving outside its own plane.

873. As we consider this movement, we conceive as possible that all the surfaces imaginable within a solid space can be felt, that is, they can be terms of the action done in us by a body. To help us understand this, let us imagine a solid cube. If I touch all six faces of a cube of very hard material, pressing as firmly as I like, I perceive simply the limits of a solid space shaped like a cube, that is, corporeal surfaces. This gives me only an imperfect idea of the body because all I have perceived are surfaces enclosing and terminating a solid space; I have perceived only the body's limits, not its solid extension.

Next I take a cube of soft material, such that I can change its form or break it into parts. If I shape or divide it, there is only one result: more and more surfaces are revealed, which I did not feel before because they were not uncovered from within the cube and were certainly not surfaces. As I continue to divide it up, I have to conclude that the solid cube presents not only a corporeal surface externally, but has the ability to present more and more surfaces internally. Experiments and thoughts like this lead me to the concept of corporeal solidity, completing my idea of solid body, that is, of a substance diffusing its activity in solid extension according to certain laws.

Article 15.
Origin of the idea of mathematical body

874. The previous experiment taught me that, by applying force to the cube sufficient to change its form or divide it, I can obtain more surfaces from within the space enclosed by the corporeal surfaces of the cube. Examining this fact, I cannot find any reason why the exposed surfaces should be in one particular part of the cube and not in another. There is no repugnance in thinking that these corporeal surfaces are equally present in all parts, that is, in every plane imaginable

within the cube. Now the possibility of thinking of the corporeal surfaces dividing the volume of the cube in any plane, is the idea of mathematical body, which is always conceived as perfectly continuous.

Article 16.
Origin of the idea of physical body

875. As long as I think the *possibility* of finding a corporeal surface in any imaginary plane within a cube, I have the idea of a *mathematical body* (cf. 874). But if instead of this simple possibility I try as well as I can to determine the forms of a particular, real body with my touch or other senses (even with the use of instruments), I become aware of irregularities, ridges and spaces between one section and another. In this case I form the idea of a complex of tiny parts, not in perfect contact, differently shaped and interspersed with intervals and links so strongly bonded together in some places that they cannot be forced apart. I call this *physical body*.

All this explains how people born blind can form the idea of both mathematical and physical bodies by means of touch, movement and intellect.

10

THE PARTICULAR CRITERION FOR THE EXISTENCE OF EXTERNAL BODIES

Article 1.
The criterion for external bodies is an application of the general criterion for the existence of bodies

876. We have dealt with the general criterion (cf. 749) and seen that, applied to the external bodies we know, it gives us the criterion for their existence. In other words, to be certain of the perception of an external body, we must perceive: 1. a force modifying us; 2. its action communicated to us in a feeling endowed with extension; 3. an extension that is stable, that is, able to repeat the sensation (otherwise we could not speak about a substance acting); 4. an extension endowed with three dimensions. Thus it is not sufficient to perceive corporeal surfaces. We must perceive a solid space which, when divided, reveals new surfaces to our senses.

Article 2.
Applications of the criterion for the existence of external bodies

877. 1. Wet a coin and press it against a child's forehead, pretending to make it stick. It is now possible to remove it without the child's noticing. In fact he will think the coin is still there and bend his head to make it fall. But if he touches his forehead he realises: 1. that he experienced something there; 2. that the substance producing the experience is no longer present, because the substance's presence involves a constant experience and the possibility that the feeling can be repeated and reinforced, granted the necessary conditions (cf. 876, no. 3).[109]

---

[109] Sensation in the nerves lasts some time even when the cause has been removed, as in the case of red streaks left in the eye caused by gyrating fireworks. Consciousness of the sensation indicates a cause but not the actual presence of the cause. This must be due to a judgment, which, if all its necessary conditions are not

2. We could touch what looks like a rod of solid silver and be deceived about its solidity; we might look inside and find another substance, or a hollow.[110]

11

THE SUBJECTIVE AND THE EXTRASUBJECTIVE
IN EXTERNAL SENSATIONS

Article 1.
The necessity of this distinction

878. After observing and describing *extrasubjective* perception of bodies by touch, we should follow with observations on the other four senses to see what perception reveals for each one. But before doing so, we must carefully distinguish the *extrasubjective* and *subjective* elements present in every sensation, so that nothing subjective remains in the extrasubjective element. When this has been done, the extrasubjective perception will stand out clearly and indicate for us the extrasubjective value of each sense.

Article 2.
Some truths recalled

879. We have demonstrated two things:

1. Sensations are in us, not in external agents (cf. 632 ss. and 672 ss.). [. . .]

2. Sensations are in us as the term of actions done by something other than ourselves. [. . .] In every sensation we experience a passive modification or disturbance within us, of which we are directly conscious, that expresses the term of an

present, is misleading. Sensation however does not deceive us as regards the existence of the part affected in our body; sensation is the result of a modification of the fundamental feeling and of a cause producing the modification.

[110] Here too it is our judgment, not the sensation, that misleads us, because it includes more than the sensation; in the example, it includes the inside of the rod.

external action. By their nature, therefore, sensations, although in us, inform us of something outside ourselves. We must either deny the difference between activity and passivity, or accept that to be conscious of an experience in us is to be conscious of an action done in us, but not by us.

Article 3.
Human intelligence analyses sensations

880. Consciousness tells us: 1. that we are modified; 2. that this modification is an action done in us, not by us. It tells us these two things simultaneously, with a single voice, as it were. Reflection then analyses this united evidence of consciousness, recognising the two things and considering each one separately. Next, the understanding applies the concept of substance to our consciousness of the action done in us, not by us. In this way it isolates and makes its object the external things on which it then meditates and reasons.

Article 4.
The general principle for discerning what is subjective and what is extrasubjective in sensations

881. The principle for accurately distinguishing the subjective and extrasubjective elements in sensations is: 'Everything contained in sensations considered in themselves (and not according to the way they are produced) is subjective; everything contained in the concept of our passivity, attested by consciousness, is extrasubjective.'

Article 5.
Application of the general principle in the search for the extrasubjective part of sensations

882. Applying the principle, we discover the following extrasubjective parts in sensations:
    1. Consciousness tells us we are passive in sensations, that is, we perceive a *force in act*. Our understanding then

sees in this action a *being different from itself*, that is, a body. *Force* then is the first part of the extrasubjective perception of bodies.

2. Consciousness attests that the disturbances and forces we feel are multiple. *Multiplicity of bodies* therefore is the second part of our extrasubjective perception of bodies.

3. Consciousness again, and reason, tell us that a *force* is actively present in every point of a sensation without exception. We are thus led to the conviction that there is a continuous extension. This is the third part of the extrasubjective perception of bodies.

883. The *force*, a property of bodies, is not any force, capable of acting in our spirit. It acts in a particular way, determined by the subjective effects it produces in us, that is, by the subjective part of sensations such as pleasure, pain, heat, light, colours, etc. Now, corresponding to all the different kinds of sensations and effects of this force, there must be, in bodies, *aptitudes* or powers for producing them. These powers proceed from the *force* which is the essence of body, and is the body itself. The first quality of bodies, therefore, generates many other qualities, that is, causes all those aptitudes in which it expresses itself in its different effects (determinations of the force).[111]

884. *Multiplicity* is not a real property of corporeal nature except in so far as it is possible to imagine it in the continuous extension with which bodies are endowed. In fact, real *multiplicity* is accidental, a relationship of many mentally conceived bodies.

885. Finally, *extension*, especially when united to *force*, is the source of a great amount of information about corporeal properties. Because extension includes *mobility, shape, divisibility, impenetrability*, etc., all these properties are both real and extrasubjective, that is, in bodies themselves, not simply in us.°

---

[111] These determinations explain the element we have so far ignored in order not to complicate the argument. It has been included in the word 'corporeal', used to qualify 'force'.

Article 6.
The difference between primary and secondary properties of bodies

886. The famous distinction between *primary* and *secondary* properties of bodies has its foundation in nature. But it would be better to call the former *extrasubjective* and the latter *subjective*, although *primary* and *secondary* are not out of place because we form the idea of body with the extrasubjective properties and apply the subjective properties as accidents of bodies.

Article 7.
Application of the general principle to find the subjective part of sensations

887. All that forms sensation considered in itself is subjective (cf. 881). Hence if we remove from sensations multiplicity, extension, and the *force* producing them and making them subsist (and anything else discovered through analysis of these three parts), anything left that we can observe is subjective.

We may note that feeling in the human being has a unity, that is, the unity of the feeling principle that gathers and unites its various modifications. Moreover, it is reasonable to believe that the nature of this feeling principle, and of the animal fundamental feeling, generates the different feelings, establishing and determining the nature of each. Nevertheless, we do not know sufficiently the nature of the principle and the feeling to understand this connection. The many, various changes undergone by feeling seem to us arbitrary and independent of each other; we cannot deduce them *a priori*.

888. I do not know whether this is due to my ignorance or whether, in this case, something lies hidden and mysterious to the human race. I have to be satisfied with indicating the many, varied kinds of sensations as basic facts without explaining them. I do not need to explain the laws that govern the generation of such different, unpredictable feelings from a single first feeling.

But it does seem to me that something is in fact hidden from us, because our imagination cannot pass from one kind of sensation to another which we have never experienced. A person born blind never gains an image of colours with the help of the other senses. Generally speaking, it is impossible for anyone born without one of his senses to use the sensations of the other senses, even if they are particularly powerful in him, to form an image of the sensations he has never experienced. It appears undeniable therefore that at least external, acquired sensations have something incommunicable, and are completely separate from each other. Their noticeable simplicity would lead to the same conclusion.

889. On this basis, it seems to me that the first subjective element is the pleasure diffused in the sensitive parts of a body animated by the fundamental feeling. The nature of this pleasure, produced by our body, is determined by the *state* of our body itself, granted the presence of life. The *modifications* of the fundamental feeling are certainly determined by the *state* of our body but, as I have said, to investigate the laws governing this fact is beyond my powers.

890. Because the various parts of the body have a different *state*, they receive impressions in a different way, and modify the fundamental feeling differently. This varying *state* of the parts of the body was wisely ordained by the creator in such a way that different organs were fittingly designed to determine various kinds of sensations. Hence the wonderful structure of the eye is designed to receive certain modifications of feeling, different from those received in the ears, nose and palate.

891. Besides the *modifications* of the fundamental feeling presented by these sense-organs, modifications also take place in different parts of the body, according to their constitution and composition, or according to some particular organisation. The sense of hunger, of thirst and of sleep, of the sexual drive, are all different in kind. But they are not considered as senses because the particular name of sense is reserved for what helps our understanding in a very special way to acquire cognitions of external things.

892. The special condition and organisation of each sense-organ makes it capable of receiving the particular kind of

modification of the fundamental feeling for which it was designed. However, the modification does not take place unless, in addition to a good organic system, a stimulus acts in the appropriate way. Light is needed if the eye is to give colour-sensations; hearing needs air, the nose needs odour-particles and the palate taste-particles. There has to be an appropriate, suitable cause relevant to both matter and form of the organ, so that the organ can undergo the change necessary for bringing about a particular kind of sensation in the fundamental feeling.

893. A simple *cause* however is not enough; it must also act in the *particular way* necessary for stimulating each of the four senses.[112]

894. Thus, to produce special sensations, three things are necessary, in addition to life: 1. the right quality of organisation, and the suitable condition of the organ; 2. the right kind of *agent*; 3. an appropriate manner of action by the agent.

895. Consequently the effect, or subjective sensation, produced simultaneously by these three principles, is certainly not an indication of the condition of one of them only. It is a mistake to think we can establish the quality of the external cause from the subjective sensation.

For example, the sensation of heat is subjective; it is in us, not in the external body producing it.° It is not therefore a suitable measure of the quantity of heat. We can be persuaded of this if we put a very cold hand into water that is not so cold; the water will seem warm. The same will happen when a hand that feels very hot is immersed in lukewarm water; the water seems cold. The reason is the different state of the hand due to the necessary change in the fundamental feeling.

Article 8.
The extension that can be felt by touch

896. Although we have seen that the basic sensations of touch and the particles corresponding to them are extended

---

[112] In the sense of touch there are a great variety of sensations according to the type of touch. Without previous experience, no one could imagine the peculiar sensation of tickling, a sensation that makes us laugh even against our will and has no connection with any other sensation.

and continuous, we cannot conclude with certainty that touch can perceive every minute extension. It is true that every smaller space assignable in a basic, continuous sensation must be felt; but we cannot attribute to each tiny space considered in itself what is said about it considered as an ideal part of the continuum.

There could be a law stating that sensation never takes place below a certain minimum extension. If so, observation is powerless to affirm anything with certainty except about possibilities or probabilities. For instance, there is no contradiction in affirming on the one hand that we can think of an indefinitely small sensation and on the other that such a sensation must necessarily have some extension. Because we cannot reasonably exclude either of them, their possibility must be granted.

897. However whether sensation is of such a nature that its extension can be reduced indefinitely, or whether it has a *minimum* extension, there seems no doubt at all that it is usually much more acute than the *awareness* of the sensation itself. As a result, sensation feels spaces so minute that we are not aware of feeling them. [113]

The fact that the *sensation* of touch is far more acute than our *awareness* of the sensation is evident in those born blind. It is commonly said that their sense of touch is *more acute*. It is known that they can distinguish coins, playing cards, the quality of cloth and even colours by touch alone; they can sense the breathing or movement of anyone silently approaching them, even at a distance. They can indeed do wonderful things with their sense of touch, but not, I think, because it is *more acute* in them or because nature has endowed them better. What has been developed is their *awareness* about sensations. Their sense of touch is the same as that of others, who may or may not be blind. [114] But blind people, not having the distractions of sight, need to profit

---

[113] This further emphasises the distance between *sensation* and *understanding*; *awareness* is an act of understanding, not of feeling. *Awareness* is only intellective attention given to what we feel or understand.

[114] We must also note that animals have a certain power over their nerves. With this power they extend and apply their nerves to receive sensations better. Its use can be perfected by skill and by habit.

from their sensations of touch. They acquire very sensitive attention and recall relative to all the different impressions on their touch, including delicate impressions which escape other people. It is not exaggerated, therefore, to believe that if awareness could make even further progress, human beings would realise that their touch, although limited, is a sense of unbelievable delicacy [App. no. 17].

898. As we have observed, it is more difficult to be *aware* of sensations when they are motionless and hardly change. When we wish to note the unevenness of a surface with our hand, it is not sufficient to press our finger on one spot only. We may feel the minute differences in the surface but not be *aware* of *feeling* them. To be aware of them we move our finger firmly over the surface. Because this action affords us sharper sensations of the uneven surface, it is easy to be aware of them and, through them, of the unevenness.

899. Hence a solid body which we are *aware* of feeling, is different from one we actually *feel* by touch. The body we are aware of may perhaps be perfectly continuous and smooth on the surface, while the body we touch is possibly uneven, with high and low points, as any powerful microscope will reveal. As I have said, it seems we cannot put a limit to the acuteness of our touch. The microscope, while revealing the high and low points of the surface, also reveals the body as joined at several places and composed, too, of small, apparently continuous spaces. This is not the continuity of elementary bodies we have spoken about, a continuity which we believe escapes the most acute attention. Nor can we call it true continuity, because elementary bodies can be so close to each other that we cannot observe any interval between them. Nevertheless, the perfect adhesion of elementary bodies is not impossible or absurd, in my opinion, for there is nothing impossible about a true contact.

900. But let us leave this dangerous, unobservable world. A solid body perceived by touch and *adverted to*, has a shape we can distinguish fairly well. We ignore the unevenness of the surface and use our imagination to shape the body in the way we find most convenient for mentally conceiving it. This explains the regularity of shapes offered by touch. We perceive them easily because of their simplicity, which

presents enough distinction and information for our purposes; we are quite satisfied.[115]

Article 9.
The extrasubjective sensation of the four sense-organs

901. Our eye perceives light directly and light informs us about external things.[o] I am concerned with the eye only in so far as it perceives light, its immediate agent, not as it indicates distant bodies that do not touch it. We have seen that the three parts of the extrasubjectivity of our senses are energy, multiplicity and extension.

Energy is felt equally by all the senses, has the general concept of agent only and in itself presents nothing determined. We must now see how we perceive, with the other four senses, multiplicity and extension, the parts that in some way determine the agent's nature.

902. As regards extension, we note that the four senses are touched and affected by bodies so minute that if only one were to strike our senses, it would be impossible to isolate and observe it. No one can see or touch particles of light or fire or air or smell or molecules of food stimulating our sense of taste, because they are so tiny that we cannot note or advert to them. As regards multiplicity, we find particles crowding in on our organs in such numbers that even if we could identify their size we could never determine their number clearly.

These two circumstances, that is, the size, shape, movement and changes that cannot be observed in the particles, and their uncountable number must cause a vivid but *confused* perception in us of the mass of particles. The

---

[115] The mind has no difficulty in grasping regular shapes, like triangles, squares and any figure with a perceptible number of sides, because their component elements are few. On the other hand, if we greatly increase the number of sides, we can no longer *advert* to them, although we perceive them all equally with our *sense*. If the sides are of varying length, it is even more difficult to have a *distinct idea*. Imagine the surfaces of a solid are all different from each other. The differences and multiplicity are beyond the power of our attention. The shape is too complex for our mind because it is conceived only by means of conceiving the unity of the parts. These, however, are so many and different that we are unable to keep them simultaneously before our mind, or to give them the amount of attention we could pay to a smaller number.

extrasubjective part of the four organs under discussion must be, as it were blind, and lacking in *differentiation*.° Hence, although the extrasubjective part of these sensations is vivid, they offer to our understanding little that is clear about their immediate agents, and seem to present something more mysterious than what is offered by the sense of touch. In fact, when the understanding receives only a few clear perceptions, mystery seems inevitable. We should also note that the understanding takes its perceptions from the extrasubjective part of sensations which, confused at its origin, renders our intellections confused and vague.

903. The difference of these four organs from touch should be carefully noted. Touch perceives larger solid bodies;[116] the particles of such bodies adhere to each other either through real contact or very close proximity (I believe both cases are true). They therefore present to touch a large, single *shape*, with high and low points escaping observation. Thus the extension of large agents acting on the sense of touch is easily identified and their regular shape easily conceived. On the other hand, the particles that impinge on and stimulate the four senses, are scattered, indefinable, moving at great speed, never remaining in the same place or state. They move about haphazardly in all directions, disappearing in the air on which they arrived. In short, even if they were only small in quantity and of a size we could advert to, they would still escape observation because of the tremendous speed and instability of their continual movements.

904. Another comment must be made which will clearly demonstrate that the immediate agents of the four organs are of such a kind that their size and shape cannot be observed[117] nor present us with a distinct perception. Without this perception, all the sensations of the four organs will necessarily be confused, and therefore, mysterious, although pleasant and vivid.[118]

[116] Even liquids, in so far as they act on the sense of touch, occupy a definite solid space, and present precise, determined shapes to our observation because, although mobile, they are nevertheless stable, large and regular.

[117] It is *size* and *shape* that give us a distinct perception of an agent, as we have already said, because they are the *extrasubjective* parts of sensation.

[118] How vivid they are depends on the particles producing a strong impression in the organ through their vast number, speed and perhaps, in the case of light, their

We have distinguished two parts, the subjective and the extrasubjective, in adventitious sensations, and have seen that an external body can make an impression and stimulate a sensation on any sensitive part of our body. We have also seen that the affected part must be distinguished from its surrounding parts into which the movement, together with the sensation, sometimes spreads in sympathy. But this kind of sensation, spreading from the touched parts, contains nothing *extrasubjective*, because the spread and communication of the movement experienced by the sensitive nerve differs from the impulse or kind of disturbance initially experienced by the nerve. The disturbance causes the nerve to pass from rest to excitation. This first impression or disturbance indicates that a force has been applied, while on the other hand the communication and continuation of the movement present no new disturbance or force, except that of the parts themselves of the nerve. These parts pass the movement to each other through the force they have received proper to them. But because this force passes from one part of the nerve to the other, it follows, as I have already said, that the whole sensation propagated by consent can be referred only to that feeling part of our body which allows movement of the parts and feeling to pass through it. The increase of the accompanying sensation is subjective only, or at least certainly not united with the perception of an external body; it remains in the stimulated nerve as in its source and matter.

905. The special nature of the four organs must be now noted. A single particle of air vibrating in the ear could definitely not produce a sensation of sound; only the entire body of undulating air causes this sensation. In the same way, although I do not know if a single unit of light could move the

---

elasticity, for light impinges and rebounds in the briefest of time without a very strong impression. The result of any strong impression must be a pronounced movement or perhaps a vibration of the nerves causing a large *subjective* sensation, as the soul feels the effect of the quivering nerve. In general we can establish the following fact given by observation: 'A very pleasant sensation is produced in a nerve when it is stimulated by rapid, frequent vibrations which do not damage or sever the nerve.' Now every time the stimuli are very small and many, they can do this, provided their number is not excessive and their impact moderate. Thus a carpet of roses or any soft material is very pleasant to lie on, and every soft surface is pleasant to our touch, in the same way that colours can please our eyes and sound-waves our ears.

visual organ, I do believe that, in order to have a sensation of colour, a certain quantity of light must act upon our eyes.

Similarly it seems to me that a sensation of taste or smell is not aroused by virtue of small, flavoured or odorous bodies but by great numbers of particles striking the taste buds and nostrils and causing such a movement that they produce a frequent, general vibration which alone occasions the sensations. If this is the case, and it seems probable to me, we can no longer say that each one of the minute acting particles must have produced some sensation of taste, smell, etc. All we can say is that each tiny body, despite its minute size, has made its impact. But this is not yet sensation. Taste, smell and other sensations begin only when the vibration along the length of the nervous membrane or cartilege has been propagated and reached the level of agitation required for the sensation to take place.

If this is the case (and it cannot be doubted relative to hearing), I believe that the four kinds of sensations would generally take place through sympathy among the parts, that is, through communication of movement. This would make the *extrasubjective* part of the sensations still more hidden and confused. We would be dealing with unobservable parts, and the sensation would be stimulated not so much by the impulse they imparted, as by the agitation following in the affected part of our body. If both impulse and consequent agitation together gave sensation, one mixed with the other would be almost indiscernible.

12

ORIGIN OF THE IDEA OF BODIES THROUGH THE EXTRASUBJECTIVE PERCEPTION OF SIGHT

Article 1.
The eye perceives a coloured surface

906. Let us imagine a human being standing still with eyes open. Vision in this person is limited to a variously-coloured

surface adhering to his eyes, without background or perspective.

Article 2.
The coloured surface is a corporeal surface

907. Because the body is an agent producing feeling with an extension mode, feelings located at points in space are corporeal actions. But our coloured surface is a feeling extending over a surface. It is therefore corporeal.

Article 3.
The coloured surface is identical with the retina of the eye affected by light

908. All senses are touch (cf 744, 745) and as such are subject to the laws governing touch; they differ amongst themselves only through their accidental phenomena. Our study of these phenomena showed that the sensations of our four organs possess, as a general characteristic, highly developed subjectivity with limited, confused extra-subjectivity (cf. 887-895). Such phenomena, therefore, are simply the mode of these four species of sensation; and indeed touch itself furnishes similar phenomena (*ibid.*), although not so distinctly. Phenomena of this kind add nothing that is capable of altering the common laws to which touch in general is subject.

In touch, however, the touching surface of the external body forms a unity with the touched surface of our body. As a result, the same surface is felt simultaneously in two ways: in our body, subjectively, and as the term of perception of the external agent, extrasubjectively (cf. 841). It is clear, therefore, that 'the coloured surface perceived by the eye is identical with the surface of the retina touched by the light.'

We have to consider carefully the fact that the eye perceives the coloured surface in the same way as touch perceives hardness and resistence in an extended body. In corporeal vision, therefore, we must distinguish: 1. the sensation of the retina; 2. the entire confused perception of the innumerable particles of light which fill the retina in which they are spread.

Article 4.
The coloured surface we perceive is as big as the retina touched by light; but the colours are distributed in that surface in fixed proportions

909. This extraordinary, but irrefutable truth is a corollary of the preceding affirmation. Nevertheless, it is sometimes called in doubt as a result of inadequate observation, because of our habit of attributing to bodies perceived visually the same size that we perceive in them through touch and movement. Later we shall explain how this habit arises and show that it depends upon our judgment about the sensation of sight, and not upon the sensation itself.

910. For the time being, we first notice that, whatever the size of the agents perceived by the eye, the eye indubitably perceives them in a definite proportion relative to one another. For example, while my eye receives all the colours of the agents in its view, it can also receive those of another person's eye. But the pupil is perceived as considerably smaller than the person's body, which in its turn is perceived as smaller than the room in which he is standing. The reason is that the pupil occupies less of my retina than his body, and his body less than the light-filled room. The eye, therefore, perceives the *relative sizes* of bodies that are equidistant from it, although it does not perceive their absolute size.

People born blind who later gain sight can confirm these observations. In the first moments of their use of sight, they experience a sensation adhering to the retina of their eye, but no distance or real distinction of external bodies. What they perceive is a painted canvas, that is, the surface of their retina covered with varying light (cf. 811).

Article 5.
The coloured surface cannot furnish the idea of solid space, even through the movement of colours taking place in space

911. We have already seen that the eye perceives movement. But any change whatsoever, taking place in the coloured surface we perceive, is reduced to change in the surface itself. The succession of coloured surfaces provides no

idea of distance or depth; pictures succeed one another in the eye like the scenes offered by a magic lantern. By itself, therefore, the eye cannot form an idea of three dimensional space.

Article 6.
Colour sensations are signs of the size of things

912. So far we have supposed that only the eyes have been used, but not touch or movement, to discover what the eyes contain and what occurs in them. We have tried to find what term the eye can achieve when left to itself. We saw that, without movement or touch, a person would perceive a coloured surface adhering to his eye; it would be no larger than the retina affected by light, and would stimulate sensation (cf. 909). We also observed that in this tiny surface colours are spread out and divided in a certain order, not haphazardly; the same can be said about the movements taking place in them. The colours have certain relationships, corresponding precisely to the relationships in the size of external things furnished by touch (*ibid.*).

The constancy of these relationships of proportion and the order maintained in the movements of the perceived colours is of great benefit in permitting the colours to act as signs by which we may learn the true size[119] of things, of distances, and of quantities of movement in our own bodies.

913. Let us examine what takes place relative first to the size of external things, and then to distances and quantities of movement. External things transmit light to our eye from every point of their surface. Larger things transmit a greater number of rays which, when the things are equidistant from the pupil, cover a greater area of the pupil. Things seen at the same distance, therefore, are indicated and depicted by sizes proportionate to that which they possess in themselves.° The pattern of things imprinted by the light on our retina, resembles a map; its scale, although less than the reality, perfectly preserves the proportions between the parts found in reality. In the same way, external bodies are depicted in a

[119] That is, those provided by touch, as we have seen, and will explain more fully in the next chapter.

smaller scale on our retina without changing the proportions in any way. The eye and light co-operate so well in drawing visible things on a lesser scale but in constantly equal proportion that the instruments used to reduce a larger to a smaller scale are only an imitation of what is done more perfectly by nature.

914. This example of the map is very helpful for our present purposes. When we look at a map, we pay immediate attention not to the colours or other qualities reproduced there, but to the scale of what we see, which indicates the real size of the area depicted. In the same way, it is not the quality of the colours that provides true, immediate knowledge of what we see in the variety of colours perceived by the eye in any sensation; colour, as such, is the subjective[120] part of sensation, as we have seen. The size and proportion of the different coloured spaces is the extrasubjective part, which indicates the size of exterior things. It offers a *true likeness* of them: a small triangle or square truly resembles a large triangle or square; the proportion between a city and a house is equal to that between the two symbols, which stand for the relationship between the city and the house.[121] In the same way, the eye indicates the size of things through a *likeness* of the sensation to them, and not through their other properties.

Now, if we wish to see how we come to know the size of things from the colour sensations experienced in our eyes, we

[120] Colours also indicate the qualities of things, although as the subjective part of sensation they have no *likeness* to things. But on the basis of our experience, they do serve as *signs*. The written word, for instance, is a sign of the spoken word to which it bears no resemblance, although a *portrait* is the sign of the person whom it resembles. Colours thus enable us to know innumerable things - whether fruit is ripe, whether a human being is healthy or sick, what kind of mood another person is in, to mention only a few. Yet colour bears no resemblance to ripeness, health, depression or other qualities which it indicates through association of ideas. Only experience, which has shown that colour in a given thing indicates certain qualities, enables us to judge the qualities of a thing from what we see of it. Sensation, therefore, as *subjective* can be a sign, but not a likeness of external things; as *extrasubjective*, it is a *sign bearing a resemblance* to things.

[121] I would like to state categorically, once and for all, that I am speaking metaphorically in referring here and elsewhere to the marks formed on the eye by colours. There is no question of impressing on the eye real marks or dots serving as objects to be seen by others, but of subjective sensations, indicated by those dots. If I want to speak of a yellow sensation of a certain size, I speak of a yellow mark - and so on for other colours. I do not want my use of figurative language, intended to facilitate the argument, to be a cause of equivocation.

have to begin by employing our touch. Here we suppose that, with this sense and with movement, we have already perceived external bodies along with their absolute extensions and their proportions. Using touch and sight simultaneously, anyone can notice an extraordinary relationship between the parts of bodies perceived by touch, and the colours perceived by sight. My hand, held out to touch a body, removes a colour from my sight; every point that it touches is a spot hidden from me because my hand covers it. By repeating these experiences, I finally learn that the sensations of touch and sight are stably related to one another, and realise that a touch-sensation outside myself corresponds to every coloured point in my eye. If one of the light-marks affecting my retina is larger, my hand can move further with its touch to cover it. Touches like this are continuing perceptions of external bodies, and serve, as we have seen, as a measure of their size. Because every coloured point of the eye corresponds to the touch-perception of a body, and every more or less large light-mark corresponds constantly and proportionately with the touch-perception of different sized bodies, it must and does occur that the marks on the eye from different rays of light are sure indications and signs of external bodies and their size, which only touch perceives immediately. We thus form a habit of passing with extreme rapidity of thought from sight-sensations to persuasion about external, touchable bodies. This habit, which never ceases in us, is strengthened and developed to such an extent that we confuse and exchange the signs with what they signify and say as soon as we perceive a light-mark with the eye: 'I see a body, a touchable object,' instead of: 'I perceive a light-mark, which assures me of a touchable body[122] outside me.'

When we look at a map, we know the size of the places

[122] Notice that we never stop to consider *signs* once they are well-known and their use habitual. We go directly to the things signified which we appear to see and perceive in the signs themselves. Signs seem so identified with the things they indicate that it becomes very difficult to distinguish one from the other. Hence we say, for example, that 'we have heard some truth or other from so-and-so, an expert in his field', as though we had heard the truths themselves and not simply the words alone, which bear no resemblance whatsoever to the truths we have heard. We speak of a portrait as though the person herself had been depicted, and give it her own name, because we no longer confine our attention to the portrait. We *think the thing in its sign*; and this occurs universally in all our operations as intelligent beings.

indicated provided we have a clear idea of the scale on which they are depicted. However, it is much easier to measure the size of things on the 'map' supplied by the eye than to recognise almost intuitively from a topographical map the size of the area under examination. The reason is clear: our visual map is always before us and, with the help of touch to correct and test what it shows, is being continually applied to various situations.

915. There is another difference between seeing a country on a map and perceiving external bodies through the perception of the retina invaded by varying colours of light-marks from the light refracted by bodies and reflected to the pupil. The map is totally separate from the country shown on it, without any lines, so to speak, of communication with the country. On the other hand, the picture in the eye has an admirable, physical connexion with bodies perceived by touch: rays of light emanating from bodies join them to the impressions experienced by the eye. It is not a question, of course, of the eye being drawn outside itself by these rays of light passing from the bodies to itself, nor of its perceiving anything other than the extremities of the rays. The extremities are changed with lightning speed and accuracy by every movement in the bodies that communicate them to the eye, especially by hands touching the bodies. Because experience teaches children that they have a light-sensation for every point touched by their hands, the points of light felt by their eyes are commensurate with those touched by their hands. They are thus led to identify visual measure with that of touch by superimposing one on the other, point by point, as it were, line by line, surface by surface. Experiences of this kind, provided by nature herself, allow us to find without difficulty in the coloured light-marks of the eye, the same measure of bodies as given through touch-perception.

916. Yet another difference between a map and its countries, and between tactile bodies and the retina speckled with colour, will help to explain the fact under consideration. The countries and the map are both simply terms of sight, one larger than the other. An external body and colours, on the other hand, are both terms of touch, but of touch in two different parts of our body. One of these parts, the pupil, is

extremely delicate and far more complex than the part connected with ordinary touch. This difference has given to sight its own particular name, separating it from touch. Now as long as we are dealing with two terms of sight such as two triangles, one much larger than the other, their likeness enables one to be a sign of the other. Nevertheless, their unequal sizes cannot be easily disregarded; there is an obvious difference between the triangles. This is not the case with the coloured surfaces perceived by the eye and the surfaces perceived by touch, both of which manifest extremely different sensible qualities. Their likeness in form and their diversity in size cannot be easily noticed without, so to speak, superimposing one on top of the other. But nature prevents this and provides instead a kind of special, deceptive superimposition so that, when our hands touch visible bodies, we seem to superimpose the apex of pyramids of light in our eye on the objects we touch. In fact, however, we superimpose the base of the pyramid which we do not perceive. What happens is that we mentally connect the apex we perceive with the base we do not perceive.

This explains why it is more difficult for us to recognise the difference in size between what is seen and touched than to believe in their equality.

Article 7.
Our sight, associated with touch and movement, perceives the distances and qualities of movement in our own bodies

917. Let us now imagine we are in motion with our eyes open.° The changes caused in our sight sensations by movement consist in constant variation of colour, and passages from shade to light and vice-versa. If you look from a distance at the colour and form of a great building, it will perhaps appear as an indistinguishable whitish point against the blue of a high mountain behind it. As you move towards it, the white point grows bigger and gradually takes shape as its outline becomes sharper. As you get near it, you see it in all its size. Your movement causes the points or marks of the coloured surface (the only thing your eye sees) to expand, become distinct and take shape. But these changes are in

constant relationship with the different movements you make, as we have seen.

Movement has no likeness to colour; the two are as different as taste and sound. Nevertheless, the constant relationship of colours, especially of light and shade, with movement, allows the variation of colour to present a clear sign for knowing and measuring movement itself.

918. Colours thus become a kind of language used by nature to speak to us of distance and size. This natural language is taught in the same way as the language we learn from one another.

In artificial language we use words to express ideas, although words are material sounds without any likeness to ideas, which are thoughts belonging to the spirit. Words are functional *signs* of our ideas. As soon as we hear them, force of habit brings to mind the ideas they represent. We form a single object of thought from ideas and words. This comes about because of the constant, analogical relationship we have created between things which differ as greatly as ideas and articulate sounds; it is this relationship which enables words to function as we have described. The same thing takes place with colours as a result of light and shade. They become quasi-words indicating the distance of things from us, and the movement carried out or required to approach things; they are analogous to what they signify.

Another likeness will help to explain more easily the perception of distance by the eye, or rather by animal perspicacity. Colours impressed upon our retina can be considered equivalent to letters of the alphabet which I write on paper but have no similarity, nor even material resemblance, with the sounds called words caused by use of my speech organ as it sends out variations in air-waves. Nevertheless, despite the lack of similarity, the written curves and strokes and dots and crosses call forth words and ideas for the reader through the constant relationship, partly arbitrary and partly analogous, between the ink marks and the sounds indicating ideas. This relationship is a rule according to which thought passes with extreme rapidity from the perception of writing on paper to what the writer wished to convey.

The same is true of colours and movement. Although they have no natural resemblance, their analogous relationship enables us to use colours as signs for knowing and measuring movement, as an animal does with its natural instinct.

919. Just as we have to learn from society how to speak and write, so we have to learn from nature how to discern distance and movement with the eye.[123] After learning the art of reading distance with the eye, and the use of colours as signs of movement, we gradually perfect our habit of interpreting the signs until we think that with sight we see distance immediately and measure the movement needed to travel it. The truth is, however, that we never see anything with our eye except a surface, although the speed with which we unite the idea of extension in depth to the various colours of this surface is such that the surface finally escapes our attention. We then believe we see depth immediately, just as a reader thinks he perceives the words immediately, or a listener thinks he receives images and ideas with ears that perceive only words.

Article 8.
Smell, hearing and taste compared with sight

920. These three species of sensation cannot be signs as precise and general as colours enabling us to know the presence and distance of bodies, because smells, tastes and sounds do not mark off for us a corporeal surface as distinct and as continuous as that provided by the eye. Instead, they offer indistinct, changeable, perfectly homogeneous and uniform corporeal points. Moreover, because the normal objects of touch do not have the same relationship with the

---

[123] Accurate observation is needed of the time required by children to learn the connection of the size furnished by the eyes and that coming from touch and distance. It should be noted that such a connection can be obtained in two ways, instinctively and intellectually. Hence, perceiving the proportions between these sizes depends upon educating: 1. the *sensitivity*, which takes place in animals also; and 2. the *understanding*, which is proper to human beings. Sensitivity learns about the connection practically through associations of *sensations, phantasms, feelings, instincts* and *habits*, all of which in human beings are accompanied by judgments. Experiments with children should help to distinguish the progress of each of these faculties, but this is extremely difficult.

ears, palate and nostrils as with the eye, these sensations cannot be authenticated, as it were, by touch.

921. However, hearing does furnish a variety of sensations which, although without the intimate connection of colours to touch, are governed by fixed, simple laws which enable such sensations to be available for the formation of language. As the eye becomes a natural, although limited, language through touch (things seem to speak to us directly through ordered colours), so hearing offers a means for the discovery of a universal language.

13

THE CRITERION OF BODILY SIZE AND SHAPE

Article 1.
The criterion of the size of bodies is the size perceived by touch

922. When we wish to know if a thing is true or false, we have to compare it with the genuine, certain notion of the same thing. The power we possess of perceiving a thing immediately, rather than its sign or image, is that which gives us this genuine, certain notion or essence.

We have already seen that extension is a mode of the fundamental feeling.[124] Hence the fundamental feeling is a power whose immediate term is not only matter, but also extension. It is the fundamental feeling, therefore, that gives genuine, certain extension, and with it the first measure of every size.

923. But the extension of the fundamental feeling is partly commensurate with extension (cf. 841). As a result, touch also furnishes the genuine, certain size of bodies and, because of the impossibility of an immediate application of the

---

[124] The philosopher who declared our body to be the measure of all things would have made a truly remarkable affirmation if he had confined his assertion to the size of spaces and bodies.

measure provided by the fundamental feeling, becomes in fact the measure used.

924. On the contrary, the eye and other senses, in so far as they differ from touch: 1. do not perceive immediately the size of distant things; 2. do not perceive their distance, but only signs of distance. The size of things presented by the eye has to be compared and rectified with that given by touch. If sight is not to be the source of error for us, we must continually relate the size we see to that offered by touch. This is the fixed measure provided by nature for comparison and emendation of visual size.

Article 2.
Application of our criterion to illusions about the visible size of things

925. We are used to making very rapid judgments as soon as we receive sight-sensations. We take these sensations as signs, but because they allow us to discern almost automatically the size of bodies, we also seem to perceive size itself through sight. This false judgment is made by practically everyone, and it would not be out of place to call it a common sense error [App. no. 18].

Errors of this kind lead to research which becomes entirely superfluous once the error has been dissipated. Let me give an example of such a pointless inquiry. With my eyes open, I can behold immense vistas. Amongst many other things making up the panorama, I catch sight of another person, dwarfed in comparison with the rest of the scene. His two eyes are tinier members of a tiny body. In each of them I notice a little black hole behind which is stretched a small, delicate and extremely sensitive background, called a retina, where light carries out its marvellous task of stimulation. On this very restricted backdrop which forms the final clothing of his eye, the other person sees me and everything else, just as I, in a similar, small, nerve-sensitive space, see him and everything else — earth, sky and immense universe. Nevertheless my eye, which sees the other person's eye, or itself in a mirror, tells me that the screen receiving the colours of so many things is no broader than a tiny line, although the things depicted in it appear immensely greater than it. How can it receive such vision? Does it deceive me by showing me objects of an immense size, when the impression it receives is so small?

The difficulty vanishes totally if we keep in mind that, as we have shown above, the eye perceives neither size nor distance, but only their signs from which the mind with a rapid judgment passes to conceive distance, while the animal acts with the shrewdness of habitual instinct as though it had conceived distance.

Signs do not have to be of the same nature and measure as the things they indicate. They enable us to know size provided we know the relationship between the size of the signs and that of the things. In the case of the eye, we know this relationship habitually because through touch we grasp the real size of things and form a habit of comparing them with the apparent size administered by the eye.

926. Another possible difficulty merits every attention. The eye is also an organ of touch, and light really touches it. Why can we not apply the law of touch to the eye? This law states that when we size up a body with our hand, which is a very suitable instrument of touch-sensations, we measure the body with the hand itself, using it as a basic unit superimposed upon the body to make the comparison. In this superimposed touch we have distinguished the sensation in the hand from the perception of the external body, and have already seen that the extension of the sensation in the hand is the measure of the extension of the body that has contact with the hand. Hence the *subjective* sensation of our own body is the measure of *extrasubjective* perception, that is, of the external agent compared in such an operation with our body. We apply this law to our eye touched by particles of light. In this case, our eye will have: 1. a *subjective* sensation of different parts of the retina as touched by light rays of varying breadth; 2. an *extrasubjective* perception of the particles of light. It will measure what acts upon it with the extension of *subjective* sensation, that is, the thinnest rays of light, or at least the extension of the bundles of rays that work like artists' brushes upon the screen of the eye. If we now confine our attention to the sensation of sight considered as touch, we cannot avoid noting the smallness of the depicted images and

realising that they are smaller than the small aperture of the eye which is, as it were, the general scene or picture whose various parts are obviously smaller than the whole. Noting, as we must, the smallness of the images received in the eye, we must also feel the relationship they have with the eye itself. It is true that these tiny images can be signs of the true, tactile size of things, after we have learned to use our touch, just as the marks on a map are signs of the size of a territory when we know the scale of the map, but this does not weaken the validity of our first knowledge, through which we compared the little images in the eye with the eye itself and, like every other object of touch, measured them with the eye according to their own, real size. Nevertheless, we have no inkling of this in our experience.

927. The difficulty may be solved as follows. The marks in the eye should not be called *images* until we have noted, through touch, that the colours impressed upon the eye are signs of external bodies. Only touch can tell us this. Because the colours tinting the eye form only light-marks which do not of themselves signify or represent anything, they are neither images nor signs for us prior to the use of touch. But the simultaneous use of touch and sight enables us to discover the constant relationship between the size furnished by touch and that provided by the marks in the eye. Because these marks vary as bodies vary to the touch, they become signs for us, and appear true images of bodies.[125]

Although the eye, of itself, perceives only sensations or, as I have called them, certain colour-marks felt only in the retina, the use of touch allows these marks or sensations to function as signs of distant things and to acquire a new state or, better, relationship with us through which we consider them totally different from what they were previously. In fact they seem to take on another nature.

The *marks* or sensations on the retina, therefore, and the visual *images* are the same thing, as far as their own being is concerned, but two things as seen by us. In other words, when we consider the sensation as a mark felt in the eye, and as an image of something external, our attention is brought to

[125] I say *appear*, because their only likeness with external things lies in their *extrasubjective* element.

bear on two entirely opposite terms: first, upon the *mark* we feel, that is, the sensation in the retina; second, upon the mark as *image*, when we move on directly to the thing represented and consider it as the only term of attention, without resting in the sign.

When a person sees a portrait of a friend, he thinks immediately of his friend without stopping to examine the picture in its own being. He ignores the canvas, types of paint, and other elements that compose it. This is possible because the mark felt in the eye is changed into an image through the intervention of touch and, as an image, immediately stimulates our attention to move well away from the portrait in its search for the object of which the mark is an image. But we cannot understand this most important fact without practical conviction of the supremely important distinction between *sensation* and *advertence* to sensation upon which we could say the whole of philosophical knowledge rests.[126]

928. The law governing advertence is as follows: 'That which we advert to is the term of our intellective attention.' Advertence of something arises in us when our attention moves towards and terminates in the thing in such a way that it becomes the final object of our attention. The intermediate links through which our attention and thought pass without making the links their *term*, are perceived fleetingly, but not *adverted to*. If we want to advert to them, we have to turn back and pass rapidly over the road we have taken so that the links we have previously ignored may become terms of our attention. We *advert*, therefore, to that which involves and terminates our act of attention; the many other things we feel and perceive remain outside our attention and inadverted.

In our present case, when the sensations experienced in the retina of the eye have acquired the quality and state of images, they cannot of themselves be terms of our attention because, as we have said above, images of their nature draw us outside themselves by becoming guides directing our attention to what they represent. An image provides a special relationship

---

[126] Depending upon circumstances, I call advertence: *observation, attention, consideration* and *awareness*. All these words express an intellective act, fixed upon a sensation, which forms an idea and adverts to the sensation [. . .].

between two things, one of which serves as a scale or means for directing our thought to the other; an image, as such, moves our attention from the nature of the thing acting as image towards the object represented, which then becomes the term of attention. The sensation on our eye, once it has become a sign and quasi-image of external things, no longer holds our attention and advertence, but directs it to another term. Thus the sensation itself remains unobserved and inadverted.

929. Another consideration may be added: 'Our advertence is attracted more easily by distinct than by confused perceptions.' If we now ask what makes sense-perception distinct or confused, we find three obvious reasons for its heightened clarity. Our sense-perception is more distinct when bodies perceived by sense are: 1. fewer in number; 2. of sufficient size to be grasped in their entirety; 3. more stable in the forms they present to sense. But particles of light are innumerable, incalculably small, perpetually mobile, and as such capable of providing only a vivid, but altogether confused perception as they simultaneously strike the retina. Moreover, when we perceive a body in a confused manner, we seem scarcely to perceive it at all, and often say, for example, that we perceive nothing if all that we see are spaces of air illuminated by uniform light.

On the other hand, our touch-perception is by nature extremely distinct, a characteristic it shares with the vivid signs of perception furnished by the eye. These signs are quite different amongst themselves, and possess extraordinary definition in their minuteness. Consequently, while we advert scarcely, if at all,[127] to the immediate perception of particles of light and their variety in the sensations on our eye, we pay great attention to observing the bodies furnished by touch in so far as the sight-sensations signify them to us. Observing bodies in this way is immensely useful in life's daily contingencies and far removed from pointless consideration of light-marks in the eyes.

---

[127] I say 'scarcely, if at all', rather than 'not at all', because everyone can notice some sensation in the eyes. We feel light falling upon our eyes, and find quite a difference in our pupils when we close our eyes. But, as I said, we do not advert to what takes place in our eyes when we have so many beautiful things to look at.

Article 3.
Application of the criterion to visual illusion about distant bodies

930. If objects delineated by light in the pupil are at different distances, they do not maintain their proportional size; more distant objects send a smaller image to the eye, and closer objects a larger image. This is due to the converging rays of light, whose angle relative to the eye, where it arouses sensation, is more acute according to the distance from which they start. The result is a smaller vestige of the object than there should be. This kind of fallacy does not, however, affect the sensation which, as such, tells us nothing of the object. It is the judgment made by our mind that deceives us as we infer the size of exterior bodies from the sensation of light taken as a sign by the judgment.

931. But this error also is soon corrected. The images coming to us from various distances follow another kind of proportion which serves to distinguish the distances themselves. Apparent size now becomes a sure sign and measure of the distances of bodies in so far as the image in the eye increases in size as the distance diminishes, and vice-versa. Apparent sizes and their distances bear a constant inverse relationship to one another. The constancy of this relationship is the foundation of the art of perspective.

Spontaneous movement and touch indicate true distances. Habitual observation enables us to know the relationship between the apparent size of bodies, and their distance measured by touch and movement. We then learn to pass with great speed from one to the other, and to note immediately, from the apparent size, the distances of the bodies from one another, at least approximately.

If we stand at the end of a long drive of trees, we see an apparent decrease in the size of the trees on both sides. It is this which makes us aware of the ever-greater distance of the trees from one another, and finally of the distance of the first tree from the last.

Once I have become used to relating the height of the trees to their distance I no longer err. Decreasing size becomes for me the effect of distance and nothing else. I amend the disproportion of apparent height, and by mentally positioning the trees at the same distance, I know that they are of the same height (granted they are in fact equal).

Article 4.
Application of the criterion to illusions about the position of things

932. Although light imprints bodies on our eyes upside down, we see them right way up because this reversal of the seen bodies is not and cannot be in contradiction with the various parts of the images themselves, nor with touch-perceptions. It contradicts only the fundamental feeling by which we feel the eye, and the modification of the fundamental feeling by which we feel our eye subjectively.

933. First of all, I note that if I perceive a bodily image upside down, the different parts of the image do not contradict the perception. The eye, by fixing its attention only on the image, cannot perceive that it is upside down. In fact, when I turn a vase, for example, upside down, I notice its new position relative only to surrounding bodies which remain right way up. But let us assume that all the surrounding bodies, and we ourselves, are turned upside down in the whole image without any relative change in its parts. In this case, it would be impossible for us to become aware of the new position of the vase and ourselves. Nothing would remain to serve as a sign of what had occurred. As we have seen, movement cannot be felt of itself, but only through the relationship between bodies which have been moved and perceived by us. The rotation of the earth, inverting us each day, proves the point. We have to discover this inversion through reason rather than through feeling because of the fixed position of our bodies relative to other things. The same is true about our eye. Whatever position images take in our eye, whether they are the right way up or upside down, they could never be recognised for what they are by the sense of sight alone. They revolve together and retain their natural proportions while we ourselves, as seen, revolve with everything else. For the whole world revolves, and because there is no change or contradiction between the

different parts of the visual image, it is impossible to notice the inversion of particular bodies through the upside down position of their images; if the eye changes the images, everything changes together. It is like our incapacity for feeling or noticing the inversion resulting from the daily rotation of the world.

934. All the eye can do is to notice things upright in their true, natural positions relative to one another; even the touch itself cannot give us any indication of the eye's upside down view of things. The position of the images on the eye, whatever it may be, cannot be in contradiction with the position of bodies felt by touch. The eye sees the relative position of bodies as it is; touch also senses the same relative position, and nothing else. For example, what is positioned above my head (this relationship establishes the position of things) is there whether I perceive it by sight or by touch. This is true whether I am standing upright, lying down, or standing on my head: the surrounds are at the same point for eyes and hands. There can be no contradiction, therefore, between the position indicated by sight and by touch whatever direction may be proferred by the images traced on the 'screen' of the eye.

935. This is not the case relative to the fundamental feeling and the acquired sensation which makes us perceive the sensitive 'screen' of the eye. Here the images do contradict the position of bodies as it is given by touch. Let us suppppose that an image is felt adhering to our eye so that we have an image-perception joined to the sensation of the whole eye and superimposed upon the retina. This is what takes place in touch-sensation, which is always twofold because it is superimposed upon the felt surface of the hand that touches the surface of the exterior body so that one measures the other. In our supposition, I would feel the image upside down in my eye, although this means only that its position is the opposite of my eye. If I were now to have in my eye the image of another eye, the latter would be upside down with the eyebrows underneath, relative to my eyebrows which hold the opposite position, that is, above. If then the tiny eye depicted in my pupil were perceived by me immediately by touch, it would be an *extrasubjective* perception opposed, as

far as position was concerned, to the *subjective* perception of my eye. Why, therefore, do I not notice this contradiction between the *subjective* and *extrasubjective* parts in sight-sensation?

936. The difficulty is completely resolved by our observations on sight-sensation in the preceding article. We observed that when the eye is considered as touch, that is, as a sense that perceives colours immediately, we can no longer rightly speak of it as perceiving *images* but only colour-*marks*. Now as long as we consider colours perceived by the eye in themselves, without reference to their nature as *signs*, their position upon our eye means nothing to us. Consequently, reflecting on them relative to the position of the eye itself must be extremely difficult, if not impossible.

Moreover, when the colour-marks have changed into images, we no longer give them any attention, as we said. We use our eyes continually for the sole purpose of knowing exterior bodies, not for knowing what happens in our eyes. As a result of this continual attention to external objects that we see, we are incapable of concentrating our attention on the eye and on the change that it undergoes.

937. In the second place, although the extra-subjective light-sensation is strong, it is still not easy for us to measure the size of the very restricted subjective sensation. Moreover, it is impossible to advert to its position relative to our sentient eye. In fact, to know and advert to one position of the image relative to my eye rather than another, I must: 1. note the position of the colour-mark; 2. note and advert to the position of my eye; 3. compare these positions; 4. note the extremities of the mark representing to me the extremities of the external thing; 5. note and advert that the part of the mark representing the top end of the external thing corresponds to the low part of the eye, and viceversa. All these operations are extremely difficult, and probably impossible. To avoid an endless task, it would be well for me to comment only on the difficulty of the third step, where the position of the colour-mark is compared with the position of my eye. I feel this position with my fundamental feeling alone, and feel the position of the mark with the acquired sensation. We have already seen how difficult it is to advert to the fundamental

feeling, and this difficulty would be compounded if we had to advert to the relative position of the parts felt in the fundamental feeling with the clarity, distinction[128] and firmness needed to compare it with the position of adventitious sensations or of the colour-marks we are discussing.

938. [. . .] As far as I can understand, it is impossible, even with the most acute advertence, to succeed in noting through sight alone this extraordinary fact: 'When we take the shape of the sensations as signs of external bodies, the lowest point relative to the eye indicates the highest point of the external thing, and vice-versa.'

Article 5.
The criterion of the shape of bodies is their shape as perceived by touch

939. Touch, united with spontaneous movement, perceives extension immediately (cf. 837-875). Hence it is this sense that perceives the limits of extension, size, shape.[129] It follows that the shape of things perceived by touch and movement is the criterion against which to compare the shape ministered by sight.

Article 6.
Errors about the shape and size of bodies occasioned by sight

940. Light enables us to perceive distant bodies because they refract and reflect it to us in such a way that its modifications are proportioned to the size, shape, distance and other qualities or conditions of the bodies themselves. But rays of light can be deviated or altered as they pass from bodies to ourselves if they meet something on the way, or can

---

[128] I also think it altogether impossible to advert distinctly in the fundamental feeling to the *relative* position of its parts without the help of acquired sensations. Can one say, in fact, that the fundamental feeling has clearly distinguishable parts?

[129] Space does not change shape for the the same reason that it does not change size. Two different shapes are only two independent pieces of space. One space, therefore, can never be transformed into another. A shape in space cannot rightly be said to change into another. If succeeded by another, it is not what it was. The second is an altogether new shape, not the first transformed.

become accidentally united. In these cases, the impression they give does not correspond to the shape we already know and use as a faithful guide to judge the bodies, which we now judge falsely because the light does not faithfully present them. Hence the reason for such optical illusions as branches bent in water, or pebbles appearing as rocks in very cold climates where the condensed air acts as a magnifying glass, and other mistakes discovered and corrected by touch.

14

THE EXTRASUBJECTIVE PERCEPTION OF BODIES BY MEANS OF THE FIVE SENSES CONSIDERED IN THEIR MUTUAL RELATIONSHIP

Article 1.
The identity of space unites different sensations, so that one body is perceived

941. Sensations of smell and taste have a very confused extrasubjective perception and consequently cannot serve as signs indicating distant bodies. The distinct perception of distant bodies comes from the differences we perceive in their size and shape. Smell and taste particles striking the relevant organs do not follow any law of proportion to size and shape of external things. However they do help in some way. We habitually note, for example, that the scent of a flower

disappears when the flower is taken away. The scent becomes for us an *indication* of the fragrant object which it recalls because the scent-sensation is associated with the idea of the body known through touch and sight. Although taste and smell are not by nature signs indicating bodies present to our touch, artificially they can become signs indicating any thing or any thought.

942. The same can be said about sounds which, however, lend themselves far more effectively to intelligent use in the formation of languages.

943. Sight-sensations, however, are arranged and ordered harmoniously by nature itself, as we have seen. Consequently they become signs, not of anything whatsoever or any thought, which demands ingenuity,[130] but of external bodies perceived by touch. This occurs because of the relationship of the different sizes and shapes of sight-sensations with tactile bodies and their distances.

The proportional sizes and shapes of sight-sensations represent perfectly the size and shape of bodies we can touch and, because of long habit, are considered as only signs of the sizes and shapes that touch presents, and whose place they take. In this way the sizes and shapes given by sight become space itself occupied by distant, external things. But various colours depict these signs and shapes which, if considered the same as those of external bodies, necessitate the projection of colours to outside objects. In a word, the coloured signs of the sizes and shapes received in our eye are taken as the sizes and shapes of the external things themselves, so that we consider as coloured the sizes and shapes of the external things we touch.

944. As a result we are not satisfied with calling the impressions on our eye signs of external things or signs indicating something. We prefer to call them *images*, as if the light, on bringing colours into our eye, first looked at the bodies and then, like a painter making a portrait, chose from them various tints, shadings and outlines to make its own creation.

[130] By means of writing, human ingenuity indicates all human thoughts through sensations of sight and in this way gives hearing to the deaf, so to speak, and speech to the dumb.

Article 2.
The visual perception of bodies is what most engages our
attention

945. After we have formed the habit of judging distant
bodies by their colours so that bodies and colours can be
reduced to the same space to form one thing (as far as we are
concerned) (cf. 941-943), visual perception becomes
attractive, pleasant, rapid, helpful, clear,[131] precise, and
attracts our attention much more than the immediate
perception of bodies by feeling or touch and movement. We
are so occupied with our visual perception that we no longer
think about other ways of perceiving bodies, persuading
ourselves that we know everything by our sight alone. What
we cannot see, we do not know, and even touch-perception
appears empty and useless.

946. Not only the mass of people but thinkers are subject
to this error. Philosophers, who do not suddenly cease being
ordinary people, allow themselves to be so charmed by the
clarity and attraction of sight that they reduce all their
arguments about perception and cognition of bodies to this
single sense.

Article 3.
Whether, in sensations, we receive the image of corporeal
things or perceive the things themselves

955. [. . .] A close bond exists between sensation and the
perception of an external body. But the connexion does not
come from the nature of sensation or from feeling in general;
it comes from the special nature of acquired sensations.

We have shown that the fundamental feeling[132] exists before

---

[131] Sometimes it provides us with a sensation that we notice and distinguish more
easily than touch. Touching a delicate rose petal can give us such a weak sensation
that we do not distinguish it from the feeling in our fingers, although our eye notices
the petal straightaway.

[132] It might be asked whether 'myself', considered alone, contains passivity, and
therefore perception. The answer to this question would necessitate analysis of
'myself', which is outside the purpose of this work. If, however, such an analysis
were to reveal passivity and perception, it would not concern the perception of
external bodies we are discussing. The present argument does not seek to establish
generally 'that sensation can be deprived of all perception', but 'that sensation or
feeling can exist without the perception of external bodies'.

all acquired sensations. The soul is united to the body by means of a wonderful bond, an intermingling, so to speak, called *life*, and it diffuses the feeling of life into the extension of the whole sensitive body, called its matter. Because an external sensation is a modification of this first feeling and cannot be thought without it, the contrary claim that 'myself' and its animal feeling depend for their existence upon an external sensation, is not true.

956. We can now indicate how, and with what limitations, external sensations are joined to the perception of bodies.

Touch gives an immediate communication with external bodies. The four senses of sight, hearing, smell and taste, in so far as touched, give an immediate communication with their own stimuli, that is, with the minute particles affecting them. The sense of sight (and proportionately the other three senses, as we have explained) indicates distant bodies that do not touch it. It has no immediate communication with them but makes them known by means of signs or *feelable species*.

957. We cannot say that the senses, even when touched and proferring an immediate communication with bodies, fully perceive bodies themselves. They perceive only certain corporeal elements, two of which are force and surface extension.[133] To complete the perception of a body, *solidity* or extension in three dimensions must be added, or at least the possibility or expectation of finding new tangible surfaces, according to a fixed law. Touch itself, joined to movement, discovers and perceives new surfaces within the given space and thus an *expectation* arises in us of being able to discover new surfaces according to the same law. In this way the sense-perception of external bodies is completed.

958. Of itself, therefore, the sensation of touch does not give a full, complete perception of bodies. It perceives some corporeal elements and should more correctly be called, as we have said, *corporeal perception* rather than perception of bodies. It is completed through an association of many touch-sensations.

959. In this sense, it would not be out of place to say that we perceive bodies by means of certain traces or impressions

[133] The *fundamental feeling* of our body is the only way we feel a solid body completely, that is, our own; in itself, no external sensation does the same.

that they leave in us as the inchoate perception we have of them.

960. Although this *corporeal perception* comes immediately from bodies, it is nevertheless in us, in our sensation, an effect of bodies upon us. Because our sensation is characterised by a *passivity* which extends to the whole *surface* encompassed by the immediate sensation, it makes us aware of this passivity, that is, indicates something outside us. To be aware of the surface in which the passivity is diffused is to be aware that whatever is outside us is *extended*. In fact, as long as we are thinking of the external body acting on us, its extension and that of our sensation are identical; thus there is an immediate communication between the body and us. But once the body has been removed (even by abstraction), it is the extension of the sensation that gives us the extension of the body. Considered separately, then, the sensation becomes a *similitude* of the body because it has an equal extension. In this sense we can say that we know bodies by means of *similitudes* that they leave in our senses or in our imagination. This proposition can thus be reconciled with the one that says we communicate immediately with the external world through the senses, although it is dangerous to use it without some kind of explanation.

15

THE RELATIONSHIP BETWEEN INTELLECTIVE AND SENSE-PERCEPTIONS OF BODIES [. . .]

961. There is no modern philosopher I know of who has not confused, at least occasionally, *sense-perception* and *intellective perception*. This difficult distinction needs careful explanation, therefore, which I shall attempt in this chapter. [. . .]

962. First, we must pay careful attention to the fact that the term of feeling is always something particular. With this in mind, we can discover the properties of both sense-perception and intellective perception, since one of its

consequences is: 'Whatever is universal in the perception of bodies, must be attributed to the intellect, not to feeling.'⁰

When I mentally perceive a body, that is, when I judge as existing an *object* having the nature of body, I have an intellective perception of body. But I could not think it like this unless I had the universal notion of *existence*.

963. What is involved in sense-perception? With the fundamental feeling we feel our body as something that is one with us. This perception, although complete, is difficult to observe and analyse. So let us turn to touch, which is the second way by which we attain sense-perception of bodies. The sensation of touch, in itself subjective, is also *corporeal perception*: 1. in so far as it is a term of the action of something outside us; and 2. it presents this term as an extended surface.

Repeated, varying sensations of touch, promptly helped by those of sight, unite to give our sensitivity the expectation of finding, by the use of movement and force, new surfaces under any perceived surface. Feeling in general is also subject to this law of the *instinctive expectation* of similar feelings, as experience shows us. It is due to a habit or inclination formed in the sense-organs, a kind of instinct to repeat acts similar to those that have been done many times and expect similar results. This instinctive *expectation* of new corporeal surfaces, after the first surface has been removed, perfects sense-perception.

964. Let us now see what the understanding does to complete its perception of bodies. When, through the senses, our spirit has received the corporeal elements so far described, the understanding completes the perception in the following way.

The experience we undergo in a sensation has two aspects: from the point of view of the term, ourselves, it is *experience*; from the point of view of the principle, it is *action*. Action and experience indicate the same thing under two different, opposite aspects. *Feeling* perceives what we are talking about simply as *experience* and the *expectation* of new experiences; only the understanding is able to perceive it as *action*, while adding nothing to it. The understanding considers the thing *absolutely*; sense perceives it in a particular *respect*, that is, *relatively*. Understanding originates in us, particular beings, but directs its attention to things in themselves; sense never moves from the particular subject, ourselves, to which it belongs.

It is, therefore, the work of the understanding to conceive the action of another being. But to conceive an action means to conceive a *principle in act*. Thus, when the intellect perceives an action, it always perceives an *agent* as such, that is, a *being in act*. But it does this by means of the idea of being that belongs to it. When it perceives the *agent* as a being different from ourselves and *endowed with extension*, it has *perception of bodies*.

We see that to perceive a body the understanding does nothing more than consider what the senses present. But it does not do this relatively to ourselves as feeling does; setting us aside and ignoring us, it adds the universal concept of being. The intellective perception of bodies is, therefore, the union between the intuition of a being (agent) and sense-perception (experience); it is a judgment, a primitive synthesis.

965. But if we set aside judgment about the actual presence of bodies, we are left with their simple possibility. This is their *pure idea* or *simple apprehension*.

16

THE NATURAL DISHARMONIES BETWEEN THE PERCEPTION OF OUR BODY AS CO-SUBJECT, AND AS AGENT OUTSIDE THE SUBJECT

Article 1.
The difference between the two principle ways of perceiving our body, that is, as co-subject and as an agent outside the subject

983. Our body is felt subjectively and extrasubjectively like any other body. It is the same entity felt by us in two ways.

But what distinguishes extrasubjective from subjective perception? When a being is perceived as *outside the subject*,[134] an *agent* is felt. In the perception of a being as *subject* or, to be more exact, as *co-subject*, the *one who feels* is felt; the feeler feels himself in and with the being. Now to be active and to be passive are contraries. The same nature, therefore, is perceived in both ways but in different and opposite respects. First, it is perceived as *something acting* that produces but does not feel the sensations; second, as *something passive* that feels but does not produce the sensations.

984. These two aspects are so opposed to each other that they have nothing in common. Consequently what is perceived in these two ways is presented as two entities, two different natures; they are not different levels but different *aspects* of the same thing, one of which directly excludes the other.

It is not simply the case of an idea of an acting body being the opposite of an idea of a passive body, but of the action and passivity particular to sense. If we consider our passive feeling, that is, our feeling of pleasure or pain, we have in the external principle producing the feeling the concept of an agent. If we consider the feeling in its term, that is, as terminated and experienced in itself, we have ourselves, modified and experiencing.

Article 2.
The similarity between the impression of external things and the sensation that follows

985. An external body touching a sensitive part of our body produces movement in that part, that is, an *impression*. This impression, caused by the external body, is either perceptible

---

[134] I refrain from saying 'as an object' because the body is only an *object* relatively to *intellective perception*, in which it is apprehended as a *being*. *Sense-perception* perceives only an action outside the subject. Strictly speaking, the *object* of intellective perception cannot be said to be *active* but only *present*. We do indeed use our intellectual activity to perceive the object, but this activity produces nothing in the object except the act with which we perceive it. The perceived object, which we cannot change and over which we have no power, is what *forms* our cognition. [. . .]

to our sight and touch or can be argued to. When a needle pricks my hand, I can see and touch the wound and notice the change in my body. If the impression is not large enough to be seen or touched, I can deduce it by analogy. Thus the impression made by light on my eye or the movement of my optic nerve is so minute and faint that I am not able to advert to the tiny particles with my sense of touch.[135] In the same way, the very faint impressions that the minute particles make on my organs of smell, taste and hearing cannot be noticed by sight and touch, and are perhaps too small for any microscope. But knowing the mechanical actions of bodies, I can reason that the minute particles must be acting on the eye, nostrils and palate, producing small irritations and alterations.

The idea that we have, therefore, of the *impression* of external bodies is the same as that of any impression, for example, on wax, or of a mark left behind or any movement in our body. These effects are terms of our touch and eyes, like the changes of our body, and give rise to sensations.

986. It is my opinion that *impressions* like these do not have the least similarity with *sensations*, considered in their subjective part, even if sensations follow immediately upon the impressions. In fact there is a real opposition between them. An imprint, a feature, a movement, an external body, perceived (with the touch) is an *agent* producing sensation in our organ. *Sensation* on the other hand is a kind of *passivity*; *the one who feels* is feelable to himself. But *something acting* is the opposite of *something passive* (cf. 983) and therefore an *impression* made on a sensitive body, causing *sensations*, has no similarity at all with sensations in their subjective part. An impression is of its nature entirely the opposite of sensation; the one excludes the other just as 'yes' excludes 'no'.

To make the difference clear, let us suppose a ball-bearing is pressed into a sensitive part of a person's body so that half of it forms a hemispherical impression in the skin. The person clearly feels two things: 1. the part of the body where the impression is made, and 2. the ball-bearing itself or agent. The *feeling* in the affected part is different from the *perception*

---

[135] The movement of the iris under the action of light is not an effect of light only but depends on other physical principles and on the spontaneity of the soul.

of the ball-bearing; they are two simultaneous feelings, referred to the same spot, but quite different.

For example, anyone who feels discomfort in his arm, *feels passively* what he is experiencing. When however he perceives the ball-bearing, he feels what *is acting*. These two feelings are opposites and cannot be confused. The part of the arm he feels affected is the *concave* surface where the bearing is being pressed, so that a body of *concave* form is felt. The part of the bearing he perceives is the convex surface pressing into the skin, so that a body of *convex* form is felt. A feeling is being experienced in the *concave surface* of the arm; a body undergoing an experience is felt. No sensation is referred to the *convex surface* of the bearing; it is not a body undergoing an experience but an insensitive body causing the experience. In sensation therefore an external body (extrasubject) and our body (co-subject) are inconfusible opposites. The perception of the external body is the sensation itself but only as term of an action coming from outside.

Let us apply this distinction to *sensation* and *impression*. The word 'impression' means something perceived by us as external *agent*; the word 'sensation' means something perceived in us and by us as *subject*. In the case of the ball-bearing, the impression (leaving the sensation aside for the moment) is perceived in exactly the same way as the bearing that in itself feels nothing. The person in our example, feeling discomfort, sees the hollow made by the bearing and then touches it with his finger; in this way he is seeing and touching the impression.

When he touches and sees the hollow, he certainly does not touch and see the *sensation* he has experienced and is experiencing as a result of the hollow. The sensation itself is neither visible nor touchable; it can be felt only through an internal feeling of the soul, only through itself.

After seeing and touching the hollow a few times, he says to those about him: 'Look at the impression the ball-bearing has left.' He calls an *impression* what he touches and sees or what is offered to his touch and sight. The meaning he is giving to the word 'impression' is that of a modification experienced by a body in the arrangement of its parts, a modification perceived by us with our sense-organs, particularly of sight and touch. This is not a sensation but an external term of our sense-faculties.

Is what I see and touch, that is, an *impression* made on a body by the action of another body, similar in any way to the sensations of touch and sight with which it is perceived? All the by-standers perceive the *impression* with their touch and sight equally with the person receiving it, who also experiences the sensation accompanying the impression.

987. We must note carefully that when the person perceives the impression in his arm with his touch and eyes, new sensations take place, and these can be analysed in exactly the same way as the sensation of the ball-bearing. In fact when he touches the hollow in his arm, he has simultaneously a feeling composed of two basic parts or feelings: 1. a feeling of his finger, at the point where he is feeling with it, and 2. a feeling of the little hollow, which he is touching. We can say about this twofold feeling what we said previously about the feeling of the arm and of the ball-bearing, that is, the finger is felt as *co-sentient*, and the hollow as *acting*. He feels his finger with a sensation referred to a convex extension; he feels the hollow with a sensation referred to a concave extension.

The sensation he experiences by touching the hollow is not referred to the hollow but to his finger. Both his finger and his eye perceive the hollow as having no feeling; relative to his touch and eye, the hollow is only a term of action. His touch and eye is subject, or rather belongs to the subject. The hollow experiences no sensation but makes my eye and touch experience a sensation.

The hollow, as presented to the eye and external touch, is called an *impression* but in itself has no feeling. It is completely outside the sensations of touch and sight, and is in fact the opposite of sensation. Hence there is no similarity but only opposition between the *sensation* as subject and the *impression*. An impression therefore cannot be seen in any way as a degree of sensation, nor a sensation as a degree or kind of impression.

Article 3.
Materialism rebutted

988. All materialistic arguments are based on the confusion between *impression* and *sensation*, because the opposite natures of these two things are not distinguished. Materialists search for a similarity between them, explaining sensations by means of impressions or finding sensations in impressions. They do not take into account the meaning given to names like 'impression', 'movement', etc., which as extrasubjective words indicate agents without feeling. These words have been coined to express things external to our senses and perceived by them, not things with feeling. Sensation is excluded by definition from things indicated by these words.

Materialists, and others inclined to the same error, try to explain sensation by reducing it to a *movement* of parts or an *impression*. This is to abuse terms and confuse ideas in a manifest contradiction. The *movement* of parts and *impressions* does indeed need *sensation* to be felt, but *sensation*, precisely because it is sensation, does not; sensation cannot be seen or touched or compared to anything seen and touched.

Article 4.
The dividing line between physiology and psychology

995. The difference between *sensation* and *impression*, between our subjective feeling and what we see and touch or perceive *extrasubjectively*, establishes the dividing line between physiology and psychology. Physiology and medicine are and can be only the product of *external observation*, that is, of observation made by touch, sight and the other senses. Psychology on the other hand is founded on *internal observation*, that is, of all that takes place in our consciousness. Physiology and medicine deal with the body as an external *object* but the purpose of psychology is the spirit and what belongs to it as *subject*.

Physiology investigates the natural state of the human body, the different effects to which it is subject, the classification of these effects, their uniformity, that is to say, the laws of the body's operation. All these effects, movements, modifications and laws to which the body is subject, are only *terms* of touch, sight and the other senses, and objects of the understanding. Thus in these sciences the body is considered as something purely external and objective. The same can be said about medicine: it uses continual *external observation* to note the diseased changes or modifications in the human body and the remedies necessary for good health.

996. It is true that in these sciences we must pay attention to what takes place in our consciousness, but that is not their aim. If they turn their attention to human feelings, to the force that can be exercised on the body by an intense application of the spirit, they do so for the sole purpose of knowing the effects of such actions. If these sciences take into account the effect different habits of the body produce on the soul and on intellectual faculties, they do so to discover a way of restoring the body to that health which enables it to serve the spirit. In all these researches the physiologist and the doctor observe the body through external observation and therefore purely as an *object*.

On the other hand the psychologist uses another kind of observation, internal observation. The facts of consciousness are the objects at which his observation stops; he considers 'myself', the subject. And if he concerns himself with the body as an *object*, he does so only through the relationship between the object and the subject. But this science does not terminate in the object; its proper purpose and concern is the consciousness of the spirit, related to which all other things are only means and aids.

997. We can therefore conclude that even if the surgeon's knife were able to reveal the minutest fibres in animal bodies and if the most powerful microscopes imaginable had been invented to reveal the hidden structure of bodies more perfectly than ever before, it could never replace internal observation of the facts of consciousness. The science of psychology would not profit in the least from these discoveries.

Article 5.
[. . .] The union of soul and body

998. It is impossible to find any likeness between body and soul as long as the former is restricted to its guise of term of our external senses. But without some likeness between the two, there is no possibility of mutual communication. It is even possible to demonstrate the inherent repugnance of communication if the body is seen simply as the term of the external senses.

1001. [. . .] External observation, however, is not the only way in which we come to know our body. Interior observation also contributes to revealing the body in a very different light from that presented by the external senses. Through interior observation, we come to see its inner, essential properties. Thus it becomes *matter* and co-cause of the fundamental feeling.

We need, therefore, to consider ourselves and the content of our awareness by reflecting upon 'myself' without allowing our external imagination to intrude in any way. Our concept of the union between soul and body cannot arise from any other source.

1002. In the feeling of 'myself', therefore, we find a force different from 'myself', but felt by it. As 'myself' feels this force, it diffuses its own sensation in an extended term. This feeling, to which 'myself' is drawn by natural force (relative to which it is passive), is a fact. Consequently, the union of soul and body should have been considered as a *fact* derived from observation of our own experience. As a primitive fact, constituting our very nature, its light dispels every difficulty we experience about admitting its existence as a fact.

Article 6.
The relationship between *external* body and body as *co-subject*

1003. Subjective and extrasubjective perception, therefore, provide two different and in some ways contrary concepts of body as *co-subject* and *extrasubject*. The opposition arises simply from the limitation of these mutually exclusive concepts which furnish contrary propositions about body. For example: *the body is in the soul,* and *the soul is in the body*; both are true, but refer to opposite concepts of body.

It is true that *the body is in the soul* in the concept of the subjective body, because in this case the body is only something *acting in 'myself'* (in the soul). It is true that *the soul is in the body*, when the body is considered as foreign to the subject and the soul is considered in the effects it produces in this extrasubjective element.

1004. We have to emphasise 'in the effects it produces' because the soul, considered in itself, is a *subject* which can never be a term of feeling, nor measured in relationship to space. If the intelligent soul is considered in itself (as a subject) and compared with a body or with anything extended, we can add a third true statement: *the soul has no place* because it is simple.

These distinctions help to eliminate a great number of difficult questions to which there are no solutions except by determined efforts to clear up inexact language.

Article 7.
Matter of the fundamental feeling

1005. When we dealt with the fundamental feeling, and with the subjective part of sensation as a modification of the fundamental feeling, we said that strictly speaking such a feeling can never have an *object*, but only *matter* in which it terminates. We perceive external *objects* and call them 'bodies' when thought is united with the operation of the senses, although we also realise that one of these perceived bodies, which we call 'mine' is the *matter* of our feeling. What difference is there, however, between *object* and *matter*? This problem requires careful investigation.

1006. Our body, whether in its natural state or modified, is *matter* of our interior feeling in so far as it is felt by this feeling. It is *term* and *stimulus* of our individual sense-organs in so far as it is perceived by them; and it is also the *object* of our understanding. Consequently, the *matter* of feeling is something halfway between pure *subject* and the *term* of sense. It is not the sentient subject because it is itself felt, nor is it a pure *term* of sense because sense cannot exist without it.

1007. The first difference, therefore, between the *matter* and *object* of any power is that the object is not necessary for the subsistence of the power while matter is a constituent of the power which, without it, could not be conceived mentally. It is true, for instance, that although there could be no sight without light, the eyes nevertheless subsist and can be thought of irrespective of light. The same is true, *mutatis mutandis*, for the other organs. The stimuli, therefore, are not *matter* of the organs, but simply *terms* of their acts, and *objects* when the understanding has perceived them.

1008. The difference between matter and object can only be understood through a correct concept of a *power*. As we know, every power is a *first act* which, given the necessary conditions, produces various other acts dependent upon differing conditions. The first, constant act is called power relative to the secondary, adventitious acts. Every power, therefore, is an activity held in check as it were, ready for action. With this in mind, it is easy to see that as every *second act* needs a term for it to take place, so a *power* or *first act* needs its own internal term without which it could neither be nor be thought. Similarly, because a *power* is something stable, while its operation is adventitious, it must have a stable term along with which it either remains in existence or perishes. If the term of its *operation* is removed, the power remains; but if the term of the power is removed, the power ceases to exist.

1009. *Matter* is a stable term, proper to certain powers, with which it forms a single reality. Because this term is joined with the powers, it helps to constitute them and cannot be thought without them. This explains why it is not called simply *term* (a name common to everything in which the acts finish externally), but matter. Nevertheless, this characteristic of indivisibility from the power is insufficient to constitute the *matter* of the power because every power has a term, but not matter.

1010. The second difference between the *object* and the *matter* of a power is that the object as such is neither receptive of action nor capable of being receptive of action.[136] On the other hand, the matter of any power is mentally conceived as modifiable, that is, having no activity of its own relative to the power. The objects I know do not stimulate my mind, but allow it to know by informing it; the impression of external light, on the other hand, is a forceful action, stimulus and term drawing my sensitivity to the act of sense-perception. Generally speaking, objects of knowledge, which have no active state relative to cognitive powers, are in a state of mere presence to them, while the terms of our practical powers are definitely passive. Now if the term of the *first act*, which constitutes the power itself, presents itself to us in an *impassive* state of simple presence to the power which does nothing except receive it, I call it 'object', not just 'term', although it is such. I do not call it 'matter', because this word includes the concept of experiencing something, or modifiability. I also call it 'form' of the power, and thus indicate it as an object which, constantly united with the subject, posits it in a first act called 'potency', that is, a power causing many other operations. Hence we have called *the idea of universal being*, the *objective form* of the intellect. Our body, as felt, on the other hand, we have called *matter* of the feeling in so far as it is 'a stable term of the first act of our feeling, bereft of activity relative to the completed act of feeling.'

1011. However, the *matter* of the fundamental feeling has a third, truly noble characteristic. As we have said, it is a term without activity related to the completed feeling, and *capable* only of presenting itself to the feeling as a passive term. This capacity or *passive susceptibility*, however, is very imperfect because matter resists, with a certain inertia, acceptance of the state that the activity of the feeling could offer it, and thus serves as a brake to the perfect operation of the feeling.

---

[136] Normally speaking, we say that iron struck with a hammer is the *object* of the action of the hammer, and the same is true of every other term acted upon by any force or instrument. From an etymological point of view, this would appear correct ('ob-jectum', thrown against), but this manner of speaking depends upon the way we conceive the fact and how the notion of object is added by the intelligence. But prescinding from this, the two material instruments *have* nothing outside themselves. Striking one another adventitiously, the two forces unite, contrast and modify one another, but they are not *objects*, the concept of which demands sameness and impassibility.

Nevertheless, we cannot say that this inertia must be a force relative to and in contrast with the feeling. We must note that readiness to be moved easily denotes perfection when there is a question of movement that improves the nature of what is moved. The capacity for receiving improvement is an intrinsic activity. On the contrary, incapacity for receiving improvement indicates a lack of what I would call seminal activity, as it were, an activity and hidden power without which development cannot take place. The lack itself is an obstacle to the perfection that could be communicated to a being. *Matter*, therefore, does not offer a real, active resistance to feeling, but incapacity or inertia.

It would not be correct to object that this is merely abstract speculation. Observation provides the ground for such a description of *matter* because it shows that the fundamental feeling does not expand in an 'empty' extension (as it were), but in one where it experiences certain resistances, and even changes and disturbance, according to stable laws which: 1. constitute the relationship of the sensitive body with external bodies; and 2. constitute the relationship of the sensitive body (matter) with 'myself', the act of feeling.

But we ought to reflect even more on the perfection of the feeling than on that of the body. The feeling would be more perfect, the more it were capable of possessing a perfect body obedient to its will. If, therefore, harmful alterations take place in the body and the feeling suffers as a result, we may indeed posit a force in the body, but it will be such as to harm the feeling. As we showed, the feeling with its matter forms a single thing, or a single power. The force of its matter is therefore the passive, imperfect part of the power, not its formal, perfect part. This is the chief reason for calling our body, in so far as it is felt by us, the *matter* of the fundamental feeling.[137]

1012. At this point, a difficulty presents itself. In this work, I have described the body as something acting on the spirit, in which it causes and excites the fundamental feeling.

[137] We have to distinguish carefully between the *principle* of an act, and its *term*. It is undeniable, although difficult to conceive, that the principle can be *simple*, while its term is *multiple*. The extension in which a sensation is diffused with its term does not entail diminished simplicity in 'myself' as feeling principle. The reasons set out above (cf. 672-691) leave no room for doubt about this [. . .].

How is it possible now to describe the *matter* of the fundamental feeling, which is the *body* itself, as passive and inert relative to the action of this feeling?

In the first place, we have to remember that the *matter* of the fundamental feeling is not the body with all its qualities. The fundamental feeling, in its matter, perceives the body only relatively to the special organs in so far as the body offers itself as a passive and inert term of the feeling itself. The *activity* the body may possess for producing the feeling is not comprised in the *matter* of the feeling. But we have to reflect carefully to see how this is possible.

1013. 'A force working in a given way on a being can draw this being to an act terminating in the very force that has stimulated and encouraged it, so that the force becomes passive relative to the act which it caused. Moreover, it can stimulate an act terminating outside itself.' Let us examine the first of these two cases.

It is clear that I can put in motion a force producing some effect upon myself; for example, if I pick up a knife, I may easily cut myself. This truth can be seen even more clearly in the case of a spiritual agent which moves with remarkable spontaneity, as our experience shows. In fact, we only need an occasion, rather than a cause, to stimulate the spirit whose interior activity comes into play spontaneously, granted the necessary occasion and causes. Our body may possess a force drawing the spirit to an act of feeling which, at the same time (because it also is an activity), may turn back to the body as to its necessary term. In fact, the laws according to which the spirit is first moved to feel are unknown, at least to me. Nevertheless, it is not absurd to conjecture that their hypothetical existence flows from the very nature of the spirit. In all the beings of which we have experience in the universe, we constantly find two things: 1. that they follow certain laws in their operations; 2. that these laws are not arbitrarily imposed upon them, but result from their nature.

If we apply the same observation to the spirit, it is not unreasonable to think that the active nature of the spirit is to operate under certain conditions. One necessary condition for the fundamental feeling, as we can see from our analysis of feeling itself, is the existence of an organised body. Given a body rightly organised, it could happen that the union and feeling result from a law inherent in the very nature of the spirit. What is certain, however, is that the body can be passive relative to the fundamental feeling which it originated and encouraged, and of which it was undoubtedly a necessary condition. Considered under this respect alone, the body is called 'matter' of the fundamental feeling. The activity moving the spirit to feel is the *principle* of the feeling; the body enfolded by the spirit is its matter and term. And although reflection on our experience shows us that we are passive when we feel, because of the external agent acting in us, the activity itself cannot as such be the matter of our feeling. Following this line of thought, we may understand a little better the ancient distinction between *matter* and *body*.

1014. In the second place, we note that although the *body* is capable of receiving in itself the activity over the spirit of which we have spoken, this concealed activity is less noticed than other bodily qualities, especially *extension* and *inertia*. We shall understand this better by setting out in order the propositions we have already demonstrated.

1. The various ways of perceiving *bodies* offer such different perceptions that bodies appear to be *different entities*.

2. These *different entities* arise: a) partly because subjectivity plays a great role in the perception of bodies, causing them to exist as different *proximate terms* of perception (the variation depends on the different 'mix' of subjectivity); b) partly because one kind of perception uncovers properties of a body that remain hidden in other kinds of perception (so that the body seems to be a different being). Perceiving an external body with our organs, we obtain what we may call 'blind' qualities, rather than perceive the body's aptitude for being the matter of feeling, which we recognise only through our own feeling.

3. Consequently, the word 'body' takes various meanings as we use it to describe what we perceive in different ways.

4. The normal meaning attributed to 'body' depends upon what we perceive of external bodies with our five organs, because we easily advert to this *perception*, while

perception originating in the fundamental feeling or in the subjective sensation is very difficult *to reflect upon* and *distinguish*.[138]

Observations of this kind enable us to understand why 'body' is not used, commonly speaking, to indicate the intimate force with which it acts upon our spirit, causing the spirit to react and bring about union. Here, we may usefully observe what happens in acquired sensations from which we normally obtain the idea for which we invent the word 'body.'

1015. When an external body acts upon an organ, it simply produces a change in the sensitive form of our organ or, more generally speaking, causes movement in it. Given this movement, the spirit feels a new sensation which does not, however, stimulate it to some totally new activity. The law governing its feeling of the body is: 'The spirit feels the body in the sensitive state in which it finds it' (cf. 705 ss.). When an external body acts upon a living body, therefore, it changes the living body's sensitive state while the sensitive principle, following this change according to the law governing its own action, now feels the new state of the organ. But there has been no radically new action of the body on the spirit. The action here can be reduced to that between our own body and an external body whose mutual activity follows the mechanical, physical and chemical laws common to all inanimate bodies. But the spirit does not unite itself to any new body while this is happening, and no new body acts upon it. Its own body's action, which it has not experienced in any new way, was present antecedently to what occurred. In an acquired sensation, therefore, all that can be perceived and noted of bodies is *external action* of the kind that external bodies exercise on one another. Because the action of our own body on the spirit is not comprised in this sensation, the action is not normally associated with the word 'body' which is generally reserved for the mutual extrasubjective action of bodies according to mechanical, physical and chemical laws.

---

[138] Moreover, we have to reflect that with the external organs we perceive qualities absolutely necessary to a body, although unhelpful for discerning the nature of the *corporeal principle*.

It is not difficult to see, therefore, how the word 'body' is void of any meaning indicating activity on the spirit.

1016. In the third place, the *activity* we have attributed to the body does not derive from the nature itself of the body, commonly so-called. This needs careful attention, and justifies common sense when it excludes from the meaning of 'body' the activity we have been examining. Generally speaking, therefore, the word 'body' offers no indication of activity, especially on the spirit.

1017. We can see this more clearly by examining the nature of the action of bodies among themselves and on our spirit.

1. *Movement*, which each body receives from outside, is not essential to bodies. However, the action done by *external* bodies on our organs seems to depend entirely upon movement. *Resistance* is simply the division of movement in the various parts of the body. *Adherence* between the parts only presents us with a law determining the number of parts amongst which movement has to be divided. The action of external bodies upon our own, therefore, as we normally experience it, is an activity received by the body but not essential and proper to it. Hence the body is truly *passive* relative to the activity of movement, because it only receives and communicates the movement.

1018. 2. It seems evident, if we go on to speak about the action of our body on the spirit, that this action is not comprised in the nature of the (extrasubjective) body, but is received by the body from some principle outside itself. If the aptitude for acting on the spirit were essential to our body as such, every body would have to be thought of as animated. But our normal concept of body tells us nothing of animation. Although the body *acts* on the spirit, it does not do so through an active principle demanded by its nature as body, but through an activity it has received. Relative to this activity, therefore, the body is an *inert, passive being*, which receives but does not give.°

In the fourth place, (and the following observation seems to me the most important of all those made so far), the *body*, according to its common concept, does not as such act on the spirit, but receives this *activity*. But could it not receive this activity from the spirit itself? As we have already seen, 'One being can stimulate activity in another, which can in its turn act upon the being which stimulates it.' We have already applied this to the action of the body, but could it not be applied much better to the action of the spirit?

1019. Meditation on this problem offers the following probable result:

1. For some kinds of action, the human spirit is determined by certain conditions, one of which is the existence of a body suitably organised for the spirit. This, however, requires no action on the part of the body, but depends upon a state of the body received from outside.

2. When such a perfectly organised body has been harmonised with the spirit, it seems that the spirit, now possessing the necessary condition for carrying out the action we have indicated, acts with this body, activating it with what we call 'life', and enabling it to acquire the final properties of a living body.

3. This activity received by the body is such that the body in its turn reacts upon the spirit, drawing it to the act called 'fundamental feeling.'

4. The fundamental feeling, pervading the body, makes it its *matter*, that is, its seat, its mode of being, its extension.

5. The body, as *matter* of the feeling, retains its inertia, remaining subject to the action of other external bodies. When the *matter which is felt* changes, the feeling changes, not however through any new action of the *matter* on the spirit, but through the law obliging the spirit to conclude its act in its matter, which is the passive term of the act.

PART SIX.
CONCLUSION

1

SUMMARY

1020. The basic powers of the soul are two senses, one for particular things, which constitutes the power normally called 'sensitivity', and one for universal things,[139] which constitutes the power normally called 'intellect'.[140]

1021. Every power, or potency, is a particular first act, constituted by an inherent term essential to it. This term is called 'matter' if it is *passive* relative to the power, and *form* if it is, as object, in a state of *mere presence* relative to the power. This presence is such as to constitute the power in act (cf. 1006 ss.). The essential term of sensitivity is its *matter*; the essential term of the intellect is its *object* and *form* (cf. 1010, 480-485).

1022. Sensitivity is *external* or *internal*. External sensitivity has body, that is, extended corporeal matter, as its essential term. *Internal* sensitivity has for its term the feeling of 'myself' and the idea (cf. 473-479, 630-672). The fundamental feeling of one's own body constitutes the power of *external sensitivity* (cf. 721-728). The simple feeling of

[139] [. . .] [I do not mean] that anything can be *universal in itself*. Every thing, in so far as it is, is singular and determined. A *universal*, therefore, is something through which many things, or rather an indefinite number of things, can be known. *Universality* is a mere *relationship* found only in *ideas* which, as we have seen, are things with which we know an indefinite number of other things. From this point of view, we call an idea a 'species'. It is true that at first sight there appears to be something besides ideas that can be called 'universal' and in this sense a *portrait* perhaps seems universal because it represents all its look-alikes. But this is misleading: the portrait is universal only in so far it is joined to an *idea*. It is only through the *idea* of the portrait that the mind is able to compare the portrait and the people it resembles, and to find the likeness which does not exist in the portrait but in the single *idea* with which the portrait and persons resembling it are thought. It is the unity of the idea which constitutes the likeness between similar things, as we see in our example of the portrait and the persons resembling it [. . .].

[140] We have reduced the power of understanding to a *primitive sense* (cf. 553-558).

'myself' constitutes the power of *internal sensitivity* (cf. 692-720); the feeling that perceives the idea of being in general constitutes the power of the intellect (cf. 480-485).

1023. If the *matter* of the sensitivity is removed, the *sensitive being* no longer exists. If the *form* of the intellect is removed, the latter ceases, but the concept of *sensitive being* remains intact. Hence, the *idea of being in general* is a true object, and distinct from the sensitive being. But the term of the sensitivity is constitutive of the sensitive being and, because indistinguishable from it, cannot be called 'object' (cf. 1010 ss., 409-429).

1024. Perception and intuition require something distinct from the perceiving subject, and are therefore essentially extrasubjective; sensation requires only *matter* (cf. 449, 742-752). Hence the intellect is an *intuition*; the sensitivity is simply a *primitive feeling*.

1025. All these powers exist in my fundamental feeling prior to their various operations, that is, in the feeling of myself together with my body (sensitivity) and my intellect. This intimate, perfectly *one* feeling unites the sensitivity and the intellect. It also possesses an activity, which I would call 'spiritual sight' (rationality), by which it sees the relationship of the sensitivity and the intellect. This function constitutes the *primitive synthesis* (cf. 528-555). But if we consider more generally the activity originating from the intimate unity of the fundamental feeling, that is, if we consider 'myself' as capable of seeing *relationships* in general, we call it *reason*, of which the *primitive synthesis* becomes the first *function* (cf. 622, 480-482). If we consider the same activity under the special respect of the union that it brings about between a predicate and a subject, it is called the *faculty of judgment* (cf. 388).

1026. The *primitive synthesis* is the judgment with which *reason* acquires *intellective perception*. But we cannot rise to any operation unless we are given some stimulus, or *mover*. *External sensitivity* is the first power drawn to operate by the stimuli of external bodies upon our organs (cf. 514 ss.). When *external sensitivity* has been aroused by these stimuli it informs our consciousness of a passivity coming not from our own body, but from a body separate from ourselves. This new feeling, that is, the modification of our fundamental feeling, becomes *sensitive perception* as the term of an external action, although previously it was simply feeling and a fundamental perception through which the soul is united to the body (cf. 630-691).

1027. The *first matter* of human cognitions ministered by *sensitivity* consists therefore:

    1. in a feeling of 'myself', perceptive of the body (fundamental feeling);

    2. in the sensations or modifications of this feeling;

    3. in the sense-perceptions of bodies.

1028. When reason considers these things in relationship with *being* in general, and produces *intellective perceptions*, it adds *universality* to the particular changes experienced in our spirit, and under this aspect is called the *faculty of universalisation*. All *direct acts* of reason depend upon this special power (cf. 490-500). *Reflexive acts* are proper to *reflection*, another *function* of *reason* (cf. 487-489).

1029. The objects of reflection are all acts of our spirit, in so far as it reasons, and terms of these acts. Thus, there is some impropriety in applying the word 'reflection' to the direct application of our understanding to sensations (cf. 511 ftn.). The *objects* of reflection, therefore, are:

    1. a feeling of 'myself' as perceptive of the idea of being in general;

    2. the acts of the faculty of universalisation;

    3. the acts of reflection, and its terms or results.

Reflection has two operations, *synthesis* and *analysis*; it separates and unites (cf. 490 ss.). The faculty of *abstraction* (cf. 494 ss.) pertains to *analysis*.

1030. External stimuli excite *external sensitivity*. Physical instincts, by moving the phantasy initially, arouse the faculty of *universalisation*. Corporeal images awake the power for dividing ideas from perceptions. Only language, received from society, can draw the faculty of *abstract ideas* to its act and furnish human beings with dominion over their own powers, that is, with the use of *freedom* (cf. 483 ss.)

1031. *Free activity*, that is, the dominion over one's own powers acquired through the abstract ideas furnished by language, provides the final impetus to the development of all one's powers, and opens the way to the indefinite growth of the different human faculties.

2

LEARNING TO UNDERSTAND WHAT HAS BEEN SAID ABOUT THE ORIGIN OF IDEAS

1038. [. . .] It is not easy to grasp the theory we have developed about the origin of ideas. Reading about the theory is certainly insufficient; careful observation of one's own human nature is also required. Without such observation, it is possible to be misled about one's understanding of the book and to form a very mistaken view of what has been said.

But there is one helpful and fairly easy way to comprehend the argument. If four points are thoroughly examined and understood, the rest will follow. And although these four points are certainly not the most difficult and mysterious elements of human nature, they offer a path opening on to belief in the most wonderful truths. In a word, if we are prepared to accept as fact what has fallen under our own certain observation, even though it remains inexplicable and mysterious, we shall be able to penetrate ever deeper into the hidden secrets of the intelligent spirit which we come to observe free of all doubt.

1039. The four points we have to make are four distinctions which will serve as a sign differentiating those who have understood the theory from others who have read but not grasped it. They are:

1. the distinction between *sensation* and *sense-perception* (cf. 740-748);

2. the distinction between the *idea* of something and *judgment* of the thing's subsistence (cf. 402-409);

3. the distinction between *sense-perception* and *intellective perception* (cf. 961 ss.);

4. the distinction between *an act of the spirit*, and *advertence* to that act, for example, between feeling and adverting to feeling (cf. 548 ss.).

If these distinctions are noted carefully as facts concerning the human spirit, and their application becomes easy through constant use, the theory we have outlined will be faithfully understood and the effort made to write this book with all clarity will be rewarded not by infusing truth, which is impossible, but by helping others on the way to truth.

Appendix

1. (442).

All this teaching may be found in the corpus of knowledge handed down to us by our predecessors. St. Thomas (*Contra Gent.* III, 46) teaches that our soul needs an *intelligible species* in order to know itself, just as it does to know other things. 'Intelligible species,' as I shall show later, is to be understood simply as a *universal idea* which the soul (this particular being) adheres to as its genus, or rather its major predicate. The soul, therefore, is known through the light of the *acting intellect* (the *idea of being*) in the same way as other beings. Here, too, St. Thomas distinguishes between *matter* and *form* of knowledge. With its feeling of self, the soul provides only the matter of knowledge. This matter, informed through an innate light, becomes true knowledge. St. Thomas says: 'Natural knowledge is that which comes about through something placed in us by nature (*naturaliter nobis additum*). Of this kind are the indemonstrable principles known through the light of the acting intellect. If we knew the soul by means of the soul itself, this too would be natural knowledge. But in things known to us by nature, there is no error... Man does not err in his knowledge of principles. There would be no error, therefore, about the substance of the soul if this were known to us *per se*. But it is obviously false that the soul is known *per se*.' He goes on a little later: 'What is known *per se* must be known prior to everything known mediately. *Per se* knowledge, like the first propositions related to conclusions, is the principle of knowledge related to mediate knowledge. But if the soul were to know its own substance through itself, it would be known *per se*, and consequently would be the first thing known and the principle of knowledge of everything else. But this is obviously false. The substance of the soul is not admitted and presumed as something already known. It has to be investigated and deduced from the principles.'

These quotations show: 1. that St. Thomas admitted knowledge of the principles prior to particular knowledge of the soul; 2. that knowledge of our own soul is impossible without knowledge of the principles; 3. that the first principles are known *per se* and immediately through the innate light which, as we have shown elsewhere and go on repeating, can only be the idea of being; 4. that the soul, known through the same principles governing our knowledge of other things, is neither the *first known* nor the *principle of knowledge of other things*. It cannot, therefore, be the source whence we deduce universal ideas and principles [...]. Rather, knowledge of the soul has to be deduced from the universal principles.

Aristotle recognised this truth when he said that the possible intellect *knows itself in the same way* as it knows other things (*De Anima*, III, 45).

2. (453).

[. . .] Sensation is an *experience* which on analysis always yields three elements: that which experiences; that which causes the experience; the experience itself. I note also that while a thing is indicated through *experience* relative to the one who experiences, the same thing is indicated through *action* relative to the agent. This difference in relationship with experiencer and agent enables the one thing to become two for our mind. The same thing takes on different and contrary aspects related to the experiencer and the agent.

It is now clear that *sensation*, as passive, is not a means of perceiving the one thing in itself devoid of relationships, but of perceiving it as experience, that is, related solely to the experiencer without reference to the thing as action. The subject of sensation feels itself, and undergoes an experience which does not originate in itself, but terminates in some other being as in its cause. It is true that the purely sentient subject does not perceive itself and what acts upon it as separate beings, but this does not prevent us from mentally distinguishing in the sensation: 1. a relationship with the sentient subject as sentient; 2. a relationship terminating not in the sentient subject, but in some other being.

We have reserved the word *sensation* to indicate the sentient subject as sensing, and the phrase *sense-perception of bodies* to indicate sensation itself as an experience necessarily related with something extraneous to and different from the sentient subject.

Hence: 1. *sense-perception of bodies*; 2. *intellective perception* (cf. 417, 418). As I have said on several occasions, *sense-perception* is subject to the action of our spirit, which takes and envelops bodies themselves. But we cannot say the same of *intellective perception*, except in so far as sense-perception serves as *matter* for intellective perception.

3. (453).

Intellective perception of bodies bears no likeness to *sensation*. But has *bodily sense-perception* any likeness to the *intellective perception of bodies*? I maintain that there is a strict association between these two perceptions, but no likeness.

In *bodily sense-perception*, it is not the body which is perceived, properly speaking, but a *passive experience* terminating in an outside agent. In *intellective perception of bodies*, the opposite is true: the body itself is perceived as an object acting in us. The two *perceptions* are contraries, a *passive experience* and *action* are contraries.

Passive *experience* and *action* are opposed as such, but the understanding, when disregarding the particular, contrary relationships they contract, considers them as one and the same thing.

The nature of the understanding is to perceive things in themselves; it is not limited to perceiving their relationships. When the understanding has perceived the thing we are discussing (that is, the change taking place in us) as it is in itself, it also finds an association between *passive experience* and *action*; it has perceived their link, the thing which is capable of two contrary relationships. This explains the association between *bodily sense-perception* and the *intellective perception of bodies*.

4. (453).

Philosophy sometimes holds back from mysteries, and

sometime leads to them. Is philosophy, therefore, opposed only to certain mysteries and not to them all? I am speaking, of course, of the tendency shown by a certain kind of philosophy, not by the individuals professing it. When a person gives his adhesion to a school or method of philosophy, he absorbs its spirit unconsciously, following it blindly in the hope of reaching a happy conclusion. I say this in order to be fair to everyone, even while I indicate the nature and tendency of a certain kind of philosophy to avoid some mysteries and embrace others. The mysteries it avoids are those which impose the existence of something spiritual. When such a philosophy reaches a point at which it must stumble without the aid of a spiritual entity, it declares; 'No progress can be made here,' and creates a *mystery* by positing an inexplicable difficulty. At this point, our philosopher is quite capable of praising his own modesty, and of accusing others of presumption. He is governed, however, by a secret prejudice which excludes spirit as unnecessary, and reduces everything to matter.

What happens if a person begins from an unproven proposition which he accepts absolutely to the exclusion of its contrary? He will proceed freely without any 'elevated' notions until he can no longer advance without admitting something spiritual. Then he stops, and says that philosophical prudence requires him to retreat. Arbitrary, voluntary limits of this nature, dependent upon blind faith in the unintelligibility of what he dislikes, first limit knowledge by forbidding human beings the free use of their reason, their highest faculty. It goes on to destroy philosophy and science by rendering human knowledge impossible. The more one meditates, the more one sees that eliminating the spirit from the universe renders human wisdom vain and absurd. Intelligence, cut off from the divine, loses its human quality. Modern scepticism, indifference, selfishness and epicureanism are the inevitable result of the philosophy we are speaking of. But even as they boast of their status, sceptics reason, cynics feel, egoists love and epicureans rise from their baseness. Caught in this appalling contradiction, human beings stand self-condemned. Human nature, and the truth which mingles with it, cannot be filed away and forgotten.

5. (490).

What St. Thomas teaches seems to agree with this. But we must understand clearly his manner of speaking. He teaches: 1. Feelable *phantasms* are only likenesses of things; 2. the intellect perceives things in their essence: 'The quiddity of a thing is the proper object of the intellect' (*quidditas rei est proprium objectum intellectus*: S.T. I, 85, art. 5). If the intellect finds only *likenesses* of things in the phantasms, but nevertheless perceives things themselves not their likenesses, as St. Thomas says, the intellect must supply the *things*, the beings. The intellect, therefore, posits beings while sense, according to Thomas, posits only the likeness of beings. An attentive reading of the following passage would show that my interpretation is correct: 'Because phantams are LIKENESSES of individuals — they do not have the human intellect's mode of being — they have no power to imprint anything in the possible intellect.' Of themselves the phantasms cannot communicate anything to the intellect. But St. Thomas explains how they can be brought to do this: 'The acting intellect turns its attention to the phantasms and BY ITS POWER a certain likeness results in the possible intellect (*ex conversione intellectus agentis supra phantasmata*); this likeness represents THE THINGS OF WHICH THEY ARE PHANTASMS, but in relationship to the nature of the species.' The species (idea) produced by the acting intellect does not represent the phantasms, likenesses or effects of the things - it represents the *things themselves*. If, therefore, the *things themselves* are not in the phantasms, the acting intellect must form the pure ideas of those things on the occasion of the phantasms by its own power (*virtute intellectus*), through the innate light, because it sees being (the nature of the thing) focusing on the phantasms, and thus the thing itself. The expression 'the intellect turning its attention to the phantasms' (*converti supra phantasmata*) can only mean 'to add being to the phantasms received by the spirit.' We have sensations; we are conscious of them immediately and say: 'Some being has produced these feelings in me.' Thus we turn to the phantasms and form the likeness or the *species* of the being that has produced the images, not of the phantasms.

It may be claimed that for St. Thomas it is the acting intellect, not our spirit, that turns to the phantasms. But this way of speaking has its origin in the fact that the acting intellect supplies *being*, through which the *species* are made. Strictly speaking, this operation must be attributed to the human being himself. St. Thomas was in fact very careful about accuracy of speech and expressly points out that 'properly speaking, understanding is not a function of the intellect but of the soul through the intellect' (*Intellegere proprie loquendo, non est intellectus, sed animae per intellectum*) (*De Verit.* q. 10, art. 9, ad 3 in contrar.). This expression is valid for all the operations of the soul's powers. Hence it is better to say that our spirit turns to the phantasms it feels, and, where they are, sees a being (supplied by the acting intellect). The *species* or idea of the thing is formed by the primitive synthesis, or first step taken by *reason*.

We should also note that this turning of the acting intellect to the phantasms has the same meaning as St. Thomas' other phrase: 'to illuminate the phantasms' (*illuminare phantasmata*), that is, to envelop them with the *light* of the acting intellect which is precisely *being* (cf. App. no. 6). Relative to my point, St. Thomas concludes: 'In the same way we can *abstract* the intelligible species from the phantasms, [but this] is not because some form previously in the phantasms is afterwards numerically the same in the possible intellect (as though it were a body moved from one place to another)' (*S.T.* I, q. 85, art. 1, ad 1). According to St. Thomas, nothing is moved from the phantasms into the intellect; only on the occasion of the phantasms does the intellect form the *species* in itself, that is, sees by the light of *being* it possesses the *beings* which produce the phantasms.

6. (495).

St. Thomas often uses the phrases, *illustrari phantasmata, abstrahere phantasmata*, to indicate two operations of the acting intellect (*S.T.* I, 79, 4; I, 85, art. 1, ad 4). What is the proper meaning of the metaphorical expression, *illustrari phantasmata*? If I am not mistaken, it corresponds, as I have suggested, with *universalisation*, that is, the operation which forms ideas when phantasms present themselves and thus enables feelable things to be understood. Undoubtedly *illustrating them* is a very happy way of describing what our intelligence adds to felt things through the idea of being which alone makes them intelligible, or clear to the intellect. However, some passages of aristotelian philosophers could render this interpretation doubtful, and lead us to believe that the two phrases do not always possess a clear, precise meaning. It would even seem that the phrase *to abstract* is often used to indicate the *universalisation* of ideas.

Nevertheless, careful consideration would seem to show that the passages in question can be given an adequate meaning. For example, this is how St. Thomas describes the two operations, *illustration* and *abstraction*: 'The phantasms are *illuminated* by the acting intellect, and the intelligible species *abstracted* from them by virtue of the acting intellect. They are *illuminated* by the acting intellect because its power is such that what is intelligible is abstracted from the phantasms, just as the sense part gains in strength from being joined to the intellect. The acting intellect abstracts the intelligible species from the phantasms in so far as, through the acting intellect, we can consider the nature of various species stripped of their individuality, in accordance with the likenesses informing the possible intellect' (*S.T.* I, 85, art. 1, ad 4).

What does he mean when he says that the sense part gains in strength (*efficitur virtuosior*) through being joined to the acting intellect, and moreover gains the power which renders the phantasms capable of undergoing the abstraction that provides the intelligible species, or ideas, of things? It is not difficult to recognise the nature of this power if we know what enables us to abstract the specific *natures* of things (the ideas), and I think I have shown what this is. As I said, the sensations or images (*phantasmata*) are united to the *idea of being* and to the *judgment* on the thing's subsistence. In this way, *intellectual perception* is determined according to the individuals perceived by the sensations (*phantasmata*). The specific ideas of things are drawn precisely from the intellective perception (through a twofold type of abstraction: first, that by which the judgment indicating real things is removed; second, that by which *individual conditions* are set aside) in order to arrive at universal, pure and isolated *ideas*. It seems clear that St. Thomas' *illustrated phantasms* correspond perfectly to what I have called *intellective perceptions*.

7. (500).

It is certain, however, that in many places Plato spoke hesitatingly about his ideas. It seems that for him ideas were abstract, that is, ideas of things without accidents. But this way of speaking (for which I shall explain the reason later) does not detract from his basic thought. St. Thomas, in explaining Plato's work, uses words which hint at my own interpretation of Plato's ideas. For example, he says that Plato makes the species *substances of individual things* (in Aristotle's *Metaph.*, book 7, less. 16). Individual things considered in their perfection differ, and to each of them corresponds an idea, an exemplar, used by the creator of the thing to mould and form it, and to form and mould new individuals, provided these can be reduced to their unique common type. This interpretation of Plato seems to me to be confirmed by everything Aristotle says (in *Metaph.*, book 8, less. 16) about the way in which Plato arrived at his teaching.

Moreover, a statement of Plato about *species* and *genera* gives weight to the sense I attribute to him. He speaks about predicating something common to several things, but in such a way that it is applicable first to one thing rather than another (*secundum prius et posterius*). In this case, what is common cannot exist *per se* and separately from the things to which it is attributed; and this is proper to genus. But if what is common is predicated equally of several beings, it exists *per se* outside the beings to which it is attributed; and this is proper to *species*. According to Plato, therefore, individuals of a *species* must be perfectly equal, at least in their positive characteristics, without differing in dignity. I conclude that by his *species* Plato meant *universal*, not abstract, *ideas*; these universal ideas contain all that is perceived in an individual except the reality of the individual, or the matter and, more generally speaking, the *subsistence* which is never contained in ideas, as I have shown (cf. 401-403).

If Plato's *species* are understood in this way, it seems to me that some of Aristotle's objections can be dismissed. For example, Aristotle's attempt to prove against Plato that the *matter* must form the *species* of things (*Metaph.* book 8) now appears a simple equivocation, a misunderstanding. When we think a corporeal thing, we certainly think of the matter composing the thing, but our idea of the matter is not the matter itself. If *species* means idea, *matter* does not enter into *species*. St. Thomas, in order to dispel the equivocation and in some way defend Aristotle, said that matter, which formed part of the species, was not the same matter as the *proper principle of the individual*, but a kind of *general matter* (that is, the *idea of matter*): 'Flesh and bones are found in the concept of human being, but not the flesh and bones of the living Socrates and Plato' *(Contra Gent.* II, q. 92).

In any case, it seems that in other places Aristotle saw that the principle of *species* is the *universalisation* of an individual (I have already indicated this) and not the *abstraction*. Cf. book 8 of the *Metaphysics*, where he compares *species* to *numbers* and says that any unity increased in number immediately changes its species.

8. (528).

In some passages of St. Thomas it might seem that the *matter* of our knowledge is supplied only by the exterior senses without any contribution from the internal feeling of 'myself'. But if we compare the various observations he makes on the subject, his mind appears very clear: the matter of our knowledge comes from two sources, external sensations and the internal feeling of the soul itself.

St. Augustine had said: 'The mind knows itself through itself because it is incorporeal' *(De Trin.,* book 9, c. 3). Clearly he teaches that the soul has a feeling, or rather is itself a substantial feeling, and therefore supplies the understanding with a *matter* of knowledge that can in no way be furnished by the bodily senses. Aristotle, whom the Scholastics had adopted as their guiding star (where he was not opposed to the christian faith), took another view. According to him, 'the intellect understands nothing without the corporeal phantasm' (*De Anima*, book 3, com. 30). St. Thomas' acute mind saw that Augustine's teaching was true from one point of view, and Aristotle's from another, and he tried to reconcile the two.

First, he established that no *species* offering a likeness of the soul could be drawn from phantasms; no idea of our soul, which is completely different from corporeal nature, could therefore be gained from corporeal phantasms: *anima non cognoscitur per speciem a sensibus abstractum, quasi intelligatur species illa esse animae similitudo (De Anima,* q. 10, art. 8). Secondly, he thought the best way of discovering how we know the nature of the soul was to examine the approach used by philosophers in their discussion about its properties. He observed that in meditating on the nature of the soul, they first examined its *acts*, especially its ideas. He says: 'Because the human soul knows the universal nature of each thing, they (the philosophers) noticed that the *species* (idea) with which the human being understands is immaterial. And because the intellectual species is immaterial, they realised that the intellect must be something independent of matter. They went on from there to learn about the other properties of intellective power' (*ibid.*). St. Thomas concludes that the abstract *species* (ideas) of material things were necessary to the philosophers' knowledge of the soul's nature not because the species could supply a likeness of the soul, *sed quia naturam speciei considerando, quae a sensibilibus abstrahatur, invenitur natura animae, in qua huiusmodi species recipitur (ibid.)* [but because, by considering the nature of the species abstracted from feelable things, we discover the nature of the soul in which this species is received]. Thus it was not the sensible phantasms, but the species formed in us by the acting intellect, as we have seen, that provided information about the soul. This species, of a completely different nature from phantasms, supplies a starting point for discovering the nature of the soul.

This was *scientific* knowledge of the soul, reducible to a *definition*. But there is also a *natural* knowledge of the soul.

Each of us is conscious of having, or rather being, an incommunicable, *personal feeling*, and of perceiving the feeling expressed in the word 'myself'. We know that this feeling is not found in any way in the corporeal qualities of extension, and so on. These are all extrasubjective; 'myself' is the subject itself.

This kind of knowledge did not, it seems to me, escape the attention of St. Thomas. To understand his mind, we must keep before us the expressions he uses to indicate the two kinds of knowledge I am discussing, *scientific* and *popular*. The former is founded on argued reasoning; the latter consists in immediate perception.

St. Thomas, therefore, declares that we cannot say we know the *nature* of anything if its specific or generic difference is unknown; only by means of this difference can we form a proposition containing the definition of the thing (*cum res speciali aut generali cognitione definitur*). Only scientific knowledge enables us to know the *nature* of the soul. But in speaking of what I would call *popular* or natural knowledge, St. Thomas calls it 'that by which the soul knows itself individually' (that is, *quantum ad id quod est ei proprium* [relative to what is proper to itself]). This kind of knowledge corresponds exactly to what I call *perception of our soul*, which takes place for the first time when we say to ourselves: I AM. It is composed of the feeling of 'myself' (matter) and of the idea of being in general (form) and nothing more. We do not know expressly any differences it may have with other things, nor do we compare it with other objects. This kind of knowledge, according to St. Thomas, is such that it makes known only the *existence* of the soul, not its essence (*per hanc cognitionem cognoscitur an est anima; — per aliam vero — scitur quid est anima*).

Before proceeding, I would like to make an observation about calling *perception* 'knowledge by which we know the soul exists.' Aquinas himself puts the following objection: 'We cannot know that something exists unless we first know what it is' (*De Verit*. q. 10, art. 12), and answers it: 'In order to know that something exists, it is not necessary to know what it is by *definition* (that is, to know it scientifically), but what is meant by its name.' Here St. Thomas is describing ordinary knowledge expressed by the way people name things. In our case, this knowledge is reduced to a global *perception* of the thing, without either comparison with other things or the realisation of the differences necessary for forming a perfect definition of it. I point this out to allow the reader to reflect that St. Thomas' knowledge 'by which something is known to be' (*qua scitur aliquid esse*) does not express the simple *existence* of the thing. We could not know the thing without sufficient information to distinguish it from all other things with which it shares existence.

We are now in a position to note the harmony between St. Thomas' teaching on knowledge *qua cognoscitur an est anima* [by which the soul is known to exist] and mine on *perceptive* or *natural and popular* knowledge.

Following the teaching of St. Augustine, St. Thomas affirms that 'the essence of the soul is always present to our intellect' (*ipsa ejus essentia intellectui nostro est praesens*). To perceive this essence, our understanding needs only to posit the act by which it perceives the essence of the soul. He concludes: *anima per essentiam suam se videt, id est, hoc ex ipso quod essentia sua est sibi praesens, est potens exire in actum cognitionis sui ipsius* [the soul sees itself through its essence, that is, it has the *ability* to arrive at knowledge of itself because its essence is present to itself] (*De Verit.* 10, 8). He likens this knowledge to knowledge in our memory saying that *sicut aliquis ex hoc quod habet alicujus scientiae habitum, ex ipsa praesentia habitus est potens percipere illa quae subsunt illi habitui* [someone who has a habit of knowledge, can perceive the things subject to the habit] (*ibid.*). And this direct knowledge that the soul has of itself without phantasms, he calls *habitual.*

For the understanding to come to *actual* knowledge of the soul (St. Thomas continues), a sufficient reason must be provided by the acts of the soul itself. 'Therefore I say that, as regards the actual knowledge by which anyone considers his soul in act, the soul is known only by its acts. A person perceives that he has a soul, that he lives and exists because he realises that he feels, knows, and performs other vital operations' (*ibid.*). No one can doubt this.

Let me conclude with an observation. Forget for a moment

reflex knowledge of ourselves and remember we are speaking only of direct, immediate knowledge, the perception of us; our soul is only our own feeling of this us. Now it is clear that we can perceive ourselves intellectively only by our acts. But some acts are essential, like feeling and the act of the acting intellect (with which we perceive being) — both St. Thomas and Aristotle accept this last act — and, because they are essential, we can never lack them. We could, therefore, have actual perception of ourselves even in the first moments of our existence if there were some stimulus to draw our attention to ourself. But as long as such a stimulus is missing, we are left only with the power to acquire this knowledge: *est potens [anima] exire in actum cognitionis sui ipsius* [the soul has the capacity to produce an act of knowledge of itself].

9. (554).

If anyone denied that the name *cognition* could be applied to the single, innate idea which our spirit intuits directly without any judgment, I would not dispute the matter. This seems to have been Aquinas' view, and I hope to be able to throw some light upon it.

St. Thomas teaches that our mind understands and knows only through phantasms. Now it is very important to grasp what he means by this. He observes that it is proper to the human mind to know things themselves (*quidditas rei est objectum intellectus*). But the mind knows things through their *idea* or species. The intellect, therefore, knows real things, but through ideas which are the means of knowledge (*non quod cognoscit, sed quo cognoscit*). He can say, therefore, *ad cognitionem duo concurrere oportet, scilicet apprehensionem* (the idea), *et judicium* [two things are required for knowledge, namely apprehension and judgment], which brings the mind to the real thing (the mental word). In this case, our simple apprehension, that is, the pure idea without any real, felt thing, would not be something we understood, but only the *means* of understanding. This is precisely the state of the mind which possesses only the idea of being without having received any phantasm through sense. It cannot be said to know anything because as yet it understands nothing; it has only a *potency* for knowing and understanding. As St. Thomas says: 'As a potency, it cannot know anything except relative to its object, just as vision is meaningless without colour. Phantasms, therefore, are related to the possible intellect as feelable things are related to sense. The intellect, although it may have some intelligible species, does not actually consider anything according to that species except in the presence of phantasms. Hence our intellect, in its present state, needs phantasms to really think' (*De Verit.* q. 10, art. 2, ad 7). St. Thomas admits that the intellect can have some *idea* or intellectual species antecedent to phantasms which, however, it needs in order *to know* in the restricted sense of the word.

10. (565).

Retinet [memoria] nihilominus scientiarum principia et dignitates ut sempiternalia et sempiternaliter, quia nunquam potest sic oblivisci eorum (dummodo ratione utatur), quin ea audita approbet, et eis assentiat, non tanquam de novo percipiat, sed tanquam SIBI INNATA et familiaria recognoscat [The memory retains forever the principles and standards of the branches of knowledge because of their everlasting quality. It can never forget them (as long as it uses reason) because in giving them its approval and assent it recognises them as INNATE and familiar. These principles are never something newly perceived] (*Itin. mentis etc.* c. 3). This is a very acute *factual observation* of the type neglected by modern sensists, despite their lip-service to facts which, even if neglected, can never be entirely ignored.

St. Thomas is of the same opinion as the author of the *Itinerarium. Prima principia, QUORUM COGNITIO EST NOBIS INNATA, sunt quaedam similitudines increatae veritatis* [The first principles, KNOWLEDGE OF WHICH IS INNATE IN US, are certain likenesses of uncreated truth] (*De Verit.* q. 10, art. 6, ad 6). He often repeats this teaching, as in the following passage: *In eo qui docetur, scientia praeexistebat, non quidem in actu completo, sed quasi in rationibus seminalibus secundum quod universales conceptiones, quarum cognitio est NOBIS*

NATURALITER INSITA, *sunt quasi semina quaedam omnium sequentium cognitorum* [Knowledge is already present in the student, but not completely. It lies there in seminal notions because the universal conceptions whose knowledge IS NATURALLY PRESENT TO US are like seeds containing all that we shall ever know] (*De Verit.* q. 11, art. 1, ad 5).

My interpretation of these passages requires that 'innate' and 'naturally present to us' be understood in the sense that the first principles are present in our first acts of reason or (and it comes to the same thing) when we first use *the idea of being*, which alone is innate strictly speaking and corresponds to St. Thomas' *acting intellect*. In order to see the truth of my interpretation it is sufficient to compare what St. Thomas says above with the following: *In lumine intellectus agentis nobis est quodammodo omnis scientia originaliter indita, mediantibus universalibus conceptionibus, quae statim* LUMINE INTELLECTUS AGENTIS *cognoscuntur, per quas sicut per universalia principia judicamus de aliis, et ea praecognoscimus in ipsis* [All knowledge is placed within us originally in the light of the acting intellect, through universal conceptions which are known immediately BY THE LIGHT OF THE ACTING INTELLECT. These universal conceptions are as it were universal principles through which we judge of other things already known in them] (*De Verit.* q. 10, art. 6).

11. (621).

St. Thomas deduces the idea of substance in the same way as I do. First, he establishes that the proper object of the intellect is *being or common truth (objectum intellectus est ens, vel verum commune)*. He concludes that everything is knowable in so far as it is, in so far as it has an existence of its own. This is my conclusion also. It is in fact absurd that what is not could be understood: *Unumquodque autem in quantum habet* DE ESSE, *in tantum est cognoscibile* [Each thing is knowable in so far as it draws upon BEING] (*S.T.* I, q. 16, art. 3). It follows that things are understood through their *substance* because substance is that by which they are beings. This accounts for St. Thomas' other declaration where he states that *substance* is the object of the intellect precisely because the object of the intellect is being: *Quidditas rei est proprium objectum intellectus* [The proper object of the intellect is what makes a thing what it is {*quidditas*}] (*S.T.* I, q. 85, art. 5). Another acute observation, drawn from the same principles, is that the *truth* in things is their *substance* and their very being: *Verum autem quod est in rebus, convertitur cum ente secundum substantiam* [What is true in things is interchanged with being in the realm of substance] (*S.T.* I, q. 16, art 3). The truth of things is their relationship with ideas in the intellect, which however can only be of their substance, because this is the object of the intellect. It follows that truth, in so far as it is shared by things, is their substance. Note that *quidditas*, in the quotation above, has been equated with *substance* because of the meaning given it by St. Thomas in this place. On the other hand, it is always true that the quiddity or essence of accidents can only be understood related to substantial quiddity or essence.

12. (622).

I would like to add a few more words about St. Thomas' teaching. It is important that the philosophical principles on which he bases religious teaching, so profoundly needed by human nature, should be understood perfectly.

I have already noted that the intellect cannot be the power which *universalises* sensations; only the soul can do this through its *unity* and *simplicity*. On the one hand, it experiences sensations; on the other, it possesses the vision of being, and unites these two things in itself. If we examine the use made of the *acting intellect* by St. Thomas, we shall see that the power of the soul uniting these two things is what he calls the *acting intellect*. Consequently, the *acting intellect* corresponds to what I have called *the faculty of primitive synthesis* or the first function of *reason*. St. Thomas also notes a *particular reason*, which he calls the *cogitative force*, whose power lies in descending to particular matters and regulating them: *Mens regit inferiores, et sic singularibus se immiscet movente* ratione particulari, *quae est potentia quaedam individualis quae alio nomine dicitur* cogitativa [The mind governs the inferior faculties, and thus influences individual things with its own 'particular reasoning power', that is, with a certain special capacity we call 'cogitative'] (*De Ver.* q. 10, art. 5).

As he says, *reason* is the power of the soul that, after coming into possession of sensations and phantasms on the one side, and of possession of being on the other, joins these two extremes. This energy of the soul then becomes St. Thomas' *particular reason* or *cogitative capacity* when considered relative to the particulars which it has to regulate. But if it is considered as a power for forming ideas in the way described, that is, by universalising phantasms, then it corresponds to St. Thomas' *acting intellect* which he rightly calls *virtus quaedam animae nostrae* [a certain force of our soul] (*S.T.* I, q. 89, art. 4). St. Thomas' teaching will be understood more clearly if we are allowed the following observations.

St. Thomas first establishes that neither sensations as such nor corporeal images (*phantasmata*) are ideas; the *acting intellect* has to *illustrate* them in order to render them such. I have already shown how this illustration, or illumination, is simply their *universalisation* brought about by adding to them the *light of the acting intellect*, that is, *possibility* or *ideal being*. The soul considers the sensations it experiences as infinitely renewable, and hence views them in their possible or general existence, rather than in their *individual existence*. '*Formae sensibiles non possunt agere in mentem nostram, nisi quatenus per* lumen *intellectus agentis immateriales redduntur, et sic efficiuntur quodammodo homogeneae intellectui possibili, in quem agunt* [The sensible forms cannot act relatively to our mind unless they are rendered immaterial through the *light* of the acting intellect and thus made compatible with the possible intellect relatively to which they act] (*De Ver.* q. 10, art. 6). He concludes that the principal agent in the formation of ideas is neither *sense* nor *phantasms*, but the acting intellect with its innate light.

My own comment is this. If the acting intellect renders the phantasms immaterial (universalises them), it must act upon them and, according to St. Thomas' own phrase, 'turn towards them'. The acting intellect, therefore, can only be the power possessed by the soul of beholding, in the possible being that it intuits, the sensations it experiences. The following passage shows clearly that the nature of the *acting intellect* is as I have described it. St. Thomas shows that the *acting intellect* makes phantasms immaterial. This takes place through the unity of the subject, that is, of the soul which on the one side has the phantasms, on the other the power of the intellect. He says: 'Although the intellective soul is immaterial in act, it is potentially DETERMINED to specific things.' This *immateriality* in act on the part of the intellective soul indicates its intuition of being in a universal act, free from corporeal limitations and determinations. St. Thomas does in fact teach that we know the immateriality of the soul by its ideas which we find to be universal (*De Ver.* q. 10, art. 8) and therefore immaterial. He continues: 'The phantasms, although certainly likenesses of some species in act, are only potentially immaterial', that is, they are not universal, although they can be universalised by our spirit. 'There is nothing to prevent a SINGLE, IDENTICAL SOUL which is immaterial in act', that is, in so far as it has the idea of possible being, 'from possessing a certain power enabling it to render immaterial in act (to universalise) the phantasms by abstracting from the individual conditions imposed by matter. THIS POWER IS CALLED THE ACTING INTELLECT. At the same time, the one, identical soul may possess another receptive power called *possible intellect* because it is capable of accepting such universalised species' (*S.T.* I, q. 79, art. 4). These words show clearly that for St. Thomas the *acting intellect* is the power by which the soul *applies being* to sensations, and hence is proper to the soul in so far as it feels both its sensations and the completely universal idea of being.

We can now reach some conclusions about the nature of the acting and possible intellects. The soul possesses an innate *light* which is the idea of being in general. This idea can be considered in two relationships. First, the soul uses and applies it in order to universalise sensations. In this respect, it forms the *acting intellect*. Second, the intelligent spirit beholds it continually as the idea transforms itself in all other ideas (all possible ideas are only the idea of being furnished with various determinations). This capacity for auto-transformation enables the idea to form the *possible intellect*. These considerations explain clearly the truth of the Aristotelian distinction between the two intellects: 'The soul possesses an intellect that *becomes* all things (the possible intellect), and an intellect that *makes* all things (the acting intellect)': *Est quidam intellectus talis qui omnia fiat, et quidam qui omnia faciat (De Anima,* bk. 3, lect. 10). As we said, the *idea* of being becomes all ideas: this is the *possible intellect*; and through the *idea of being* the soul forms all ideas: this is the *acting intellect*.

13. (667).

[. . .] Because of the difficulty of understanding the perfect *unity* between *that which feels* and that which is felt, I need to make a further observation about it.

This mysterious unity is found not only between a being that feels and a being that is felt, but also in any action by which one being affects another, when one is passive and the other active. We must carefully observe the fact as it is; I do not wish to enter into an explanation of it. It will be found that the fact happens as follows.

What is being *experienced* is the *term* of another being's action. Now the experience, purely as experience, is in the passive being but it is also *term* of the action. Considered as term of the *action*, it is in the *active* being. It is impossible to posit two *terms* of action, one outside, the other inside the agent, as though this were a fact, rather than a product of the imagination. The experience is the *effect* produced by the agent; an agent must be *acting* precisely where there is an effect and nowhere else; the agent's action properly terminates in the effect. The term of the action is necessarily joined to the action in precisely the same way as the term or limit of a stick is in the stick. The *acting being* is indeed separate from the effect it produces in the *receiving* being but this happens when its action ceases. Now, we are considering the being at the moment of its action. What for one being (which receives) is an experience, is for the other, at that moment, a *term* of action; the same thing is joined and belongs to two beings in one act, having its own direct relation to each. It is a concept of two beings touching each other, as it were — a difficult, unique concept but nevertheless true. Like any *fact*, it cannot be dismissed, much less denied; on the contrary, it should be investigated and verified with greater care.

As regards the fact of sensation [. . .], I must indicate the sense in which I accept the fusion of the *subjective* and the [...] *extrasubjective* elements into one single fact. The reader is referred to what is written in the footnotes to 453 [cf. App. nos. 2, 3, 4] where I have shown how *reflection* can break down *sensation* into two elements, *subjective* and *extrasubjective*. Sensation can properly be called *sensation* in so far as it is subjective, and *corporeal sense-perception* in so far as it is extrasubjective or term of an action outside us. All this demonstrates how *extrasubjective sensation*, which I admit, must never be confused with *intellective perception* or with the *idea* of bodies, because this is formed not only through sense but also through the intellect endowed with the *idea of being*.

Finally I point out that 'smell', 'taste', 'sound', etc. are words indicating mainly the *subjective* element, while names of the first qualities of bodies, like extension, indicate solely the *extrasubjective* element. But later I will have the opportunity to discuss all this at greater length.

14. (708).

When we had to establish the first, substantial difference between our own body and bodies different from our own, we found that the former was perceived along with us as sentient *subject*, while the latter were perceived simply as forces different from the subject. This difference was proved by: 1. a *fact* revealed by consciousness — when we say 'fact' we mean 'something self-evident', and therefore 'certain'; 2. use of the theory of *perception* already outlined (cf. 528-536), and of the *principles of substance and cause* (cf. 567-569).

However, our body can be perceived *extrasubjectively*, just like any other body. In this case, if we perceive our body as an *extrasubjective* term of our sense-faculty, we can discover secondary, but nevertheless important differences, enabling us once again to distinguish it from external bodies. This way of distinguishing our own body, considered as different from us as subject, from external bodies, supposes the truth about an *extrasubjective* term of our sense-faculty. There was, however, no need of this as long as the distinction between our own and other bodies depended upon the substantial difference between *subject* and *that which is extrasubjective*.

Three differences may be noted between the *extrasubjective* perception of our own and external bodies. These differences show that our own body is quite distinct from any external body. Galluppi sets out the differences as follows:

First difference. 'If your right hand is hot, and your left cold, and you bring them into contact, you will feel the same "self" in them both. "Myself" which feels the heat of the right hand is the same as that which feels the cold of the left. "Myself", therefore, seems to exist in both hands. But if you touch a block of iron with one hand, you will feel "myself" in the hand without feeling it in the block of iron. It does not seem to exist in the iron, which is extraneous to "myself". Contact between the two hands furnishes two sensations; contact with the block of iron only one. "Myself" looks upon right and left hands as parts of its *own* body because it has a touch-feeling in both; it looks upon the block of iron as an *external body* because it has a touch-feeling *of* the iron, but not *in* the iron. "Myself" regards as its *own* the body which it feels, and in which it seems to feel or to exist; it regards as *external* to itself a body which it feels, but in which it does not seem to feel or exist.'

Second difference. 'If you want to move your arm, you do so from within, immanently. But the block of iron will not move simply because you want it to. First, you have to move your hand towards it, and then move the block by moving your hand. "Myself" regards as its *own* the body which it can move by willing to do so; it regards as *external* any body whose movement does not depend upon its act of will.'

Third difference. 'You can move the block of iron to a place where it no longer acts upon any of your senses. But you cannot do this with your own body. At least while you are awake, it is impossible to avoid its action. "Myself" regards as its *own*, therefore, that body which is unceasingly present to it; it regards as *external* any body ceasing to modify it or not present to it' (*Elementi di filosofia*, etc. T. 3, chap. 3, 29).

Galuppi concludes from these observations that we can distinguish our own from external bodies by means of *sight* and *touch*. But both senses perceive *extrasubjectively*, and I am not satisfied with showing a difference between our *own body* and *external bodies* as differing terms of sight and touch. We must also recognise that our own body pertains to ourselves as *subject*, while external bodies are purely *extrasubjective*. This is the basic difference beteen them.

Nevertheless, the three facts indicated by Galluppi do help considerably to underline the distinction between a *subject* and something *different from the subject*, if we take their analysis one step further. In the first of the three differences, where the *hand* feels itself as sentient, we find a *subject*, while the *block of iron* which is only felt and does not feel itself, is indicative of something different from the *subject*. In the second difference, the movement that I want to carry out through my hand can be perceived not only with sight and touch, but principally through interior feeling and consciousness, which draw attention to the *subject*. The movement I impart to the block of iron is clearly noted only through sight and touch indicating *something different from the subject*. In the third difference, I feel my body united with me wherever I go, not because I see it or touch it, but principally through interior consciousness, which indicates me as its *subject*. The distance of external bodies is brought home to me by touch or the other senses indicating that these bodies are *extrasubjective terms* of my feeling powers.

15. (713).

Chronologically our thought, while adverting last of all to our interior and fundamental feeling, has to be preceded by reflection upon the *external* sensations. Understanding this enables us to reconcile different passages of St.Thomas Aquinas on the need for *phantasms* if we are to think.

Sometimes he is adamant about the necessity of *phantasms* in our thought (*S.T.* I, q. 86, art. 7), affirming: *quidditas rei materialis est proprium objectum intellectus* [the proper object of the intellect is that which makes material things what they are] (*S.T.* I, q. 85, art. 5) or *natura rei materialis est objectum intellectus* [the object of the intellect is the nature of material things]. He then concludes that *habits* are not *objects* of the intellect, but are present *ut quibus intellectus intelligit* [as things enabling the intellect to understand].

Taken by itself, this teaching appears the opposite of that attributed to St. Thomas in this book, and proved with his own words [. . .], that is, that the *matter* of our cognitions is furnished by the interior feeling as well as by the external *sensations*. Although presenting some difficulty, St. Thomas' dual approach to the subject is of great importance, and should be evaluated carefully. Let us try to explain St. Thomas with St. Thomas.

According to him, the *material thing* is not the *sole* object of the intellect, but simply *first* in *chronological* order. This is precisely what I am saying. St. Thomas asks (*S.T.* I, q. 87, art. 3) 'whether the intellect knows its own act,' which is certainly not material, and replies affirmatively. He adds, however, that it does so *after* knowing *material things*. In this, the human being differs, according to Aquinas, from angels who with their first act understand both themselves and the act with which they understand themselves. He says: 'Another intellect exists, the human one, which does not furnish its own understanding (as the divine intellect does). The essence of this intellect is not the *first* object of understanding' (as happens with the angels, according to St. Thomas). 'Its *first* object is something external, that is, the nature of material things. Hence, the *first* thing known by the human intellect is material. Only *secondarily* does the human intellect know the act with which it knows the object, and through this second knowledge come to know itself' (*Est autem alius intellectus, scilicet humanus, qui nec est suum intelligere, nec sui intelligere est* OBJECTUM PRIMUM *ipsa eius essentia, sed aliquid extrinsecum, scilicet natura materialis rei. Et ideo id quod* PRIMO *cognoscitur ab intellectu humano, est hujusmodi objectum, et* SECUNDARIO *cognoscitur ipse actus, quo cognoscitur objectum: et per actum cognoscitur ipse intellectus*). He says the same thing more clearly shortly afterwards in summing up his teaching: 'The object of the intellect is something common, that is, BEING and TRUTH, included in which is the act itself of understanding. The intellect, therefore, can know its own act, but not as its FIRST object which, in our present state, is not any being and truth, but being and truth considered in material things' *(S.T.* I, corp. ad 1). He confirms this with a phrase from Aristotle: 'objects are known BEFORE acts *(PRAECOGNOSCUNTUR*), and acts BEFORE powers' *(De Anima,* book 2, test. 33). It is clear that wē are dealing with priority in *time* alone, and this is precisely what I have been saying.

But I also observed that in order to reach the state of intellectual development necessary for reflection on one's own interior feeling, it is not enough to know bodily things *first.* It is also necessary to arrive at abstract thoughts (which is normally impossible without the use of language) and through them obtain dominion over one's attention which can then be directed at will. Only after this can a human being reflect upon himself, and advert to his interior acts. *First* amongst these acts, as we have said, is the fundamental feeling which, however, is reflected upon *last,* after advertence to its accidental acts. The *chronological* order of our *advertence* runs as follows: 1. we advert to what is feelable in a bodily sense; 2. form *abstract thoughts*; 3. advert to our *act of feeling* (sensations) and our act of understanding; 4. finally advert to the *fundamental feeling,* the first act and common root of both sense and intelligence.

It is now very easy to reconcile other passages of St. Thomas in which he makes it clear that the sources of our cognitions are not the senses alone. Some examples may be useful.

'Sensitive knowledge is not the whole cause *(TOTA CAUSA)* of intellective cognition. We should not be surprised, therefore, if intellective cognition extends beyond sensitive knowledge *(ultra sensitivam se extendit)*' *(S.T.* I, q. 84, art. 6). Amongst these things which go beyond sense knowledge, and to which only intellective cognition reaches out, first place belongs to all that is in our understanding. *Quod intellectualiter cognoscitur, per se est notum, et ad ipsum cognoscendum natura cognoscentis sufficit* ABSQUE EXTERIORI MEDIO [What is known intellectually is known of itself, and the nature of the person who knows is sufficient, WITHOUT ANY EXTERIOR MEANS, as a means of knowing it] (*Contra Gent.* I, q. 57). For example, we cannot know where our affections lie except by consulting our heart. External, material things can tell us nothing about them: *Etsi fides non cognoscatur per* EXTERIORES CORPORIS MOTUS, *percipitur tamen etiam ab eo in quo est per* INTERIOREM ACTUM CORDIS [Although faith is not known through EXTERIOR MOVEMENTS OF OUR BODY, it is perceived by the person possessing it through AN INTERIOR ACT OF THE HEART] (*S.T.* I, 87, q. 2). Again, if we knew only *material things*, we could not form any idea about *spirits*, knowledge of which has to be drawn from our own soul, as Thomas says, following Augustine: *Ex illa auctoritate Augustini haberi potest quod illud, quod mens nostra de cognitione incorporalium rerum accipit,* PER SEIPSAM *cognoscere possit. Et hoc adeo verum est, ut etiam apud Philosophum dicatur, quod scientia de anima est* PRINCIPIUM *quoddam ad cognoscendum substantias separatas (De Anima,* bk. I, test. 2). *Per hoc enim quod anima nostra cognoscit seipsam, pertingit ad cognitionem aliquam habendam de substantiis incorporeis, qualem eam contingit habere* [We have Augustine's authority for saying that our mind receives knowledge of incorporeal things through what it can know of itself. Indeed, even Aristotle says that knowledge of our soul is a certain principle enabling us to know separated substances (*De Anima,* book 1, test.2). Hence the knowledge our soul has of itself is an element in the knowledge of incorporeal substances in the way our soul needs to possess such knowledge] (*S.T.* I, q. 88, ad 1).

16. (806).

I take the opportunity of resolving a possible doubt about the distinction between an *idea* and *judgment on the subsistence of things.* We said (cf. 398-401) that any object whatsoever could be mentally conceived as endowed with all its essential and accidental characteristics, and still not subsist. Judgment of its subsistence, therefore, adds nothing to the idea we have of it. But are not place and time characteristics of a thing, and added to it when we judge of the thing's subsistence? If so, the judgment does add something that was not previously present in the idea of the thing.

I would deny that place and time are characteristics of a thing. Wherever and whenever a thing subsists, it is always itself, neither more nor less. There is no change, no addition to its nature. This needs careful consideration, and proof of it may be found in experience undergone by sensitive beings transported thousands of miles without feeling the change. This occurs because being in one place or another (and the same may be said about time) has no effect on their nature which remains exactly what it was. Place and time do not enter, therefore, into the idea of a thing.

When, however, judgment on the subsistence of a corporeal thing depends upon sense-perception, such judgment determines its *place*. If I perceive a body with my senses, I must perceive it in a determined place. But what is this *place* occupied by the perceived body? *Place*, we maintain, is something appertaining to *reality* precisely because it is foreign to the idea but at home in the judgment together with the *subsistence* of the thing of which, in corporeal matters, it forms an element.

An immediate objection springs to mind: what of the *idea* of place? It is of course true that we have such an idea, but in the same way as we have the *idea of subsistence* which, like all other ideas, is universal because it is only the *possibility* that a being subsists. Where, however, we are dealing with the particular subsistence of a being, the subsistence we think of is the idea of *subsistence* focused through a judgment on an individual. The same is true about our idea of a place. This idea is the *possibility* that an extended being exists in that place. But when we perceive a subsistent, extended being, we determine the *idea* of that extended thing by a judgment affirming its subsistence and, together with its subsistence, the place it occupies. The difference between subsistence and *place* is that the former is the act itself of the being while *place* is an abstract, that is, the *mode of the subsistence* of the being we call body.

The distinction between the content of the *idea* or *essence* and the judgment which makes known something about it (the particular subsistence), was known to early philosophers, but often forgotten (it is in fact very difficult to keep before the mind). As a result, questions insoluble without it were tackled by means of other distinctions resembling it. This resulted in serious embarrassment for science by multipying beings without necessity under the guise of such distinctions. One of these distinctions, which we have already mentioned, is that between *general* and *particular matter*. It was thought that the former, but not the latter, was necessary for corporeal things. In fact, it is not true that these two kinds of matter exist. What exists is: 1. particular matter; and 2. the *idea* of particular matter. The latter is simply particular matter in so far as it is thought possible. Because what is possible is universal, it seems to be universal matter. The same kind of distinction was made by early philosophers between universal and particular quantity, and here too the same observation is relevant: universal quantity is only the *idea* of quantity.

The term *intelligible quantity* used by these philosophers shows they had some notion of this. In book 4 of Aristotle's *Physics*, Simplicius says: 'I think it is better to say that we have a *specific* extension (Gk., *kat'eidos*, that is, according to the idea, as I have been suggesting) which can be seen in *exemplars*,' and another extension conceived mentally 'by passive discernment of an indivisible substance without parts.' *Intelligible* quantity is that described as *according to the idea*, which is seen in *exemplars*, that is, in first ideas. It is therefore the *idea of quantity*, or, if you prefer, the quantity thought in the idea, which is the same as possible or universal quantity.

17. (897).

The following observations offer further confirmation that many things attributed to the different grades of perfection in our senses should in fact be attributed to levels of perfection in our *advertence* or attention to sensations.

Observation shows that the hand is not the most sensitive

part of our body; other parts contain more nerves and are more sensitive. In fact we can say that the skin is more sensitive in all other parts of our body than in the hand where nature has wisely reduced sensitivity so that we can use the hand freely without being frequently troubled by pain. Continual use hardens our hand still more. Increase in the hand's sensitivity, therefore, is not brought about by its use except for greater effectivity and alertness of the nerves in the parts that are used more; and I have no doubt that this comes into play here. This, however, only proves the need for a greater attention or at least *sensitive* effectivity. My concern, on the other hand, is to know which part of our body can more easily make us perceive and distinguish the tiniest particles, the little inequalities of rough, uneven bodies and all their tactile differences. The answer must be the hand.

This ability does not come from greater, natural sensitivity of touch in the hand but from our habit of using the hand for that purpose and from our habit of *adverting* to minute differences in the hand's sensations. Normally, we do not learn to *advert* to them in other parts of our body. But extraordinary things are done by people who have lost their hands. Long education has taught them to be attentive to the sensations in their feet, accurately noting and differentiating every sensation. Such evidence does not lead me to think that sensitivity in their feet has increased. Rather, they have learnt to direct their attention to the sensations in their feet and note what takes place. Other people pay little or no attention at all to these sensations.

A good doctor with long experience notices the least change of pulse in a sick person; others do not. His sense of touch has not been refined specifically for taking pulses; any other person could have taken the pulse and learnt nothing. If the constant taking of pulses actually refines the doctor's touch, why does contact at the place of the vein rather than elsewhere render the nerves of the doctor's hand more sensitive? Why is the doctor's touch so sensitive to pulses but dull and coarse to the delicate engravings of an object worked in gold. If feeling the differences of pulse depended on the physical sensitivity of the skin and not on the acquired ability to advert to what is felt, the same sensitive touch could be used for everything; those born blind would not have to learn to determine the pulse by practice since they would already have a very sensitive touch.

All this is explained by *advertence* to our sensations, which is being continually improved and increases much more than the senses themselves. Our senses might improve a little even physically by use but certainly not enough to explain the great difference between senses that have been used meaningfully and senses that have not been so used. Their physical sensitivity, which depends on the texture of the organ, is given by nature and cannot be markedly changed. The sense of sight, it seems, can be improved and sharpened by practice, but we must remember that what this sense tells us about distant bodies is due to *habitual judgments* (as we shall show later). It is our ability to make these judgments that is perfected. And what sight tells us about surfaces is to a large extent due to the practice of observation. The jeweller's sharp eye, the doctor's capacity to tell at a glance how a person feels, other people's insight into character, all depend upon sharpened observation. The very subtle differences painters see in colours and pictures obviously involves skill in discerning the variations which others also see but do not advert to.

The same is true about music and the practised ear, which seems to hear many more things in an orchestral piece than the ears of others. In both cases the same sounds are perceived but with different mental attention. Another example is the acute sense of smell of tribesmen who, it is said, could identify the tracks of the Spaniards by smelling the ground. But we should be much more amazed by their constant practice in sensing minute sensations of smell and their differences.

Again, the taste buds of the palate undergo little change from frequent contact with different foods but what amazing sensitivity gourmets acquire, compared with other people, in judging different tastes! Perhaps Juvenal's glutton had dulled his palate by continual use of spices and dainty foods, but nevertheless, by applying the greatest attention to food, had so developed his sense of taste for oysters that with one bite he could say from which sea they had come.

The benefit the reader can draw from all these observations is to be convinced of the great difference between *sensation* and *advertence*, and to be persuaded that we feel an infinity of things without being in the least aware of them.

18. (925).

Most common errors, it would seem, depend upon habitual judgments formed almost involuntarily and irresistibly by the mass of people. Judgments become habitual because experience indicates an almost constant connection between the inability of ordinary people to take note of infrequent exceptions and their tendency to judge immediately; they pass from 'often' to 'always' in their judgments without suspending judgment when necessary. For example, everyone said that the sun moved around the earth, although the eye told us nothing of the real movement of the sun. People as a whole made a judgment on the basis of their sight-sensation and would have avoided error if they had not made the judgment. But could the judgment be suspended when universal experience showed the apparent movement of the sun to be accompanied by real movement? Experience did indeed show various anomalies, some of which are available to everybody's experience as, for instance, when we see, from a fast sailing boat, what appears to be moving sea. But individual examples are powerless to help the mass of people suspend their judgment. When people as a whole are ready to make certain kinds of conclusions, to urge them to suspend their judgment is like trying to prevent an avalanche on a mountain — you may foresee it, but you will be unable to stop it. Only after centuries are such judgments amended. First, some extraordinary person shows that they are wrong, only to be eliminated for his pains by public opinion. But his martyrdom does not sweep away what he has discovered. The grain of truth gradually forces its way to the surface and flourishes when humankind comes finally to realise its errors and repent of the injury inflicted on the truth and on those who uphold it.

Subject Index

7.—Criterion of the *size* and *shape* of bodies, and its application, 922–40.

DEFINITION, is the principle of every *science*, 573.—*Scientific knowledge*, that which can be reduced to a definition, 528n.—Definition at the beginning and end of scientific knowledge, 871n[105].

DEPTH, one of the three dimensions of a solid space, 838.

DETERMINATION or DETERMINATENESS, every *mode* of being, 435.—Primary and secondary, 690.—The idea of *determinate number* includes also the idea of *finite*, 790.

DISTANCE of bodies, perceived by means of the sight associated with touch and motion, 917–9,—and the criterion for not erring in this, 930–1.

DISTINCTION (the) between things is perceived by *adverting* to the sensations which we severally receive from them, 897n[113]., 900n.

DIVISIBILITY, a property of bodies comprised in extension, 885.—The meaning of the divisibility of the *continuous*, 830.—The indefinite divisibility of time is simply a mental possibility, 788.

DREAMS (from) idealists draw an argument against the existence of bodies, although dreams are a proof of it, 763.

DURATION, one of the limits of *action*, 766.—Successive duration gives the idea of time, 767.—The relation of the duration of one action to that of another gives the measure of time, 768.—Difficulty of thinking duration without *succession*, 796.—Successive duration is perceived simply as the possibility of obtaining a given *quantity* of action by means of a given degree of *intensity* in that action, 776.—Speaking of complete things or actions, durations mean their unchanging permanence in a given state, 795.—In this kind of duration, the *continuous* is found, *ibid.*

EFFECT, how it differs from an *accident*, 568.—*Immediate* effects, 855.

ENERGY, speaking of bodies, it is their *actual existence*, 588n.—In general, it is that force or operating substance with which every corporeal being is endowed, 667,—and that which is the cause of our sensations, 676.—In it the essences of bodies consists, 692.—It is limited, 677,—in two ways, in *intensity* and *duration*, 766,—which may be increased indefinitely, 767.—Their relation is invariable, 770.—Energy may be conceived in three ways, 589,—and is an element of the idea of body, 690.

ESSENCE, that which is contained in any idea whatever, 646.—Strictly speaking, *essence* means the most *universal essence*, which we intuit in the *idea of being*, 647.—Essences distinguished into *generic* and *specific*, 653,—and this in three ways, 654.—There are also *real, mental,* and *nominal* generic essences, 655–6.—The *specific essence*, in its highest sense, is what we think in the perfect idea of a thing, *i.e.*, in the idea of a thing furnished with all the perfection suitable to its nature, 648.—They are of three kinds: *complete, abstract,* and *full* though imperfect, 650n., 651–3.—Importance of distinguishing the *abstract* from the *full*, 657–9 (v. SUBSTANCE).

ETERNITY, the eighth characteristic of the *idea of being*, 443.

EVENT, an event without a cause is a contradiction in terms, 569.

EXISTENCE, of all the qualities of a thing, that which is *most common* and *universal*, 411.

EXTENSION, a primary extrasubjective property of *bodies*, 882.—From it arise in bodies other properties of a secondary character, 885.—It is real, not illusory, 846,—but does not, however, constitute the essence of bodies, since it is a mode of that feeling they produce in us, 752, 757,—and is always the term of a *force*, 817, 822n.—The extension of external bodies is united in one and the same surface with that of our fundamental feeling; hence our perception of them, 843–4.—It is furnished with three dimensions, 872.—Its conception is formed by the aid of touch combined with motion, 872.—*Subjective* extension is different from *shaped* extension, 728, 731.—The subjective extension of our own body is not known to us as shaped, unlike that of external bodies, but as a mode of our fundamental feeling, 735n.—The shape of the extension felt in us may undergo changes, through changes taking place in the shape of our sensitive organism, 808—considered as separate from body, extension is an abstraction, 820.

EXTRASUBJECT, differs from *subject* and *co-subject*, 1003.—*Extrasubjective* is all that is perceived outside the intelligent *subject*, 627.—Our own body also may be perceived extrasubjectively, 628.—The *extrasubjectivity* of sensation, 694n[51]. (v. SUBJECT)

FACT, every action joined with change, 616.—To say *fact* is to express a *certainty*, App. no. 14.—We must not take into account less than is necessary for the explanation of facts, 26,—nor more, 27.—These two rules constitute the principle of *sufficient* reason, *ibid.* n.,—which is the least possible that can be admitted, 28.

FACULTY, often used as equivalent to *power*.—*Spiritual* faculties, 410.—*Locomotive* faculty, or that by which the soul can change the *mode* of the fundamental feeling, 803,—and repeat at pleasure the surfaces of a space already felt, 838 (v. MOVEMENT).—The *active* faculty of the *rational instinct* corresponds to the *faculty receptive* of the manifestation of being, 524n.

FEELING, by itself does not constitute knowledge, 443.—Corporeal feelings, 684.—*Subjective* feeling, 704.—The feeling of our own existence an internal, permanent feeling endowed with particular qualities, 438.—The feeling of 'myself' is different from the *idea*, or the intellective perception of 'myself', 439-451.

FEELING (fundamental), importance of clearly defining this, 548n.—It

proceeds from the conjunction of our sentient principle with its term, 696.—It is different from *life*, 698,—and has its seat in the sensitive parts of our body, although we do not always advert to it, 699.—By it we perceive, subjectively, our own body, 701,—which, through its union with our spirit, becomes part of the feeling subject, *ibid.*—The fundamental feeling begins and ends with life, 705,—and is always substantially the same activity, although the state of the sensitive part of our body, and the feeling itself, may undergo modifications, *ibid.*, and 706.—This feeling by one and the same act perceives our body in two modes, the one substantial and the other accidental, ibid.—It is given us as a fact of consciousness, 708, 717.—Difficulty of reflecting upon it, 709.—It escaped the notice of many philosophers, 710,—or at least its true nature was not observed by them, 711.—Whether special organs are necessary for our adverting to it, 712,—or at least some sensible representation, 713.—In the chronological order, it is the last of the feelings we advert to, *ibid.* n.—It does not inform us of the shape and size of our own body, but causes us to know it in quite a different way, 714.—It extends to all the sensitive parts of the body, 715,—which it feels continually, 716.—Four observations on the air, the blood, the heat and the force of attraction, which go to prove its existence, *ibid.*—The existence of the fundamental feeling is proved also by the analysis of 'myself', 719.—How this feeling is to be distinguished from the sensitive perception of external bodies, 724-725.

It is a fundamental action which we feel as exercised on us, immediately and necessarily, by an energy different from ourselves, which action is pleasurable to us, but may be varied according to certain laws, 726.—Its *mode* of existence is extension, 731.—It has always this same mode in whatever state it may be found, 735.—

thing from *sense*, and are formed by the application of *pure ideas* to the same, 630.—Such are the ideas of *spiritual substance*, 631-71,—of *material* and *corporeal substance*, 672-91,—of our own body, 692-748,—of *time, space* and *motion*, 764-830.

Phenomenal ideas, which come from pure appearances, 789.

Pure ideas, which take nothing from sense, 575.—Their origin, 575.—To these belong the *elementary concepts* of *being*, the ideas of *substance*, of *cause*, of *effect*, of *truth*, of *justice*, of *beauty* which are drawn from the idea of being and proceed from the *formal* principle alone, 630.

Relative ideas, consisting of a relationship, are formed by *reflection*, 489.

Specific ideas are of three sorts, *complete, abstract* and *full*, 650.—In the chronological order we ascend from *full* to *complete* ideas, *ibid.*, n.—The complete idea is the true specific idea, the others are only its *modes*, 648-9.—The full, specific ideas are acquired first, but they then present to us an *imperfect* and sometimes *corrupted* thing, 650n.—They are formed by universalisation, 653n.—The *abstract specific* are formed from the *full* by means of *abstraction*, *ibid.*—which alone gives us the *abstract specific essence*, 650n.—The complete or *perfect* specific are formed from the abstract specific by means of *integration*, 653n.—As we cannot usually arrive at that idea, which would be the *archetype* of the rest, we use in its place the *abstract specific*, 650 and n., 652.

IDEALISTS,—The argument against the existence of bodies drawn by the *idealists* from dreams, 763.—Idealists place corporeal nature in multiplicity, 848.—Their error about the fact of *sensation*, 879.

IDEALITY (v. POSSIBILITY).

IDENTITY, or *unity*, is the fourth characteristic of the idea of being, 427.

ILLUSION, *optical illusions*, and their origin, 940.

IMAGE, what is required that we may form the sensible image of a thing, 400.—From what series of thoughts it may be obtained, 401.—Its close relationship to *sensation*, 518.—Corporeal images, the same as phantasms, 517.—According to St. Thomas, they are not ideas, but become such when *illustrated* by the *intellectus agens*, App. no. 12.

Visual images: what they are, and how distinguished from spots felt on the *retina*, 927-8, 944.

IMMANENT, the *actus primus* of a being, the same as its existence, 621n.

IMMUTABILITY, the seventh characteristic of the *idea of being*, 433,—and one of its elementary concepts, 575.

IMPENETRABILITY, a property of bodies comprised in extension, 885.

IMPERFECT, distinguished from *false*, 870n.

IMPOSSIBILITY (v. POSSIBILITY).

IMPRESSION (the mechanical) produced in our corporeal organs differs essentially from *perception*, 985.—It refers to an external agent, 986.—The impressions produced on our body are the same as those produced on other bodies, 985.—They are not sensations, but simply terms of an external action exercised on the *sensorium*, 986,—and are in fact the direct opposite of sensation, 987.—materialists' error in confusing the two things, 988.

INDETERMINATENESS, the ninth characteristic of the idea of being, and at the same time one of its elements, 434,—not, however, inherent in it, but proceeding from the imperfection of our intellectual vision, 436n.

INDIVIDUAL, its idea comprehended in that of *substance*; the explanation of the latter gives us the origin of the former, 591.—*Subsistent individuals* are thought, not by means of *ideas*, but by means of *judgments*, 590n.—Their perception explained, 597.—*Individual* things, 518.—*Individual existence*, App. no. 12.

INERTIA, a characteristic of *matter*, which does not include any idea of true resistance, 1011, 1017–18.—It is a quality of *bodies*, 1014.

INFINITE. Every *idea*, as universal, is called *infinite*, 428.

INFLUENCE (physical) between soul and body, an undeniable fact, 721.

INSTANT, the beginning and end of a possible *action* which is taken as a standard of measurement, 785n.— whatever happens, happens by instants, 780.—A series of *successive* instants does not give the idea of truly *continuous time*, 781.

INSTINCT, moves in correspondence with the faculty of feeling and of corporeal images, 518,—and is of two species, *sense* and *rational*, 524.—How far it can go in each of them, *ibid.*—The rational instinct is an active faculty, *ibid.* n.—What is meant by *instinctive expectation*, 957, 963–4.—The *physical instincts* move the *phantasy*, and excite the faculty of *universalisation*, 1030.—*Instinct* also has a kind of *attention*, which would be more properly called *application of the instinctive force* of the animal, 449.

INTEGRATION, in epistemology, is that operation or faculty by which our spirit completes the *full species*, 509n., 623–4, 650n.

INTELLECT (*Understanding, Mind, Intelligence*), the faculty of the intuition of indeterminate being, 481—or simply of the intuition of being, 545.

Whatever *material* element there is in the *cognitions* is given by the *sense*, 478.

According to St. Thomas, the understanding perceives things in their *essence*, App. no. 5.—Whether, and when, it knows its own act, App. no. 13.—In its highest part, it is outside all *time*, 799n[79].—It is the second original *faculty* of the soul, and relates to universals, 1020.—Its essential term is also its *object* and *form*, 1021–3.—Error of attributing to the intellect that which ought to be attributed to the human spirit, 511n.—The intellect is called a *receptive faculty*, 524n.

How the intellect may be called a

sense, 553, 1020.—Everything may be its object, 603.

INTELLECTION, every mental act having for its term an idea, either alone or conjoined with something else, or a mode of an idea, 505.—It is distinguished into three classes, *i.e. intellectual perceptions, ideas* properly so called, and *modes of ideas*, 506.—The difficulty of explaining these consists in assigning a sufficient cause to move our spirit to abstraction, 513.

INTENSITY, one of the limits of *action*, 766.—The degree of intensity runs in inverse ratio to the *duration*, 770.— This relationship is founded on two constant data, 771.

INTERMINABILITY and *immensurability*, properties of *space*, 821.—What they are and how we acquire the idea of them, *ibid.* and 882.

INTUITION, how distinguished from *persuasion*, 405.

INVARIABILITY, one of the properties of *substance*, 612.

ITINERARIUM *mentis in Deum*, a work of St. Bonaventure,—In it the first principles of reasoning are called *innate*, App. no. 10,—and the way in which our mind is conjoined with eternal and immutable things, 799n[80].

JUDGMENT, that internal operation by which we attribute a given *predicate* to a given *subject*, 42.—*Habitual judgments*, in which cases deceptive, 762 and n., 810n., 877n.—They are the principal source of common errors, App. no. 18.

KNOWLEDGE, every cognition consists of two parts, one *a priori*, constituted by its *form*,the other *a posteriori*, constituted by its *matter*, 474.—The *matter* of our knowledge is not, by itself, knowledge, but becomes such through union with the *form*, 480.— The *fundamental feeling*, with its *modifications*, and the *sensitive perception* of bodies, give the *first matter* of knowledge, 1027.—The *form* of knowledge consists in the idea of being, 474.

effect the movement), or without change in the sense organs, 804.—The second we can perceive only by means of external sensations, 805.—Hence our movement is not *per se* feelable, 806.—The movement effected in our sense organs is perceived only by the fundamental feeling through the alteration undergone by its matter, 807–8.—*Absolute movement* in general is entirely distinct from sensation, 809. *Continuity of movement,* not *real,* but only *phenomenal,* 814.—Real continuity of movement absurd, 815.—The objection: movement would take place by leaps, and its answer, 816–7.—Difficulty of this conception, 818–9.—Movement combined with *touch* gives the idea of *solid space, i.e.,* space furnished with three dimensions, 838.—Movement is distributed between the various parts of our body according to a law arising from their respective degrees of *cohesion,* 1017.—*Relative movement* is an affection of the matter of our sensations, and is felt exactly as the matter itself is affected, 809.—It arises from the corporeal perception of the five senses, 810, 812.

Movement enables us to know *distances,* 838n[94].

MULTIPLICITY, a purely mental entity, 848.—Its concept is relative, and does not belong to corporeal nature considered in its essence, 847.—It is a primary extrasubjective property of bodies, 882.—We can imagine it in the continuous extension with which the body is furnished, 884.

'MYSELF', the term applied to the substantial feeling proper to ourselves, 440n.—The *idea* of 'myself' is distinguished from the *feeling* thereof, 439,—and is preceded by the *idea of being,* 442.—The intellectual perception of 'myself' must be distinguished from 'myself' considered as a *feeling,* 980–1. (v. SUBJECT, SPIRIT, and REASON)

MYSTERIOUS, that which is inexplicable by us; differs therefore from *absurd,* 793.—Mysteries, which are admitted and which denied by philosophers, App. no. 4.

NECESSITY, the sixth characteristic of the idea of being, 429,—and one of the elementary concepts of being, 575.

NUMBER, one of the elementary concepts of being, 575.—Pythagoras makes numbers the exemplars of things, 507n.—Recurring numbers, 543n.

OBJECT, relatively to perception, must be distinguished from *subject* and *co-subject,* 983n.,—and from the matter of the fundamental feeling, 1006–10.

OBJECTIVITY, the first characteristic of the *idea of being,* 416.—*Objective necessity,* that which arises from the nature of the thing thought, 620n.

OBSERVATION, when not sufficient for explaining a thing, we must have recourse to the possibility of that thing, 782–3.—Observation does not show us minute actions, 784,—nor perceive very small extensions, 813.

OPERATION, in general, is considered as the effect of some being, 649.

ORDER *of ideas, intrinsic,* 649,—and *chronological,* 650n.—The one proceeds inversely to the other, ibid.—The same may be said of the chronological order of feelings relative to our *advertence* of them, 713n.

ORGANS (sensitive), 807.—The form or figure of an organ may change, 808.—The sensation felt by the organ must be distinguished from the sense-perception of the thing different from the organ, 810n[83].

PERCEPTION. There are two essentially distinct kinds of perception, *sensitive* and *intellective,* but modern philosophers have confused them, 961.—This distinction is founded on the principle that the *sense* perceives *singulars* and the intellect *universals,* 962.—How the sense-perception is formed, 963,—and what the intellect does to complete it, 964.—Intellective perception, the union of the intuition of a being with sense-perception, *ibid.*—Whence the difficulty in distinguishing between these two percep-